DATE DUE

POLITICS AND
POLICYMAKING

POLITICS AND POLICYMAKING

IN SEARCH OF SIMPLICITY

IRA SHARKANSKY

LYNNE
RIENNER
PUBLISHERS

BOULDER
LONDON

Published in the United States of America in 2002 by
Lynne Rienner Publishers, Inc.
1800 30th Street, Boulder, Colorado 80301
www.rienner.com

and in the United Kingdom by
Lynne Rienner Publishers, Inc.
3 Henrietta Street, Covent Garden, London WC2E 8LU

Library of Congress Cataloging-in-Publication Data
Sharkansky, Ira.
  Politics and policymaking : in search of simplicity / Ira Sharkansky.
    p.   cm.   (Explorations in public policy)
  Includes bibliographical references and index.
  ISBN 1-58826-084-4 (alk. paper)
  1. Policy sciences.   2. Public administration—Decision making.
I. Title: Politics and policymaking.   II. Title.   III. Series.

H97 .S5   2002
320'.6—dc21   2002018874

British Cataloguing in Publication Data
A Cataloguing in Publication record for this book
is available from the British Library.

Printed and bound in the United States of America

The paper used in this publication meets the requirements
∞ of the American National Standard for Permanence of
Paper for Printed Library Materials Z39.48-1984.

5 4 3 2 1

Contents

Preface

The argument of this book is that the nature of politics and policymaking does not allow participants to act with certainty. Most of the time, activists cannot predict even the near future, never mind what will come later. As a result, they cannot know for sure what they will produce by their statements or actions.

In these conditions, activists simplify their lives by taking shortcuts rather than surveying their options and planning carefully. Repeated use has made these devices reasonable accommodations to complexities that hinder any fulsome analysis. At times the devices appear to be simple, but they lead practitioners into further complications. Among the requisite skills of good politicians and policymakers are judging the conditions they face and deciding whether they should respond with thorough analysis or with a learned routine.

Politics is exciting. Sometimes too much so. As I work my way through the argument of this book, I am beset by war and election. Occasionally I hear gunfire, which seems to originate 300 meters across the valley from my balcony. Israel's prime minister resigned, and Israel went to the polls with the people divided on the best way to deal with an upsurge of violence. Meanwhile, the United States meandered toward a deadline while state and federal justices pondered the results of an unclear election. Fortunately, this level of uncertainty and excitement is exceptional. Most of the time, most decisions (even during periods of stress) are routine. Individuals seek simplicity where they can find it.

It is this pursuit of simplicity that is the focus of this book. It is a partial view of politics and policymaking, but one that encompasses much of what occurs. Not all politics and policymaking involve simple actions. Without recognizing the importance and prominence of simplicity, however, a description of politics and policymaking is incomplete.

This book does not offer a theory of politics or policymaking. Nor does it test propositions systematically that are meant to explain political behavior or policy outcomes. Instead, its goal is the more modest one of using numerous vignettes in order to coax the reader to think outside of traditional academic frameworks. Ideally, readers will consider the simplifying options I identify and test them against their prior experience and understanding. The stories offered here, along with parallel ones known to the readers, should clarify why politicians so often behave as they do in the face of difficult choices.

At times, activists do plan with great detail in the hope of maximizing the chance that their actions will have the desired effects. During a recent upsurge of Israeli-Palestinian violence, Israeli politicians argued the details of actions they thought appropriate. Government ministers discussed with military commanders the likely Palestinian responses to the use of particular weapons against specific targets. It reminded me of President Lyndon Johnson huddling with his generals over maps and target lists from Vietnam.

While President Johnson and Israel's prime minister and defense minister, Ehud Barak, focused on the details that fascinated them, they left other parts of their responsibility to routine administration. Moreover, these examples of intimate involvement with detail do not bode well for leaders' success with the task of government. Neither Johnson nor Barak fared well after dealing intimately with the details of their key policies. Lyndon Johnson gave up the presidency without finishing the war in Vietnam. Several of Ehud Barak's allies left his government out of protest with his management of the peace process. He resigned his office two months after the violence began in the hope of getting a better political arrangement. When he turned to the voters in search of an endorsement of his policies, he saw a large majority support his opponent. Among major parties' U.S. presidential candidates in the twentieth century, only Alf Landon received a similar level of rejection in percentage terms.

It is paradoxical that a book focusing on simplicities in politics and policymaking appears in the third millennium and draws most of its examples from the United States. High-tech prevails in the largest of the world's national economies; university social science faculties pour out publications that describe and analyze every imaginable feature of society, economics, and politics; and bookstores (virtual and otherwise) offer an abundance of how-to books dealing with proper decisionmaking.

For some years social scientists have concerned themselves with the ways that policymakers should deal with their problems. Theories of proper rationality and scanning have urged officials to take everything into consideration, or at least to focus on the most relevant of issues before making decisions. This level of sophistication sets the conditions that require simplicity. Advances in social sciences provide so much information that analysts spend much time arguing which information is important, and whether they have performed enough tests to be sure about their conclusions, often failing to complete the task at hand. In short, the careful consideration of all factors that may be relevant to a decision is seldom realistic in practice. Some academics use a "garbage can" model to illustrate that a lot of decisionmaking involves random chance by which some factors turn out to be influential while others lose out in the competition for officials' attention.

Increasingly powerful and intrusive government spawns efforts at privatization, outsourcing, and other ways of downsizing the public sector. The commonality among sophistication, governmental power, and privatization is that complexities lead people to simplify. A great deal of information about the working of society, economics, and politics along with elaborate analytic procedures does not assure certainty. The result is that policymakers take shortcuts and decide with limited information. Officials of powerful governments are not comfortable with the prospect of continuing to multiply agencies, staffs, and procedures in order to deliver the services that citizens demand. Privatization is a way to reduce government responsibilities while staying in step with political trends. In reality, much of privatization involves a shifting of formal responsibility, while continuing government finance and the government's participation in goal setting or management.

"New public management" is a fashionable label for the most recent of efforts to streamline government by clarifying objectives and being more clever in assigning responsibilities. Earlier reforms sought to achieve similar results under the headings of planning, performance budgeting systems, zero-based budgeting, and management by objectives. Each of these devices has sought to deal with ever increasing government by developing ever more complex tools to measure demands and parcel out resources. Sloganeering on behalf of reform is one thing. Often the reality is that officials continue with something close to customary procedures.

This book examines the links between the continuing growth of government and efforts at simplification. It also addresses several of the devices meant to improve decisionmaking. However, the principal targets are not the prominent fashions that have occupied the business of government reform over the most recent half century but rather the more basic phenomena that spawn simplifications. This book describes a number of methods individuals use to perform their political and policymaking activities without wrestling with all the details relevant to their work. The behaviors, we find, lack the hoopla of the latest fads, but they have emerged successful from the underlying reality of too many players with too many demands, and too many ways of obtaining information and analyses. I shall concede the problems in simple actions. The book ends with a discussion of when simplifications are worthwhile.

This book owes a great deal to others. It began with the readings indicated in the endnotes. The final product owes much to comments on earlier drafts received from my friends and professional colleagues, James Anderson (Texas A&M University), James J. Gosling (University of Utah), Jan-Erik Lane (University of Geneva), and Yair Zalmonovich (University of Haifa). Along with these readers, Laurie Milford's copyediting added considerably to the clarity of my argument.

1

On Simplicity, Politics, and Policymaking

Politics and policymaking are complicated for the average citizen, whether observer, voter, or activist. Candidates formulate their statements differently, according to the audience. For activists, just knowing the postures of candidates is difficult enough. Knowing which postures are truly important is likely impossible. Not even the candidate can predict the conditions that will develop and influence the ranking or reformulation of one position or another.

Success in supporting a candidate brings an activist only partway to having an influence on public policy. Politicking and policymaking differ in the skills they reward. To shape policy it is also necessary to know what policies exist. Government activities almost never spring up from nothing. They grow from what has come before. Those who aspire to policymaking must know something about program accomplishments and shortcomings. They should also know which politicians are likely to support what kind of change.

Potential policymakers must also be aware of the administrative organizations involved with existing programs, along with the procedures used by bureaucrats to decide who gets how much of which service. An American who aspires to shape policy need not be familiar with all of the more than 90,000 governmental units, plus uncounted millions of quasi-governmental units that participate in the shaping and administration of public policies. However, the aspiring policymaker should have more than a vague idea of which bodies are relevant to the idea at hand, and which clusters of administrators, clients, and other interested parties are likely to support or oppose it.

1

Potential policymakers should also be familiar with the variety of nongovernmental and overseas factors capable of influencing their efforts. In this age of easy travel, instant communication, and global commerce, economic influences flow quickly among countries and continents. Poor management of banking in Southeast Asia and then Russia tumbled the New York Stock Exchange as well as the markets of Latin America and Western Europe. Those events, in their turn, required recalculations of expected tax receipts and government payments for unemployment insurance and other social services.

Ranking bureaucrats and elected representatives can enhance or cripple an idea by their responses to it. Policymaking involves who you know as well as what you know. The "who" and the "what" you know includes the political and professional affinities of key administrators and legislators: what provisions are likely to attract their personal support, and what they are capable of promoting among their colleagues, allies, and antagonists. The answers depend not only on personal and political feelings and relationships but also on conditions of the moment. This is what former Speaker of the U.S. House Tip O'Neil meant when he said, "All politics is local." Politics involves the personal histories of activists and officeholders, their likes and antagonisms, their enemies and potential allies. It takes current information and analytic skill to determine what is likely to survive the rivalries in present political and economic conditions. It also requires a bit of luck that one's calculations remain valid through the changes in key personnel or in economic and political environments during the process of policymaking.

Changing policy, or changing the rules about making policy, is not likely to be quick in any democracy. Government institutions are designed to slow change. In this way they offer some protection to affected individuals, giving them a chance to voice their opposition, as well as safeguards against demagogues able to fan the passions of the moment. Governments are divided mechanisms that separate powers and require the agreement of different groups of administrators or elected officials. Proposed changes must be advertised to the public and pass through several stages of consideration before they can affect existing laws or programs. The procedural rules of the U.S. Congress, as well as other legislative bodies, govern the format for presenting a proposed piece of legislation, the referral of the proposal to a committee, the rules to be followed by the chair and members of the committee, and the allocation of time for debate in the full legislature as well as voting procedures and ways of appealing judgments about the rules made by the chair of the committee or the full legislature.

Individuals make a difference and influence the outcomes. A candidate's personality ranks among the factors that shape voting. Preferences of the chief executive, a committee chair in the legislature, or key administrator can affect the chances of a proposal becoming law. Yet the individual's role is limited by the very size of public activities. Aides orchestrate the time and attention of the chief executive with respect to most fields of policy. While the president is dealing with the details of one or a few issues, cabinet secretaries responsible for other matters may be unable to obtain an appointment with the chief executive for even a brief consultation. Among the complexities to be learned by an aspiring policymaker are the interests and idiosyncrasies of individuals occupying key positions, not to mention those of aides who control the schedule of the key persons.

The multiplicity of participants is only one of the basic traits of politics and policymaking that limit the activists who seek the most effective means of influencing policy. Another problem appears in the likelihood that there will be contradictory demands at the center of prominent disputes. Economic versus social priorities is a common problem. While some advocates demand greater benefits in the fields of housing, health, education, and environmental protection, others emphasize other priorities, or they take the more general posture of minimizing taxes and budget deficits.

A lack of substantive information limits the capacity of policymakers. Natural and social science has a long way to go. Causes of disease, economic crises, or environmental pollution are matters for dispute among experts, whose recommendations are fraught with doubts as to their effectiveness. The most obvious causes and cures of society's problems are likely to have been written into public policy. Current disputes tend to focus on those issues where information is incomplete and debatable.

The picture is not all gloomy. Dispute makes politics exciting. Political scientists as well as ordinary citizens gravitate to the more difficult issues. We choose to ignore the great bulk of what government does as predictable humdrum.

My point of departure with respect to politics and policymaking is to recognize the many elements that may be influential and the numerous calculations these elements impose on anyone seeking to shape the results of an election or the nature of public policy. This point of departure can lead in one of two directions. One would be to document each of the factors needing to be taken into account by someone who would participate and to suggest how to calculate a path toward success. But I will choose the second option, which concedes the improbability of listing all the factors likely to influence a particular campaign of politics or policymaking. This direction also admits the even greater problems of charting a course of action that will succeed. It employs the shortcuts of simple options, chosen perhaps on the basis of intuition, or learned responses to parallel conditions.

The Well-Trod Paths: Simple Ways of Dealing with Conflict and Other Forms of Complexity

Recognizing the multiplicity of political actors and demands, not to mention chronic uncertainty, leads us to the way most activists work most of the time: They choose a simple path rendered routine over the years by numerous others who have tread it with some degree of success. It is not perfectly informed as to what is likely to happen, but it may be the wisest path to choose. Not only the profound complexities involved in politics and policymaking discourage thorough planning. There is also the chronic pressure of time. Activists demand action in the immediate future, not a long analysis of how to reach goals over time.

Activists in politics and policymaking learn the simple routines from a variety of sources. Some—such as "be politically correct" and "emphasize the positive"—they may absorb from family, friends, fellow students, and coworkers from childhood onward. Some they learn on the job from seeing others succeed and fail or from talking with mentors. Some of what is described in Chapter 4—such as "serve your constituency" and "create a crisis"—can be found in political science texts and so may be learned as part of formal education.

Without a doubt, there are those among politicians and policymakers who enjoy the plotting out of strategies. They work at (1) defining their desires in a way that maximizes the chances of support and (2) planning how to maneuver through the relevant institutions and individuals. They take account of current conditions and looming possibilities in politics, economics, and social fashions. Far be it for me to limit the efforts or enjoyment of those who earn their living in this way. But I shall play the probabilities, which indicate that actors should learn the simple rules that others have learned before them. Those simple rules will guide many actions, even of those who at other times wallow in complexity. This book represents a partial view of politics and policymaking. It focuses on those elements of politics and policymaking that demand simplification. Limiting the issues that activists must worry about serves to increase the likelihood that they will succeed.

Numerous books and articles emphasize the lack of rationality or thoroughness in policymaking and purvey one or another way for officials to improve the nature of decisionmaking. It is common to advise careful planning, precise definition of one's problem and available resources, a wide net of consultation, plumbing the desires of one's adversaries, exercises to improve one's own creativity in considering additional options, and attention to the details of policy implementation and follow-up.[1] A subset of this approach concedes that it is impossible to survey everything relevant and that it is wise to honor priorities favored by those with political influence. The point is to scan options selectively, but widely, before making decisions.[2] Yet another approach is to admit that there is much that seems random in policymaking. Scholars use the model of a "garbage can" to describe what can be influential: Activists stick their hand into a metaphorical garbage can, fish around, and find themselves influenced by one thing or another, without knowing exactly why.[3]

Here I want to emphasize the variety of simple devices used by policymakers that represent the evasion of analysis. Readers seeking labels may put this book in the literature dealing with "mixed scanning," "bounded rationality," and "satisficing" as opposed to "optimizing."[4] This book also adds to the description of the "garbage can," or a view of policymaking that emphasizes the randomness by which some options seem to be adopted and others rejected.

My concern is to describe several of the many ways that decisions are actually made. I do not disparage careful planning, attention to detail, and all the other norms of comprehensive policymaking when they seem appropriate, but I assert that these norms are relevant only part of the time. My mission is to describe and explain behaviors widely used by policymakers. I also suggest some rules that may help in deciding when to employ thoroughgoing ways of policymaking and when to pursue simplicity. My work is primarily empirical rather than normative. That is, I describe what occurs rather than advocate what should occur. Yet I also verge into the normative debate, by pointing to the advantages associated with simplicity.

The reliance on simple devices for most purposes is a "rational" (or reasonable) use of an official's time and energy. The vast majority of issues do not warrant the attention of top officials. They are likely handled better by lower-ranking personnel who have become expert in their focus on a limited range of problems, or they are served adequately by the unthinking application of routine procedures learned and internalized over the years. Advocates of rationality speak of the "central minds of government" who should be highly informed about the most important of issues. There are no end of examples to document the lack of wisdom shown by the central minds of government. Often the speedy use of learned procedures is the best way of acting.

For several decades, a procession of efforts to reform policymaking and public administration have sought to deal with the accumulating demands and growing complexity of government. With more services to provide increasing populations, unwieldy government has invited the creation and marketing of one device after another. Their principles resemble one another, although the slogans used to identify them change. Privatization, downsizing, contracting, outsourcing, and deregulation have sought to limit the responsibilities of government by distributing its components to willing contractors. Often the result is continuing government involvement in setting conditions of service, providing money, and identifying clientele, leaving nongovernmental individuals—sometimes former civil servants now employed by private sector or nonprofit organizations—to do the actual work.

The centrality of budgeting in policymaking has attracted its own reforms. Program budgeting, planning-programming-budgeting, and zero-based budgeting have sought to clarify the results of financial allocations so that budget makers can make their decisions with a greater concern for productivity and efficiency. Management by objectives, reinvented government, and new public management have put together various pieces of these schemes and flogged them through commissions of inquiry, graduate programs of public administration, and international organizations. Advocates and opponents of each reform make their claims, usually supported by anecdotes and rhetoric rather than thorough analyses.[5]

In this book there is no assessment of the relative success of highly touted management reforms. Neither is there another proposal to reform government. Rather, my purpose is to describe a number of devices that simplify governing and make it manageable for participants. The purpose is not to prove the utility of one way of dealing with complexity over another. The goal is the simpler one of showing the variety of devices employed, making the point that much of politics and policymaking involves pursuing what is manageable rather than what is ideal. Critics may accuse the book of being overly pragmatic and too ready to settle for the less than ideal. Yet the persistence of simple devices and their widespread use suggests that the simple way is often the most attractive.

The Principle of Simplicity

The principle of simplicity is to politics and policymaking what Occam's razor is to explanation. It aspires to employ as few considerations as possible in order to achieve goals. Just as the famous razor cuts through convoluted explanations in order to find the fewest explanations for why something has occurred, simple rules of action in politics and policymaking employ the least time and the least analysis in cutting through the many possible ways to shape policy. These rules sacrifice elegance in the pursuit of certainty for a reasonable chance at accomplishing an approximation of desires in the time available.

Why go a simple route when a thorough assessment of conditions and a careful choice of strategy may be both more satisfying intellectually and more successful? The answer is imperfect as is the course we choose. A full calculation of options can never be complete, given the large number of actors, the conditions that may influence them, and the dynamics among them.[6] The quick and imperfect shortcut leaves some alternatives unexplored, but it has the weight of experience on its side. The simple route is likely well known among colleagues and may have been "taught" in mentoring. It is conventional and accepted as a practical way of acting.

Admittedly, there is no clear evidence on the side of the known, but simple shortcuts as opposed to the thorough examination of options do guide decisions. Social science remains incomplete and unsatisfying. We cannot know for sure if the choice of simple solutions causes serious loss, brings overall benefit, or remains neutral, with no apparent overall effect on outcomes. The details that may convince the doubter I will discuss in later chapters.

Not for Simpletons

The chief executive or a legislator occupying a key position in the lawmaking body is not likely a simpleton. Whether in a democracy or an authoritarian regime, key officials have gotten to their positions by planning; taking advantage of opportunity; and cunning, or wisdom, as well as good luck.

Once on the road to high office, and even more so once arrived, the chief executive has the advantage of an extensive staff, typically made up of individuals who are themselves skilled in spotting and using opportunities. They plan and connive, master the formal procedures of political parties and legislatures, and learn the needs and weaknesses of others within their own country and outside of it.

The exciting stuff of high stakes and difficult choices is what attracts media headlines and thoughtful columnists. Russia's 1999 war against Chechnya pit U.S. concerns for the welfare of refugees and revulsion about civilian casualties against the desire to remain on good terms with Russia and to coordinate U.S. foreign policy with principal allies yet not to be tied to the cumbersome decision processes of several European governments. Russian diplomats responded to U.S. complaints about civilian deaths by reminding the Americans of Russian opposition to American and NATO use of force in Kosovo. "When you hurt civilians in Kosovo, it was called collateral damage and when we do that, you call it a violation of human rights. . . . And you were doing it in a foreign country and we are defending our own borders."[7]

American punishment of Russia on account of Chechnya was out of the question. A principle of U.S. foreign policy has been to aid Russia through its difficult transition to economic viability and democracy, with an eye toward the massive Russian stockpiles of nuclear weapons as well as residual anti-Americanism in Russia.

Bill Clinton's policy toward China was no less problematic. He began his presidency seeking to link favorable trade terms with China's cooperation with U.S. policy in favor of human rights and against the sale of sophisticated military hardware to Iran, Syria, and other places thought unfriendly with respect to U.S. interests. Later the president began to support the long-term benefits of liberalizing China's politics by opening up its markets. The change brought out skeptics and outright opponents. Would loosening trade relations really change Chinese politics? Would it even assure U.S. access to Chinese markets? Administration critics argued that even European countries occasionally balk at honoring international economic agreements that threaten their domestic agriculture or industries. The chief U.S. negotiator, Madeleine Albright, herself admitted to some skepticism when an agreement was signed. As one *New York Times* writer pointed out,

> We have to be realistic about the prospects for change in China because there are elements of the country that will never change . . . but

what's the alternative? Let's punish China by not gaining access to its market? Who does that punish? I am cautious in making claims that a market-opening agreement leads to anything other than opening the market. It may—it could have a spillover effect—but it may not. And we've got to understand that.[8]

The cases of Russia and China show that ranking officials ponder the many sides of evolving details and options for response. In these cases, officials focused on the pros and cons of detailed options, rather than using simple routines. But when they choose to focus on certain items, they are likely to rely on nearly automated routines to deal with most other issues. Simplicity in most matters allows time and energy for those that are most interesting, dangerous, or puzzling. For readers wanting an early view of what I describe as simplifications, they include reliance on political parties to limit one's selection of personnel, incrementalism in making decisions about policy substance, and communicating by slogans, plus a number of homilies that guide leaders through the choices to be made on a daily basis.

Party and interest group leaders use a number of simplifications to solve problems. "Support our members and oppose our opponents" is one of the simplest and most pervasive. However, it does not help in cases when politicians take complex positions that are not entirely either friendly or antagonistic. Nor does this rule help when a candidate takes one position overtly but may be preparing to alter that position once in office. Knowing motives is as impossible as knowing the future. It might be a necessity of party politics to bet on the result of electing politician x, but parties and interest groups must realize that politicians are skilled at disguising their goals.

Not all simple responses are useful. Key officials are not always well informed. For instance, I heard an Israeli who served as ambassador to Washington in the 1970s talk at a small gathering about one of his meetings with the U.S. national security adviser in which he asked what changes to Israel's 1967 borders the United States would accept. The national security adviser responded with an incremental formula: that "cosmetic" alterations would be all right. When asked what he meant by "cosmetic," the national security adviser said, "no more than ten or twenty miles in any direction."

If this report is true (ambassadors have been known to embellish the truth for the sake of a good story), changes in the magnitude of ten to twenty miles could wipe out much of what might go to the Palestinians. The West Bank is hardly more than sixty miles north to south and less than twenty miles at its narrowest east to west. Gaza is no more than twenty miles long and at spots less than three miles wide. It is separated from the West Bank by some twenty-five miles of Israel as the crow flies and forty miles by road. Israel itself is no more than two hundred miles north to south and less than ten miles east to west at the narrowest point in its pre-1967 borders.

As this story indicates, the work of chief executives and their aides is not entirely incisive. They have to simplify in order to deal with many of the issues that come before them. Much of what they do is the application of routines learned from books, personal experience, and mentors who have gone before them. Indeed, much governmental work is routine. The government operates by simplified procedures meant to produce imperfect but acceptable decisions in the context of many problems of great complexity.

To Exemplify Simplicity

The approach of this book is simplicity exemplified. I aspire to clear language and an uncomplicated argument to make the point that policymaking invites simple approaches to situations that defy fulsome analysis and detailed planning. I use insights from academic writing and details from recent newspapers and magazines while avoiding jargon and elaborate formulae whose obtuseness overwhelms whatever contribution might be made.

What is called formal theory, public choice, game theory, or rational analysis has stimulated much of what lies within the principle of simplicity, even though writers in those schools might not recognize their work here. For all the value in their work, it is difficult to find room for nuance or subtlety in their writing about politics. However, nuance and subtlety are essential in political discourse.[9]

The underlying truths of postmodernism and deconstruction will also find their influence here. They teach that meaning and intentions are elusive and vary according to the perspective of the reader.[10] That will be apparent in my discussions of slogans, symbols, and political correctness. Hopefully, the message will be clear enough without resorting to the endless probing of subtexts and elaborating all the perspectives that specialists employ in order to explain the meanings in a comment or a document.

In an effort to emphasize the pursuit of simplicity yet to distinguish simplicity from that which is simplistic or superficial, I should early on set apart our endeavor from the endless supply of precepts, principles, and prescriptions that have marked much of the writing about public administration.[11] This is not a normative exercise concerned to improve the workings of politics and policymaking. I do not endorse any of what are proclaimed as ideal ways to solve problems. This book is, rather, an effort to describe and understand—that is, to analyze—behaviors that are already widely employed. It is empirical more than normative, analytic more than prescriptive. While it lists numerous simplifications that individuals use in their political and policymaking activities, it neither endorses nor condemns any of them. It asserts that individuals use them. And it cautions that some are more useful in certain circumstances than others and that none are useful at all times. Much of my concluding chapter is dedicated to the point that the essence of political wisdom is to know when to use one approach rather than another or when to avoid all simplifications in order to make an intensive inquiry into the root causes of and basic approaches to a problem.

Although my argument is actually very simple, its details may overwhelm and confuse readers. I employ numerous illustrations of the conditions that confound policymaking and the ways that individuals seek to simplify their actions. The devices I call simplifications include some of the basic building blocks of politics. Readers will recognize them from their extensive treatment in political science texts. Here I view them from an angle that may seem unconventional: as means individuals use to make their way through the complexities that surround them. Political parties simplify the choices that people make from the vast number of candidates and policy proposals available for selection. Incrementalism limits our choices for policies and program details to those that depart only slightly from the status quo, thereby easing the way we select among alternatives. We use slogans as shortcuts in communication. When we face opposition to ideas, we may postpone our decision, sometimes for so long that we end up not deciding. Other rules that policy activists have learned from their experiences include:

- Serve your constituency.
- Do as little as possible.
- Postpone the unpleasant by appeals and other delaying tactics.
- Make a moral declaration.
- When competing for support, promise a great deal.
- When bargaining, demand a great deal.
- Take a narrow view of your responsibilities.

- Ignore the inconvenient rules.
- Blame someone else.
- Be politically correct.
- Be careful what you express and how you express it; symbols may be more important than substance.
- Keep your message simple.

The following chapters include numerous vignettes that illustrate the complexities in politics and the methods used by activists to navigate these complexities. The argument will move forward in stages. Two more chapters deal with the problems that lead activists to choose simple solutions. Chapter 2 shows that a model used to simplify the portraying of policymaking actually lends itself to limitless forays of elaborate description. Chapter 2 also details the complexities involved in two stages of policymaking: the formulation of an agenda for policy consideration and the implementation of policy once it is decided. Chapter 3 describes public organizations whose structures are meant to hinder policymaking by elected officials and their appointees.

Chapter 4 provides a number of answers as to how politicians and other policymakers deal with the problems raised in Chapters 2 and 3. Chapter 4 illustrates how individuals simplify the many options involved in policymaking. Chapter 5 admits to the problems caused by shortcuts to political goals and ponders the merits of simple procedures that are imperfect but arguably the best available. The bottom line of my argument is that simplifications are widely used. They are, to be sure, evasions of prescriptions to be rational and to take everything into consideration. Insofar as they provide workable solutions to difficult problems, however, simplifications are reasonable responses to reality.

The sources employed are scholarly publications and the mass media, filtered through my forty years of experience in reading and observing politicians and policymakers in numerous countries, and occasionally participating as kibitzer or formal adviser. Many of the details come from my frequent perusal of the *New York Times, Washington Post, Christian Science Monitor,* the *Times* of London, the *Economist,* the *New Republic,* and *Ha'aretz* of Israel. Thanks to the Internet, such activity is accessible and affordable.

The journalistic sources used for many of the details should not cheapen the book. Individually, these newspapers and journals are among the most authoritative in the world. Together, they provide different views on the same basic events. In keeping with one of the themes of this book, judgment is the key to the best use of simple rules. The episodes described are not meant to be case studies. They are only partial descriptions of events. Undoubtedly other illustrations would lead to different insights. If distortions in detail or interpretation appear in individual episodes, their weight in my total discussion is small. For scholars alive today, the world media is at our fingertips, but we must judge what is reliable as well as what provokes insights worthy of passing on to others. By the same token, readers must judge what are reasonable interpretations of ongoing events.

The principle of simplicity appears to be widespread. It may be true that all politics are local in the sense that activists must be aware of the status accorded to individuals, groups, and issues. However, the prevalence of simplicity reflects a global need to cut through many details and complexities in order to bring about change.

Most of the examples used in this book refer to the United States. Some come from other sources, including my experience in Israel, but those are explained in ways to make them intelligible to wider audiences. The concern is to emphasize the widespread simplification of politics and policymaking and to illustrate this process with a number of examples from different settings.

Notes

1. Yehezkel Dror, *Public Policymaking Reexamined* (San Francisco: Chandler Publishing Company, 1968); Dror, *Policymaking Under Adversity* (New Brunswick, N.J.: Transaction Books, 1986); Aaron Wildavsky, *Speaking Truth to Power: The Art and Craft of Policy Analysis* (Boston: Little, Brown, 1979); David Dery, *Problem Definition in Policy Analysis* (Lawrence: University of Kansas Press, 1984).

2. Amitai Etzioni, "Mixed Scanning: A 'Third' Approach to Decision-Making," *Public Administration Review* 27, December 1967, 385–392.

3. John W. Kingdon, *Agendas, Alternatives, and Public Policies* (Boston: Little, Brown & Company, 1984).

4. Herbert A. Simon, *Administrative Behavior: A Study of Decision-Making Processes in Administrative Organization* (New York: Free Press, 1976).

5. See, for example, H. George Frederickson and Jocelyn M. Johnston, eds., *Public Management Reform and Innovation: Research, Theory, and Application* (Tuscaloosa: University of Alabama Press, 1999); Harvey B. Feigenbaum, *Shrinking the State: The Political Underpinnings of Privatization* (Cambridge: Cambridge University Press, 1998).

6. See Peter L. Bernstein, *Against the Gods: The Remarkable Story of Risk* (New York: John Wiley & Sons, 1996).

7. Jane Perlez, "War in Chechnya Threatening U.S. Strategy Goals," *New York Times,* November 15, 1999. Internet edition.

8. David E. Sanger, "A Deal That American Just Couldn't Refuse," *New York Times,* November 16, 1999. Internet edition.

9. See Donald P. Green and Ian Shapiro, *Pathologies of Rational Choice Theory* (New Haven: Yale University Press, 1994); Michael Laver, *Private Desires, Political Action: An Invitation to the Politics of Rational Choice* (London: Sage Publications, 1997); and Jonathan Cohn, "When Did Political Science Forget About Politics?" *New Republic,* October 25, 1999. Internet edition.

10. A classic expression of the theory of deconstruction is Michel Foucault, *Discipline and Punish: The Birth of the Prison,* translated by Alan Sheridan (New York: Vintage Books, 1979).

11. Herbert A. Simon, "The Proverbs of Administration," *Public Administration Review* 6, no. 4, 1946, 53–67; Simon, *Administrative Behavior: A Study of Decision-Making Processes in Administrative Organization* (New York: Free Press, 1976); Jay M. Shafritz and Albert C. Hyde, eds., *Classics of Public Administration* (Fort Worth, Tex.: Harcourt Brace, 1997).

2

The Mysteries of Agenda-Setting, Policymaking, and Implementation

We know a great deal about what can influence public policy, but we know very little about the extent to which each potential influence affects specific outcomes. An analyst seeking to array the conditions to be taken into account in planning a program for a particular setting can spend a lifetime pondering what is likely to influence the chances of a proposal being approved and then the chances of the program being administered as planned and actually having its hoped-for effect. When it comes down to identifying the weight of specific influences, or what will actually determine success or failure of a particular proposal, our representative policymaker, to be honest, must admit ignorance. In other words, we know a great deal in general terms about policymaking and program implementation. When it comes to predicting success or failure of a specific proposal at one time and place, there are so many possible influences that we cannot tell what happens until the story is complete. Then we might look back and unravel the tangle of influences.

The Policymaking System

I can begin to illustrate the complexities in politics by focusing on a teaching device used to indicate what influences what. The device is meant to be simple, but in the hands of teachers and students, it quickly becomes filled with a great amount of detail. What starts out clear becomes muddied with more and more elements that can influence policymakers.

For a number of years now, teachers of policymaking have employed a systems model to portray the notion of cause and effect, or

15

what is likely to influence what. One formulation appears in Figure 2.1. It includes an environment that supplies the stimuli of inputs to the policymaking process, which in turn produces policy, which leads to outcomes in society that in turn pass through the environment and feed back into policymaking at a later time.

When asked to identify the detailed components in each of the system's categories, students go on and on. In the "environment" they place a country's culture, its economic resources, rates of growth in population, industry, and income, plus political tendencies of liberalism or conservatism and support or opposition to particular ideas and programs. Religion also appears in the environment. It not only affects attitudes toward a host of policy issues, like abortion and the content of schooling, but is also a topic of policy. Countries vary in the way they support religious activities and how much resources they devote to religion. Though some may think that a separation of church and state solves the issue in the United States, it only makes the amount of funding more difficult to measure. Government support for religion exists in the tax-exempt nature of property and facilities used for religious purposes as well as in the financial resources that find their way from government budgets to education and other social services provided by institutions linked to religious organizations.

Outer reaches of the environment go beyond the country's borders and include what happens among near neighbors as well as on the other side of the world. Overseas demands for a country's industrial product can spur growth, while international depression can put a damper on the economy.

"Inputs" in the model of the policymaking system represent the transmissions from environment to policymaking. They include expressions of

Figure 2.1   A Beginner's Model of the Policymaking System

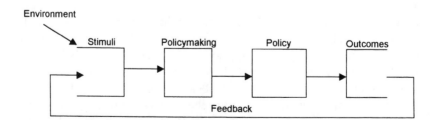

demands and the flow of resources. The flow of resources reflects tax policy as well as the wealth of a jurisdiction's economy. Specific demands reflect the political culture, the messages carried by the mass media, and the array of interested individuals and organizations who stand for, against, and indifferent to particular issues.

Into the box identified as "policymaking" students list governmental institutions and key officials, as well as political parties, interest groups, and citizen activists. In some formulations, parties and interest groups appear in both the category for environment and the category for policymaking. The political parties of key officials and interest groups close to them may be placed in the box labeled policymaking, while other parties and interest groups may gain a place in the environment.

"Policy" includes official pronouncements plus laws and regulations, budget allotments, definitions of client entitlements, and other program components. "Outcomes" are the results of these policies in the near and longer range. In the case of education, outcomes include the learning actually attained by students and further down the road the impact of that learning on graduates' job placement, earnings, and other adult behaviors that reflect education.

"Feedback" conveys the dynamism of policymaking. It includes responses to policies and outcomes, their impact on the environment, and the subsequent demands coming out of the environment for alterations in policy as well as resources coming out of the environment that help pay for policies.

Although the schematic of a policymaking system is meant to simplify learning by providing a place for different elements that interact with one another and an ordered way to think about what is likely to influence what, the possibilities of adding further details and possible interactions are likely to crowd the classroom display board and overcome the image of simplicity. Figure 2.2 shows lines of influence directly from the environment to policymaking, policy, and outcomes, without passing through inputs; it also shows policymaking and policy moving back to the environment without passing through outcomes. The point is that statements of policymakers can trigger responses from the environment even before they affect policy or outcomes.

There is no end to the additions that critics of the simple model add to the portrayal of the policymaking system. They distinguish between international, national, and local environments and portray lines of influence among them. They divide policymaking among the various branches of government, and they separate out nongovernmental actors

Figure 2.2 The Policymaking System Enhanced

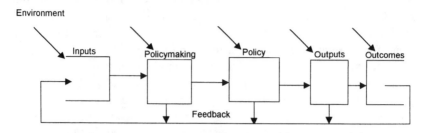

such as political parties and interest groups and quasi-governmental actors that affect the implementation of policy, such as agencies that contract with governments for the delivery of social services. Some formulations of the policy system separate "outcomes" from "impacts." Outcomes can be short-range effects of policy (such as what students learn as the result of schooling), while impacts are the effects in a longer view (such as the lifetime earnings of college graduates as opposed to those of high school graduates).

There has been limited success in moving beyond models meant to simplify reality for students to the statistical analysis of variables that represent components of the policy system. Researchers have sought to identify indicators for various components of the model, measure statistical relationships among them, and thereby estimate the influence of components on one another. Studies have compared traits of U.S. state and local governments with those of the countries of the world in order to test how measurements of environmental, policymaking, policy, and outcome traits support one or another hypothesis about cause and effect. The strongest and most consistent findings point to strong links within the "black box" of policymaking. They indicate that policy is likely to bear close resemblance to its own immediate past. In other words, incremental changes are much more common than major changes. Other findings show the effects of economic development. The wealth of a country, U.S. state, or other locality and the education of its residents are likely to show their impact on the nature of public policy. For the most part, it is the more well-to-do places, with well-educated populations, that are likely to be generous with public services.[1]

These and other findings do not rest without criticism. Findings vary with the measurements and statistical tests employed as well as with the jurisdictions examined and the time frame of the study. Perhaps the clearest conclusion of this research, aside from the prevalence of incrementalism, is the large number of factors that might influence policymakers and the problems in ascertaining in advance the weight and direction of influence to come from any one source on a particular feature of public policy.

An Especially Noisy Policy Arena

At times there is so much noise in the policy environment that a model aspiring to simplify reality reaches the limits of its utility. For example, the more than 130 organizations that participated in a sometimes violent demonstration against the World Trade Organization's 1999 Seattle meeting puzzled commentators whose job it was to describe the demands being made. Participants in the demonstrations included right-wing militia members, gays and lesbians, environmentalists, unionists concerned with job export, opponents to child labor, anarchists, and a number of looters seeming to represent nothing as much as their own desire for a television set or something else they had seen in a store window. An anti-police group also coalesced after the police responded to an earlier round of protests with tear gas, rubber bullets, and some 1,000 arrests.[2]

The Seattle meeting also presented several problems of interpretation after its conclusion. The official delegates went home without reaching agreement on significant decisions. The next week the city's police chief announced his resignation and expressed his concern for the reputation of the local police force. The whole affair might have set back the cause of international trade and the benefits it could bring to rich and poor countries. As one observer wrote, "Politicians all over America will look at Seattle and say, 'Wow, if that's what you get when you support free trade, I'm hiding.'"[3] All the groups that demonstrated might have contributed to the weakening of an international regime to regulate their various concerns (e.g., protection of the environment or workers' rights), leaving in place something closer to a free market without administrative mechanisms to protect anything.

What Affects the Policy Agenda?

If it is already clear that many things can influence policy, it should be no surprise that an impressively large number of elements can influence what officeholders consider on their way to making policy. Here it is appropriate to talk about the *policy agenda*. This is a term for the issues considered by the legislature or the chief executive or those that are debated by knowledgeable persons in the mass media. Items on the agenda may not become policy. There are usually too many ideas scrambling for attention in order to be adopted. If something does not get on the agenda, however, it has no chance of becoming policy.

There is no clear answer to the question of how something gets onto the agenda. It is part of the complexity that pervades policymaking. Very early in the process of making policy is an idea. It may be to introduce an entirely new program, perhaps something that has been observed in another jurisdiction. Or it may be a proposal to improve something that already exists in the jurisdiction. Before it is possible to move the idea to adoption, supporters must attract attention. Others involved in making policy must accept the idea as something worthy of discussion.

Some time ago, Professor John Kingdon of the University of Michigan sought to explain why some items reach the agenda of the U.S. Congress, while others never get there.[4] During 1997, representatives and senators introduced over 5,500 items for consideration and managed to enact fewer than 160 laws.[5] Perhaps much of what was proposed formally was not really on the agenda but was introduced without having a serious chance of enactment—and without the person introducing it intending to work seriously for its passage—in order to make a favorable impression on constituents. To reach the congressional agenda, an item must be something that is discussed seriously by numerous legislators or at least by the key individuals who head committees or are minority party leaders on the committees.

The situation is similar in state legislatures. Lawmakers introduced some 140,000 bills in 1999, many of them highly particularistic solutions to problems that had been featured in recent media stories. The vast majority never received serious consideration by a legislative committee, and fewer still served as the subject of debate before an upper or lower chamber of the legislature. Reports from the Maryland legislature treated the following issues as exotic proposals offered by members offended by an injustice or moved to lip service by a constituent who claimed to have suffered:

- to require tow truck operators to accept one of at least two major credit cards;
- to require health insurers to pay for wigs for chemotherapy patients who lose their hair;

- to forbid women to nurse a baby not their own without permission;
- to require hospitals to disclose to patients if they reuse disposable equipment;
- to prohibit anyone from videotaping people in a private home without their permission.[6]

Kingdon succeeded only partly in his task of explaining how items get to the agenda. He managed to identify a number of factors *capable of influencing* an item's success in reaching the agenda, but he could not measure their influence or say when one or another of the influences would carry the day or fail in the case of a particular proposal. He listed the kinds of individuals capable of bringing an issue to the attention of others. They include elected officials and their appointees as well as career bureaucrats and nongovernmental actors in interest groups, research institutes, universities, and the mass media.

Kingdon found that an item's ascendance to the congressional agenda reflects several different processes. One is a process of problem recognition, which comes about when individuals notice indicators about social conditions or problems in the working of existing programs or are impressed by the magnitude of crises or disasters. Another is a process of proposals emerging from a "policy primeval soup," or ongoing writing and discussion among experts in and outside of government. For a proposal to come out of this primeval soup and achieve serious consideration by policymakers, it should be technically feasible, suitable with respect to prevailing values and the current political mood, and in line with the budgetary resources that might be made available. The political suitability of a proposal may itself reflect a number of conditions: present fashions in public opinion, the presence of supportive individuals in key positions in administrative departments or legislative committees, and the campaigns being waged by interest groups.

Kingdon's discussion of these contributors to the policy agenda deepen our understanding of what might happen and what is not likely to happen. However, his conclusion is both honest and disappointing: "We still encounter considerable doses of messiness, accident, fortuitous coupling, and dumb luck. Subjects sometimes rise on agendas without our understanding why. We are sometimes surprised by the couplings that take place. The fortuitous appearance or absence of key participants affects outcomes. There remains some degree of unpredictability."[7]

Kingdon explained his findings by reference to the garbage can model. That is, there are lots of explanations for what among the many policy options succeeds in competing for attention and support. Yet there

is no clear and convincing explanation of what works. Problems, solutions, participants, and windows of opportunities are mixed in an ever-
changing garbage can. There is a substantial element of randomness in
influencing what emerges from the can to get serious consideration as
public policy.[8]

Learning from the Exotic

We can learn about the problems of policymaking by considering items
that receive some public attention—and thus at least minimally can be
said to have made it to the policy agenda—but show no progress toward
becoming policy. Someone said that every individual can aspire to fifteen minutes of fame if he or she does something outstanding or bizarre.
Here we see that some strange issues get a bit of attention but so far
seem a long way from being adopted as policy.

Several unusual issues have struggled to find their place on the policy agenda. At times something plops onto the agenda from nowhere
and commands a great deal of time and nervous energy even though it
may amount to very little in the end. These issues add to the noise that
surrounds policymaking. Some disturb more than others. Individuals
skilled in policymaking may know which are serious proposals intended
to shape policy and which are meant only to show dedication to a cause.
Sometimes, however, policymakers mistake a serious proposal for something taken by others as frivolous or find that a policy has been enacted
from a proposal they thought to be unimportant.

Here I present some of the issues that have found a place on the
policy agenda without so far affecting policy.

Reparations for Slavery

Rep. John Conyers Jr. (D-Mich.) has worked for years to advance the
idea of paying reparations to African Americans for their ancestors'
slavery. He has introduced a proposal in every legislative session since
1989 but has managed to get only 31 out of the 435 members of the
House to sign on as cosponsors. Even two African American Democrats
on the Judiciary Committee—Mel Watt of North Carolina and Bobby
Scott of Virginia—have declined to support Conyers's proposal. The
legislation, labeled "The Commission to Study Reparation Proposals for
African Americans Act," has never been debated in Congress.

Among the questions asked by skeptics and outright opponents are, Why should American taxpayers who never owned slaves pay for the sins of ancestors? How would you establish who is a qualified descendant? How much should be paid to each? How much would it cost the American treasury? One researcher calculates that unpaid wages to blacks before emancipation amount to the equivalent of $1.4 trillion in today's values. Others add that the gains of whites from labor market discrimination (from 1929 to 1969) approximate $1.6 trillion in present-day dollars. A number of African American leaders have opposed reparations out of concern that the money would be better spent to benefit poor African Americans suffering currently from inadequate education and other social services.[9]

The idea is not entirely out of line with what the United States and other countries have done to redress historic wrongs. In 1988, Congress authorized payments of $20,000 each to roughly 60,000 survivors of Japanese who were interred during World War II. Canada provided a $230 million reparations package to Japanese Canadians. The German government has paid $60 billion to settle claims from victims of Nazi persecution. Inuits, Aleuts, and other Native Americans, as well as survivors of a 1923 massacre in a predominantly black Florida town, have received restitution that amounts to more than $1 billion. In Australia, the government has apologized for its treatment of Aborigines and is negotiating compensation.[10]

Disestablishing the Church of England

Parallel to reparations for slavery in the United States is the proposal that has made it to the fringes of the British agenda to disestablish the Church of England. The issue reached the pages of the prestigious *Times* of London when ranking members of the Church proposed to remove the ban on Catholics serving as monarch. The ban itself began with the Act of Settlement, enacted by Parliament in 1701, as part of a complicated resolution of a civil war. Some observers thought that the issue would interest Prime Minister Tony Blair on account of his wife and children being Catholic, but he seemed inclined to avoid the issue. Aside from a few key clerics who supported the idea, the proposal triggered expressions of opposition from figures high and low. For those who would change the law, the procedural requirements are formidable. The link between Crown and Church appears in eight acts that would need to be amended or repealed by the British Parliament as well as in the laws of fifteen other countries that are independent monarchies within the Commonwealth. Conflicting feelings about the role of religion in a modern state, plus the lively sectarian conflict still seething in Northern Ireland as well as the long road to enactment, seemed reasons enough to avoid moving the proposal to the point of a serious discussion by policymakers.[11]

Is There No Limit to Government's Reach?

Some items reach the public agenda as a result of a rule announced by an administrative agency under its existing authority. The matter becomes political if those affected raise their voice in opposition and attract the attention of ranking executives and legislators.

The U.S. Occupational Safety and Health Administration (OSHA) ruled that companies are responsible for the conditions of employees who prefer to do their work at home. Opponents asked if the government's concern to eliminate unsafe conditions associated with sweatshop-like conditions in contracted sewing and other industrial work extends to telecommuters who do their work on home computers. OSHA responded that high-tech does not mean safe. A consultant concerned with telecommuting described one worker who used a wooden plank stretched across two file cabinets of differing heights as a base for his personal computer. Other workers were so surrounded by piles of paper and books that it would be difficult to evacuate quickly if a fire broke out. Many were overloading the electrical circuits of older homes or were working in confined areas with no ventilation.

OSHA officials did not clarify their intentions to the satisfaction of worriers. On the one hand, they said that when an employee works at home, "the employer is responsible for correcting hazards of which it is aware, or should be aware." On the other hand, OSHA officials indicated that they had no intention of conducting inspections at private homes the way they do at employer work sites. And they would not require employers to routinely inspect the home work sites of their employees.[12]

These reservations were not enough for organizations of employers, employees interested in telecommuting, or the White House and OSHA's bosses in the Labor Department. Only a few days after OSHA's policy became widely known, a White House official expressed "surprise and shock." Although the policy had been developed as part of a two-year process, the Labor Secretary claimed to have been uninformed and ordered it withdrawn.[13] Less than a month later, OSHA clarified its policy to exclude concern with home offices. It would, however, continue to hold companies liable for hazardous manufacturing that workers perform at home.[14]

The Fate of a Little Boy

"Feeding frenzy," a metaphor based on the behavior of sharks competing for pieces of blood-soaked food, typifies the intensity with which some issues rise to the top of the political agenda. Politicians seeking a piece of the action for themselves may treat their subject with no more respect than sharks treat the creature that supplies their meal.

One case seems to have had no lasting impact on public policy. However, it jammed the agenda for several weeks and may have dimmed the publicity opportunities of other issues. It illustrates how an issue may rivet the attention of politicians and the public but in the end serve more as public fascination than an influence on policy change. A photogenic six-year-old boy was rescued from a doomed boat escape from Cuba that killed his mother. Family members and politicians from both the United States and Cuba competed for Elian Gonzales. Members of religious sects argued whether the boy's miraculous survival from the sea—according to one story guarded from sharks by dolphins until he was rescued—signaled his status as divine and perhaps a portent of the fall of Castro's regime.[15] One U.S. senator claiming that the boy did not want to return to Cuba and had pleaded with him to prevent his return, together with a member of the House of Representatives, subpoenaed the boy to testify before Congress in order to foil efforts by the Immigration and Naturalization Service (INS) to return the boy to his father in Cuba.[16]

The plight of the Cuban child was to be torn between different wings of his family, each encouraged by political supporters in countries with a history of antagonism and perhaps too by media personalities anxious to keep a story alive. Several months into the dispute, some commentators worried about the long-term effects on the boy himself, no matter how the case would be resolved. Yet that hardly seemed to limit the intensity of family members on either side, personnel in the INS and federal and state courts, or elected officials who added their comments. The child's Cuban father had the support of the Justice Department. Department officials claimed that the law clearly granted priority to a biological parent, unless proved unfit. Presidential front-runners George W. Bush and Al Gore sided with those who wanted to keep the boy in Florida. *New York Times* legal commentator Anthony Lewis asked if we were going to be governed by law or the mob.[17] A newspaper survey of opinion in South Florida found sentiment sharply divided by race and ethnicity. Eighty-three percent of Miami-Dade County Cuban Americans supported keeping the boy in the United States, but 92 percent of African Americans and 72 percent of non-Hispanic whites supported his return to Cuba. In response to Gore's announcement of support for keeping him in Florida, a New York Democratic member of the House of Representatives, Jose E. Serrano, asked rhetorically, "Where are your family values? Don't you believe this small child should be with the father who loves him?" The Democrats' Senate minority leader Tom Daschle questioned the politicization of a family tragedy: "This is as despicable a situation as I've seen in a long, long time. Analysis of the choices facing local politicians found them being dragged into expressing themselves by the weight of 743,000 Cuban-Americans in a total county population of 2.1 million."[18]

Meanwhile, other activists cited the inequities suffered by some 10,000 Haitian immigrants whose illegal stays in the United States had produced 3,000 children who were American citizens. They did not enjoy the benefits of media hoopla. Differences in the treatment of illegal arrivals from Cuba and Haiti—having to do with Cuba's status as a Communist country while Haiti was governed by a no less miserable but non-Communist regime—worked to the disadvantage of the Haitians. As a result, Haitian parents facing deportation pondered the option of leaving their American-born children in the care of public authorities in the United States.[19]

Officials eventually took the boy into custody. This also proved controversial. Harvard law professor Laurence H. Tribe cited the attorney general for procedural faults:

> Ms. Reno's decision to take the law as well as the child into her own hands seems worse than a political blunder. Even if well intended, her decision strikes at the heart of constitutional government and shakes the safeguards of liberty.[20]

Columnist Thomas L. Friedman applauded the triumph of law over passion. He saw a highly publicized picture of a U.S. marshal demanding the boy while pointing an automatic weapon at the person holding him as illustrating "what happens to those who defy the rule of law and how far our government and people will go to preserve it." In a more general comment about those who had demanded keeping the boy from his father, Friedman wrote, "One only hopes that this affair will remind the extremists among the Miami Cubans that they are not living in their own private country, that they cannot do whatever they please and that they may hate Fidel Castro more than they love the U.S. Constitution— but that doesn't apply to the rest of us."[21] Elian disappeared from the U.S. agenda when federal courts ruled in favor of returning him to Cuba with his father, and his Miami family exhausted their legal appeals.

Why Policies Are, or Are Not, Implemented as Policymakers Expect

If winning a place on the agenda is a problem at an early stage in the policy process, achieving implementation is a problem at one of the last stages. To be *implemented* means to be administered, with actions actually delivered to target populations. Since Jeffrey Pressman and Aaron Wildavsky published a book entitled *Implementation* in 1973, the term has come to define an important topic among political scientists interested in public policy.[22] The main activity of the field is to focus on policies or programs that are *not implemented* as the researchers expect and to explain this lack of activity.

The general picture available in the literature about implementation runs parallel to John Kingdon's conclusions about the policy agenda. Researchers have succeeded in listing a variety of elements capable of affecting the nature of a policy's implementation. However, they fall short of weighing the importance of the elements or predicting the character of implementation to be expected in the case of particular policies.

One representative summary of the implementation research, by Daniel A. Mazmanian and Paul A. Sabatier, offers a flow diagram with eighteen components capable of contributing to implementation success.[23] In Jewish culture, the letters representing the number eighteen make up the word for *life,* thereby turning the number into a symbol of good luck. Not so in social science. Eighteen elements necessary assessing the implementation of a policy is too many, especially insofar as they are not precisely defined. Some of the elements themselves appear to be highly complex clusters in need of assessment. The list of eighteen appears in Table 2.1.

As a way of dealing with all the elements that might affect implementation, Mazmanian and Sabatier boil down the eighteen components

Table 2.1   Elements Likely to Affect Policy Implementation

1. Diversity of target group behavior
2. Technical difficulties
3. Behavioral change required
4. Percent of population in target groups
5. Socioeconomic conditions and technology
6. Attitudes and resources of constituency groups
7. Public support
8. Support for statute from sovereigns
9. Commitment and leadership of agency officials
10. Consistent objectives, causal theory, decision rules, and recruitment
11. Final resources
12. Formal access and evaluation by outsiders
13. Hierarchical integration: veto points and sanctions
14. Policy outputs of implementing agencies
15. Compliance of target groups
16. Actual impacts
17. Perceived impacts of sovereigns and constituency groups
18. Changes in statute

capable of influencing implementation to six conditions necessary for effective implementation:

1. Clear and consistent objectives
2. Sound theory concerned with the causal linkages relevant to the policy issue, together with sufficient jurisdiction with respect to the target population
3. Assignment of tasks to agencies that are sympathetic with respect to policy goals, together with sufficient financial resources and legal authority
4. Adequate managerial skills in the hands of responsible agencies
5. Support by constituency groups
6. Public support that continues over the process of implementation

The researchers concede that as a matter of course, "all six conditions are very unlikely to be attained during the initial implementation period for any program seeking substantial behavior change."[24] In other words, the implementation of a program that is radically new or controversial is likely to entail a struggle. Issues embroiled in controversy, those that lost the fight at the stage of policymaking in the legislative, executive, or judicial branches, are likely to remain intense and active in blocking whatever is yet to be done in terms of funding, recruiting program directors, finishing the enactment of rules and regulations, or persuading clients to take advantage of the program and comply with its requirements.

Issues recently on the agenda illustrate a number of general features that complicate policy implementation and frustrate the hopes of those who want results. They display opposing interests; problems of coordination among different units of government; problems in deciding what individuals want, who is in charge, and what to expect from officials. The devil is in the details, but the details are not necessary to someone already tuned to the argument. Readers convinced about the problems of program implementation can skip the episodes that follow.

Opposing Interests

Lack of support by constituency groups was important in frustrating the Clinton administration's "don't ask, don't tell" policy with respect to gays in the military. The policy forbid the military to ask personnel about their sexual orientation but allowed members' dismissal if they volunteered that they were gay or identified openly as gays. Gay advocacy groups reported that the policy had led to an increase in discharges of gay service members and an increase in complaints of harassment. Gays could not tolerate the silence about their sexual preference and military personnel could not prevent the harassment of personnel thought to be gay.[25] Newspaper reports indicated that ranking officials in the armed services remained convinced that gays would threaten the operation of military units. They prevented equal opportunity advisers from dealing with homosexual issues, and they put minimum effort behind training programs to limit harassment of personnel suspected of being gay.[26] A survey conducted by the Pentagon found 80 percent of service members questioned had heard antigay remarks during the past year; 33 percent said that they heard these comments often or very often. A legal defense organization reported that 1,034 gay men and women had been discharged from the military and claimed this number reflected the failure of the "don't ask, don't tell" policy.[27] For those skeptical about the policy's value, these 1,034 cases illustrate its lack of implementation.

Individuals or firms may simply ignore a law or comply in a limited way that manages to evade the spirit of the policy. A report by the General Accounting Office indicates that 14 percent of surveyed employers were not complying with a law requiring health insurance parity for the coverage of mental and physical illness. Some firms complied with the letter of the law—by not imposing different dollar limits on mental health treatments and physical health treatments—but violated the spirit of the law by setting different limits on the number of office visits or days of hospitalization for mental care.[28] However, the charge of avoiding the "spirit" of a policy is too easy. Who can be sure of the spirit of a policy? To define the spirit requires interpreting endless discourse on policy over an extended period prior to enactment.

Metropolitan areas are rich with illustrations about the problems of program implementation. Historically, cities have been the centers of economic activity. Heterogeneity is their hallmark. They have rich and poor, people concerned about the environment, and those who want to earn as much money as possible, as well as numerous ethnic groups, religions, occupations, and political perspectives. It is only natural that what some want, others oppose.

In several locales the issue of metropolitan growth presents sharply drawn examples of conflicting interests that get in the way of both policymaking and implementation. On the side of unregulated expansion are real estate developers plus individuals who want the benefits of a large lot in the suburbs, the convenience of driving to work, shopping, and recreation. Arrayed against them are the prospects of more traffic congestion and air pollution that will spoil the advantages of a suburban lifestyle.

Atlanta illustrates the problems as much as any U.S. metropolis. Set in the core of the free-enterprise South, this highly developed area has grown mostly by expansion into the undeveloped hinterland. Suburban authorities enjoy the taxes paid by new malls and office blocs that multiply the problems of traffic congestion and air pollution. In a recent twelve-month period, Atlanta suburbs grew by 94,000 residents while the central city grew by 900. Relieving traffic congestion depends on more roads. Because of high smog and ozone levels, however, the U.S. Environmental Protection Agency (EPA) has threatened to ban federal money for additional highway construction. One business leader called the federal action a "train wreck" for the region. An academic, meanwhile, made a pessimistic summation of Atlanta's policy problem: "This is a democratic, free society with a lot of wealth, which translates to private mobility. Short of extremely draconian measures which no one wants to take, there's almost nothing that will materially affect traffic congestion."[29] Without the draconian measures (that is, those not likely to be enacted), no program to deal with traffic congestion is likely to effective.

Opposing interests with implications for policymaking and implementation are most clear in the realm of foreign policy. The intensity of opposing economic and ethnic interests is greater internationally than domestically. The rule of law is less firmly institutionalized, and armed conflict more likely. Moshe Arens, a former Israeli defense minister, is fond of the epigram "The Middle East is not the Middle West." By this he means that Americans are inclined to think that conflict resolution is simply a matter of trading concessions. That may work where most people share the same language and other cultural traits—and where the most recent civil war occurred 140 years ago. It is less relevant where ethnic hatreds prevail and national armies have fought during the present generation.

A review of UN peacekeeping is Bosnia five years after the signing of an accord between Muslim, Croat, and Serb factions indicated that international efforts to pacify the area were only superficially successful, if even that. On hand were 30,000 troops from thirty-seven countries, financed by aid from international sources worth more than U.S.$4 billion. The population remained polarized between ethnic and religious factions, mostly separated into enclaves. Families seeking to return to an enclave dominated by another group had trouble receiving municipal services. There remained three ethnic police forces and numerous secret police organizations controlled by rival ethnic political parties. Criminal gangs influenced local administration. Ethnic party patronage governed the allocation of jobs, land, and apartments and was likely to determine the outcome of cases that sought resolution in court but found themselves before a judge beholden to one ethnic group or another.[30] This case suggests that deep-seated ethnic and religious antagonisms can thwart the operation of arrangements that might work in more placid settings.

The Weight of Intergovernmental Relations

Governmental bodies are not neutral players in policymaking. They reflect the interests of groups that dominate policymaking forums. Moreover, each body has traditions that can influence those coming to office.

The dispute involving Atlanta, its suburbs, and the U.S. EPA illustrates the complications that intergovernmental relations add to policy implementation in the United States. Federal, state, or local policies are likely to come up against the laws, rules, or preferences of some other level of government. It is not unusual for governmental frictions to complement political rivalries. For instance, the U.S. secretary of housing and urban development during the Clinton administration, Andrew M.

Cuomo, supported Hillary Clinton in her pursuit of a Senate seat from New York. Initially, her principal rival was the Republican mayor of New York, Rudolph W. Giuliani. When Cuomo ruled against one of New York City's programs for the homeless, a shouting match began between Giuliani and Cuomo as to who was using a public program to advance a partisan agenda.[31] Often politicians who find themselves the heads of national, state, or local entities use their formal authority to embarrass competitors in the political game.

Another feature of U.S. federalism appears when policymakers or observers seek to figure out just what works and why. State-to-state variations occur not only in laws but also in the quality of program implementation and the characteristics of program clients. In general, well-to-do states offer more generous programs than poorer states. But there are counterexamples of rich states where individual programs are not well conceived or administered as well as rich states whose policymakers put the premium on keeping taxes low rather than providing generous services. Some poor states have been leaders in the development of certain programs. The success of even the most attractive examples may be difficult to disentangle from economic or social conditions that may make them workable in one situation but not in others, as we see below in the case of a Wisconsin welfare program.

Too Many Demands from Above and Below

The problems of implementing transportation policies in the Atlanta metropolitan area reflect a more general problem of local government officials. They are at the bottom of a pyramid whose height is in Washington and whose middle level sits in the state capital. Local officials must live with the program requirements and financial constraints that come from above. And they must somehow reconcile these pressures from above with what is likely to be a lot of noisy demands from even further down: local government employee organizations and citizen groups that reflect the range of social, economic, and ideological clusters likely to be found in metropolitan areas.

New York City's problems in retaining a head for its school system illustrate an extreme case of too many demands from above and below. There have been eleven school chancellors in twenty years. In a number of other large cities, the retention problem is almost as severe with school heads averaging only two and one-half years on the job. The turnover has prompted New York critics to conclude that the head school job is impossible. Not only are the responsibilities awesome (1.1 million students, 1,100 schools, 75,000 teachers, and close to 3,700 central office personnel) but the chancellor is dependent on too many bosses. Those with power over New York City schools include the state legislature; the mayor; and borough heads who appoint the board of education, which hires and fires the chancellor, as well as thirty-two separate elected school boards that possess some control over elementary and middle schools. All this is in a city that may be the nation's most heterogeneous and politically demanding, with sophisticated advocates pursuing demands on behalf of racial, ethnic, and religious groups; gays and lesbians; AIDS victims; the homeless; environmental quality; culture; and fashion.[32] *Complexity* barely covers the range of contrary pressures found in such cases—among frustrated officials, high turnover in administrative positions, clients who complain that they are not getting what they want, and observers who record flaws in policy implementation.

The Power of Inaction

At times officials intend no implementation. Administrators use what they claim as their discretion not to implement rules that they consider problematic. We do not know the frequency of inaction that passes unnoticed in the innards of government bureaucracies. One example that has come to light is the lack of action by the Food and Drug Administration (FDA) against the technically illegal recycling of "single use" medical devices. Medical personnel claim that they can save considerable sums by purchasing used and recycled devices without endangering their clients, while the manufacturers of the single use devices chafe at the loss of business and claim that the practice is unsafe.[33]

The Immigration and Naturalization Service can be assiduous in patrolling the Mexican border against incursions, raiding workplaces in search of illegal immigrants, and incarcerating and deporting individuals with a minimum of procedural rights. When the economy is booming and employers need workers, however, the agency can be tolerant of illegal immigrants. During a period of labor shortage, sweeps and arrests of illegal immigrants at workplaces dropped sharply: from 22,000 in 1997 to 8,600 in 1999.[34]

Israel's minister of commerce and industry, Natan Sharansky, explained on a radio talk show why he was not enforcing the measure that required handicapped access to all workplaces that employ more than a minimum number of people. To him, the provision would cause the closure of numerous small establishments and cause more harm to the national economy than benefits to the handicapped.

The willingness of the FDA, the INS, and the Israeli Ministry of Commerce and Industry to skimp on the application of rules points to officials' use of discretion (whether written into the laws or not) and the weighing of benefits against costs. They may be more willing than ordinary citizens to take some risks, on the assumption that absolute safety is elusive and may be very costly. The outlays necessary for an absolutely clean environment, for example, include equipment to assure the cleanliness of air and water as well as unemployment caused when marginal industries choose to close rather than to comply. One line of research finds that citizens are likely to demand complete safety, unless their own jobs are threatened. They seem willing to exchange complete safety for a looser measure of protection that minimizes the prospect of unemployment.[35]

Some failures to implement policy reflect nothing so sophisticated as weighing benefits and costs. Poor training, overwork, and sheer laziness cause some assignments to fall by the wayside. Inquiries about the proper filing of court orders in the region around Washington, D.C., found lags of more than three months between the proclamation of restraining orders against abusive spouses and others accused of violent actions and the entry of the information into computer records meant to keep those people from buying guns. The explanation of one unit responsible for entering the information was that the state government's computers were slow and cumbersome: It took forty-five minutes to enter one report.[36]

In another case from the Washington area, more than one-third of District of Columbia police vehicles had expired registrations, and a substantial number had skipped required vehicle inspections.[37] British railroads have their own problems of overlooked regulations. One month after thirty-one people died in a rail accident on the outskirts of London when a train ran through a red light, an inquiry revealed that seventy-six trains per month were running through red lights.[38]

Now developments in international Internet commerce are foiling governments' aims to implement their policies. Germans wanting to evade their own government's prohibition against the distribution of Hitler's *Mein Kampf* have bought it from Amazon.com. According to Amazon, *Mein Kampf* was among the company's top-ten best-sellers in Germany during the summer of 1999.[39]

Even the most dense sets of controls can fail to prevent problems. Medical researchers face a number of checkpoints designed to prevent frivolous or dangerous experiments. They must obtain funds for their research and recruit colleagues or skilled assistants. If they work in a university, they face committees that must approve applications to use animal and human subjects. Corporate and hospital labs have procedures to limit danger to patients and the mistreatment of animals. Government bureaucracies have their own demanding procedures, typically requiring detailed explanations of the risks and benefits of a proposed activity, that are presented to committees of government officials and outside advisers that decide on financial grants to support research. The very multiplicity of approvals is meant to prevent conflicts of interest and easy approvals given on account of personal or financial relationships.

A team at the prestigious University of Pennsylvania employed an experimental gene therapy that seemed to cause a fatal reaction in a patient whose disease was being controlled by more conventional treatment and whose case did not seem to justify the use of a risky procedure. Inquiries into the chain of events leading up to the patient's death found the following failures in the implementation of policies designed to assure medical safety:

• Substantial incentives by a pharmaceutical company to promote aggressively the research on human subjects, despite signs of problems with animals subject to similar therapy.

• Researchers with multiple involvements in the results of their own research, including financial connections with companies paying for the research and standing to profit from products being investigated. Universities vary in the extent to which they allow staff scientists to be involved in research associated with companies that the scientists own in whole or in part and whether they allow physicians who conduct the research to recruit patients to participate as subjects. FDA approval in the University of Pennsylvania case was influenced by what was called the "stellar reputation" of the chief investigator. However, that researcher also had a substantial personal financial stake in the outcome.

• The research team also broke its assurance to the committee of the National Institutes of Health (NIH) that researchers would recruit participants only through physicians.[40] Volunteers were recruited in ways that federal officials had explicitly precluded as being too coercive, with direct appeals on a website that heralded "promising" early results from the clinical trial and said the experiment used "very low doses" of the medication being tested when in fact the doses were relatively high.

• The original consent form, reviewed by the NIH, clearly notified prospective participants that monkeys had died from a related treatment, but the final version given to patients eliminated any mention of the deaths.

• Researchers did not inform government authorities of all the serious reactions encountered by patients involved in the experiment.[41] One report noted that only 39 out of 691 serious side effects experienced by patients had been reported immediately to the NIH, as required.[42]

In January 2000, the FDA halted gene therapy experiments at the University of Pennsylvania's Institute for Human Gene Therapy after finding numerous violations of federal research regulations and failures to protect human subjects.[43] In later actions, the FDA tightened existing regulations concerned with patient safety.[44]

An article in the *Journal of the American Medical Association* summarized research about physicians who do not implement the programs of Health Maintenance Organizations (HMOs). Among the concerns were physicians who do not follow guidelines requiring them to counsel the smokers among their patients. The reasons for noncompliance included the physicians' lack of awareness about the guidelines, their lack of agreement with them, their feeling that antismoking efforts are not likely to succeed, and their feeling that they were not effective counselors in such matters.[45]

The findings about physicians square with other research about the compliance of individuals with the orders issued by their organizations. Individuals can be overloaded with too many orders, instructions, and guidelines. When questioned, the bosses can say that "we told them" or "we sent them a memo," but individual instructions must compete with other messages and other responsibilities. Employees may decide that they can only do so much. They may not notice particular instructions, or they may forget about them in the presence of many other memos. They may decide to prioritize their instructions, with the result that they seldom if ever comply with certain demands. Training programs for new employees and in-service courses for continuing employees express the need of organizations to invest in the education of their employees rather than simply issue them instructions. A classic study of leadership exercised by the U.S. president concludes that issuing orders is not sufficient.[46] Executives must take account of their subordinates' interests. Bosses may have to formulate their instructions in order to attract compliance and may have to persuade their subordinates to go along.

Against the background of numerous cases of failed implementation, officials encounter problems of public trust even when they give repeated assurances about having done their job properly. A prominent example concerned the Y2K problem, the predicted crash of computers and the services governed by them on account of misreading the date of the new millennium. In order to demonstrate that his agency had done its job of countering the Y2K problem, the head of the Federal Aviation Administration promised to be in the air at midnight on December 31. However, so many other potential passengers were refusing to fly that he had trouble keeping his promise. A number of airlines canceled many if not all of their flights. American Airlines canceled about 20 percent of its flights over the New Year, United Airlines about 22 percent, Virgin Atlantic all of its flights, and Frontier Airlines 36 percent of those scheduled for December 31, including all of those operating after 9 P.M. and 19 percent of those scheduled for January 1.[47] Israel closed its international airport during the hours before and after midnight on December 31 when it became apparent that airlines had canceled all scheduled arrivals and departures.

Who Is Responsible? Bureaucracy and Politics

From a cynical perspective, government is not likely to implement programs smoothly without a great deal of seeking after self-interest by individuals and organizations. It boils down to bureaucracy and politics.

Both "bureaucracy" and "politics" are epithets as well as nouns. Like other slogans, their meaning varies. "Bureaucracy" can refer to the large size of government organizations, which to some observers only causes waste. It can mean a hierarchy where superiors direct and supervise subordinates. The meaning that is relevant to this discussion involves convoluted procedures that can tie up a decision until numerous officials in separate organizations agree to cooperate. Delays in agreeing about rules and procedures are frequent causes of nonimplementation.

"Politics" is closely related to "bureaucracy." Used as a curse, "politics" can mean self-serving individuals who put their own interests above the common good. A political scientist might insist that "bureaucracy" should refer to the failures of appointed officials while "politics" involves elected officials. We must also assert that many bureaucrats and politicians provide commendable service and that civilized governance would be impossible without them. It is true, however, that politicians and bureaucrats do not always score high on professional competence or moral purity.

At times elected and appointed officials seem to conspire against the rest of us. A report about the failure of administrators to increase achievement in their schools faulted the unions for protecting lazy and incompetent teachers as well as local politicians who served as the patrons of individual administrators. Yet there also was a bit of sloppiness on the part of those who identified others for dismissal. When the head of one school system fired a district superintendent because of poor student performance, one of the justifications was a decline in reading scores in his area of 1.2 percent. A later inquiry found a problem in the tests, and it turned out that scores had risen by 2.9 percent.[48]

A lack of program implementation may also reflect a lack of sufficient pressure on bureaucrats or politicians. New York State used to have an oil industry. Production peaked in 1882. Now the few remaining wells produce an average of one quarter of a barrel per day. More prominent than the oil being produced for sale is the seepage pollution from wells abandoned by their owners years ago. More oil fouls the water wells of homeowners than makes it to market. Nearby residents find their water contaminated and their air smelly. Apparently the problem is too small for state politicians or bureaucrats to bother with. Without an industry or a problem prominent enough to generate serious governmental responsibility for cleanup or protection, those who suffer from pollution must bear the costs by themselves.[49]

Can a Bureaucracy Police Itself?

Bureaucracies are essential to implementation, but their workings are not always consistent with expectations. Employees operate with a narrow view of their responsibilities. It keeps them from conflict with fellow employees. Being a "whistle-blower" can be costly. Even though a number of governments have laws meant to protect individuals who report wrongdoing in their organizations, it may be difficult to enforce those protections in a situation where other employees feel that the whistle-blower broke an informal code of silence.

A subset of the problems that hinder self-policing involves the latitude given to high-ranking personnel. While the little person may feel the full weight of law and discipline, the elite may benefit from personal relationships with ranking politicians, key figures in business, and individuals prominent in society. An English proverb is that the person who steals a goose from the common is hanged as a thief, while the person who steals the common from under the goose becomes an aristocrat. An Israeli saying is that it is easy—and common—to blame a military snafu on the lowest ranking soldiers who may be the guards at the gate, while overlooking problems among ranking officers who designed the operation.

The former head of the CIA violated security regulations by using an insecure home computer to work on classified documents. The response was forgiving in the extreme. Agency heads discouraged underlings from processing formal complaints about the actions and reached an accommodation with the former director that involved his apology and the denial of a subsequent security clearance and consulting opportunities. At about the same time, a middle-ranking employee of another agency involved in national security, the Los Alamos nuclear laboratory, was jailed without bail for downloading classified material to his personal computer. At least part of the time in custody, he was kept in solitary confinement and shackles due to claims that he was an extraordinary threat to national security. Among the reasons for a delayed onset of a trial for this poor fellow was the inability of prosecutors to come up with evidence linking him to espionage.[50] According to a *New York Times* review of the case eight months into the man's confinement, the lead FBI agent in the case admitted that he provided incorrect testimony in hearings concerned with the possibility of granting bail.[51] Ultimately the government agreed to a plea bargain that let the scientist off with time already served. The *New York Times* chastised itself: "we too quickly accepted the government's theory that espionage was the main reason for Chinese nuclear advances and its view that Dr. Lee had been properly singled out as the prime suspect."[52]

Are the Courts and Prosecutors Reliable?

Among the most sensitive questions concerning the implementation of public policy concerns the enforcement of criminal statutes. Police and prosecutors have been found guilty of pressuring the accused or witnesses improperly and even manufacturing evidence to strengthen their assertions about a person's guilt. High rates of conviction or incarceration do not mean that criminal statutes are being implemented if the wrong people are in jail.

A scandal wracking the Los Angeles Police Department found at least ninety-nine individuals framed by rogue officers planting drugs or guns on them. More than thirty criminal convictions were overturned and twenty officers quit or were dismissed or suspended. The police chief estimated that settling lawsuits from aggrieved citizens could amount to $125 million.[53]

The most serious cases of these kinds involve the death penalty. If authorities err in other cases, the government can compensate the wrongly accused for time spent in prison. The action cannot make up for lost years and a ruined life, but it is more than can be provided to a person wrongly put to death. Illinois's governor announced in February 2000 that he would suspend the application of the death penalty in his state, pending inquiries into the cases of thirteen individuals sentenced to death since capital punishment was reinstated in 1977 who were subsequently cleared of murder charges. In the same period, Illinois carried out death sentences against twelve individuals. The governor hoped that those already executed truly were guilty as charged.[54]

Is the Law Too Strict?

Authorities must be convinced that a law is reasonable for them to implement it aggressively. Traffic officers are well known to allow drivers to go somewhat over the speed limit. The police are often too tolerant in the face of domestic violence, as becomes apparent when individuals with a history of complaints against them go beyond past behavior to spousal murder.

A study of Israeli city mayors accused of corruption found a high incidence of not-guilty verdicts or light sentences. An interview with one judge brought forth an explanation. The judge perceived that the mayor's job is nearly impossible. Laws enacted by the national government require local authorities to provide extensive services without the needed resources. Heads of national ministries have put more pressure on the local officials to implement programs but have not been forthcoming with grants of money. Local residents also want social services from the municipality as well as special favors. Well-to-do individuals and business firms are willing to contribute to the campaigns of local officials, or to the upkeep of municipal projects, in exchange for favors. Contractors want approval of their projects by municipal authorities, and other businesses need licenses to operate. The demands of reformers for squeaky clean government do not square with the realities of city hall. Mayors may evade or flaunt legal provisions against taking financial contributions but do so in a setting that earns the forgiveness of judges.[55]

Who Is Speaking?

Interest groups involve themselves in all stages of policymaking and implementation. They represent legitimate avenues of influence, informing policymakers and administrators about the views of citizens, professional organizations, corporations, state and local authorities, and foreign governments. Interest groups and their tactics have long been topics of political science research as well as the targets of reformers concerned that government be transparent or that citizens know who is behind campaigns in favor of or against policy proposals, candidates for public office, or efforts to shape how policy will be implemented.[56]

One tactic of interest groups is to claim a great deal of public support, but skeptics have learned to look behind the rhetoric. A group calling itself Citizens for Better Medicare describes itself as a coalition of "patients, seniors, pharmaceutical research companies, doctors, caregivers, hospitals, employers and health care experts." Critics of the group say that it does not represent citizens and is not concerned with better Medicare but is actually an alliance of drug companies set up under a legal provision that exempts it from conventional disclosure requirements. During the Clinton administration, congressional Democrats claimed that the group was concerned primarily with killing the president's proposal to expand Medicare drug benefits while offering a vague compromise plan that had little support in Congress.[57]

What Do the Statistics Mean?

Judging implementation requires agreement on what is happening. However, some indications of program activity raise more questions than clear answers. Among the problems that get in the way of smooth implementation is confusion over information.

The enforcement of laws designed to protect women from domestic battering are turning up a considerable number of women as the batterers. In Concord, New Hampshire, during the first ten months of 1999, nearly 35 percent of domestic assault arrests were of women, up from 23 percent in 1993. In Vermont, 23 percent of domestic assault arrests were of women, compared with 16 percent in 1997. In Boulder County, Colorado, one-quarter of defendants charged in domestic violence cases through September 1999 were women. A survey by the organization National Violence Against Women estimated that 1.5 million women and 835,000 men were raped or assaulted by an intimate partner in 1998, a ratio of roughly two male offenders to one female offender.

What does this mean? Researchers offer several explanations for the findings, none of which is conclusive. Perhaps police officers who enter a scene of enraged and disheveled spouses shouting that each has beaten the other arrest both and let someone else sort out the accusations. The result is one woman and one man entered into the statistics as arrested for violence. Some cases involve a woman beating another woman, perhaps a daughter beating her mother, or a lesbian beating her lover. Another scenario of unknown frequency is a women who had been a victim in the past and turned the tables on her abuser. Another possibility results from the perspective of the police officer, often a man: The officer decides to even the score by arresting the female who looks as if she gave as well as received abuse. And finally is the possibility that some women are more violent and perhaps stronger than their spouses.[58]

Are crime rates in the United States increasing or decreasing? It depends on the period chosen for analysis. The most recent period, from 1993, does show a decline, but the longer period from 1969 shows that violent crime in major cities reported to the FBI has risen by 40 percent. And there remains the outstanding character of the United States with respect to crime and firearms. In 1995, handguns were used to kill 2 people in New Zealand, 15 in Japan, 30 in Great Britain, 106 in Canada, 213 in Germany, and 9,390 in the United States.[59]

"Why something is happening" is just as important in understanding implementation as "what is happening." Controversies about New York City's tough policing practices—and claims about police influence on declining crime rates—illustrate the issue. The argument occurs against the background of claims that aggressive policing has violated the civil rights of minority communities and has produced legalized killings of suspects thought, incorrectly, to be carrying weapons.

Falling crime rates have coincided with tough policing in New York. However, crime rates have fallen even more in Boston and San Diego, where the police have pursued less aggressive tactics, and they have fallen almost as much in San Antonio, Houston, Los Angeles, and Dallas. These cities have not followed a coherent policing strategy.

In these cases, the "why" of reduced crime remains unresolved. Falling crime rates may reflect changing norms or the age profiles of populations (an aging population generally produces lower crime rates) rather than anything associated with one way of policing or another.[60]

Researchers who examine crime statistics have found cases where police departments lie in their reports to higher authorities. Some exaggerate the incidence of crime, perhaps to enhance their arguments on behalf of hiring more personnel. Some report less crime than actually occurs, in order to create the image of a peaceful locality that is a nice place to visit and shop.

Problematic statistics also occur in education. High test scores may not mean success in the implementation of educational programs. In order to boost the statistics showing the success of their pupils, some teachers and school principals cheat. They provide students with advance copies of the questions to be asked on examinations used to rank their schools and allow students to correct wrong answers.[61] The principal of a primary school in Maryland resigned when confronted with evidence that she and her teachers had intervened in state examinations used to assess school performance. Teachers had pointed to incorrect answers and advised, "You might want to look at this one again." The principal herself had asked pupils to change answers after the testing period was over.[62]

Ranking education bureaucrats and politicians have also claimed success on the basis of test scores that are ambiguous. Texas education personnel and Governor George W. Bush touted increasing scores in statewide examinations of reading and math, but researchers from the Rand Corporation and other skeptics noted differential results depending on the test used. They also found teachers pressured to spend inordinate time preparing pupils for the state-sponsored test and to excuse retarded and poor students from the test—which resulted in elevating the statewide scores. Critics also found some cases of actual score tampering in order to produce more attractive results.[63]

Corruption

Corruption appears in numerous ways, at levels high and low in the public sector. It involves police officers who beat individuals until they confess to crimes they did not commit; officials who accept money in exchange for favorable decisions; those who discriminate in favor of or against clients according to race, sex, ethnicity, or religion; and clerks who misreport events for the purpose of producing favorable statistics. Corruption means impurity, distortion, something rotten or spoiled. In whatever form it exists, it lessens the quality of policy implementation. Yet "corruption" is not something that may be clear to all who examine an action. Identifying corruption depends on the observer's perspective. Culture matters more than formal law. What is widely viewed as corrupt in one place or at one time may be accepted as conventional elsewhere.

Corruption is not only a matter for the public sector. Among the problems of program implementation are the struggles between government and business over what constitutes acceptable practice. Business firms have fudged the truth with statistics made to seem authoritative. Researchers have found systematic errors in company claims of profits and losses as well as in the official reports made to regulatory authorities.

Official reports come after unofficial press releases or executive comments. The unofficial reports are likely to influence the price of company shares on the stock exchange. Exaggerating profits or trimming losses may not be illegal if corrected in the official reports. Investors are more likely to read early newspaper reports about what the company claims than the official documents that appear later. When business executives claim to have made innocent errors in their unofficial comments, skeptics see lies. Yet some say it is appropriate to "push the envelope" of what is legal in order to obtain an advantage in highly competitive markets.[64]

The Federal Trade Commission brought a case against a popular brand of foods whose label said that consumers could get 75 cents off their next purchase. The coupon printed on the inside of the label, which was hidden to shoppers, required the purchase of at least five cans in order to qualify for the 75 cents.[65]

Hear No Evil, See No Evil

Policymakers have reacted to the prospect of bad news about program administration by forbidding its publication. Citizens cannot judge policy implementation if they cannot acquire accurate information. Censorship is an old craft, practiced by modern democracies as well as authoritarian regimes. Several governments have failed to report—or even survey—the incidence of AIDS in order to avoid frightening potential tourists. Water utilities may be lax in reporting indicators of poor quality in the hope of avoiding panic. The U.S. House of Representatives voted to forbid the EPA from identifying areas with high smog levels, seemingly to prevent the enforcement of new clean air rules that might work against local industries. The effort at censorship was largely the work of the Republican majority, but also had the support of fifty-eight Democrats. According to one critic of the majority, "They are certainly targeting the EPA's ability to do their job, which is protecting the environment and the public health. . . . Now, they're even trying to limit the EPA's ability to even know the nature and dimensions of the problem." According to a Republican who voted against his party, "The idea here is dirty air doesn't exist if it isn't officially recognized."[66]

Economic and Social Measurements: What Is IT?

Policymakers as well as administrators charged with program implementation may flounder in a confused setting where it is not clear what is happening. The U.S. government, like others, collects numerous indicators about economic occurrences, meant to guide policymakers in their efforts to minimize financial crises and unemployment, regulate interest rates, and otherwise smooth out the bumps in the economic road. Among the mysteries that have been prominent in recent years is the weight of information technology (IT) in the economy. Popular wisdom indicates that it is large and growing and central to economic progress in the new millennium. But what is IT? A few bytes from the Internet edition of the *Economist* illustrate the problems involved in measuring the incidence and economic implications of information technology:

> Measuring the size of the "new" economy is a statistical minefield. The most generous estimate comes from the Organization for Economic Cooperation and Development (OECD), which tracks the "knowledge-based economy." It estimates that this accounts for 51% of total business output in the developed economies—up from 45% in 1985. But this definition, which tries to capture all industries that are relatively intensive in their inputs of technology and human capital, is implausibly wide. As well as computers and telecoms, it also includes cars, chemicals, health, education, and so forth. It would be a stretch to call many of these businesses "new."[67]

What Is Equality?

The issue of social and economic equality is something that troubles policymakers and critics in numerous countries, yet it defies clear definition and measurement. Programs in the fields of education and income support are meant to address questions of equality. Arguments about their effectiveness depend on measures of equality and whether the differences between various groups in the society are increasing or lessening over time.

The concept of equality as used by different commentators begins with differences in income and ranges outward to notions of justice and fairness in opportunities for education, occupational status, housing, and health. Experts quarrel about measurements showing differences between upper and lower income groups, the widely used summary indicator (GINI coefficient), national measures of the "poverty line," and separate indicators for income and wealth. Differences between "income" and "wealth" are important with respect to older people, who tend to score low on monthly income but higher on indications of wealth, partly because of homes that have appreciated in value.

It is no simple task to probe deeply into equality in its various forms. This would require valuing the public services received by families at different levels of income; tracing the flow of government payments for welfare and pensions; reckoning how much families in each income class pay for indirect taxes (sales, value added, property, customs duties); taking account of accumulated wealth represented by housing, land, savings accounts, the values of governmental and private pension funds, and other possessions; and considering unreported (underground) income. The problems do not stop with assessing the formal legislation concerned with taxes and services but require an assessment of how different taxes are actually levied and collected and how services are actually distributed. Most research proceeds only part of the way along the chain of increasing precision. Few compilations struggle with the problems of differential policy implementation from one population sector to another, or questions like, What is the value of public education received in a slum school compared to that in an upper-middle-class neighborhood? or What about the uneven assessments of taxes, or the discretionary discounts on taxes provided in cases of hardship?

Israeli politicians and political activists claimed to be dismayed by a report that one-sixth of the population lived below the poverty line, and they pledged to find public resources to help poor families. What they did not emphasize, however, was the large number of religious families that affect the statistics. The commentators who picked up this issue described their poverty as "voluntary." The typical ultra-Orthodox family is large, supported by a mother who works and the modest stipend that the father brings home from his religious academy. He has chosen, with the support of the family and the larger religious community, to devote his life to the study of sacred texts. His earlier education was likely to be exclusively religious and to have prepared him only for a life of continued study. His sons are likely to continue in his footsteps, his daughters in the footsteps of their mother. They will probably each have upwards of five children, carry the burden of being poor and working hard, perhaps expecting better conditions in the world to come.[68] Should they be counted among the poor who are the normal targets of government programs to help the disadvantaged? There is no obvious answer.

The analytical problems involved in measuring equality multiply for those concerned with comparisons across national borders. Those who would judge the implementation of their own country's efforts at reducing poverty should make the comparison. Otherwise, they might be holding up their government to an unreasonable standard, such as reaching levels of equality that surpass what similar countries have been able to achieve. Yet the comparisons are tricky. Countries have non-identical public services, transfer payments, and tax rates and the exclusion of certain incomes and expenditures from taxation. They also have different definitions for reporting economic statistics, different levels of effectiveness in implementing tax policies, and different reputations with respect to the veracity of their official statistics.[69]

Is the Glass Half-Empty or Half-Full?
Perhaps the Program Hasn't Run Long Enough
for the Findings to Be Meaningful

Interpreting program results is essential for judging the quality of implementation. For a complex program with several components and numerous expectations, however, there is likely to be a mixture of positive and negative results. Commentators may be impatient to conclude good or bad, without giving the program long enough to have an influence on clients. Results, attractive or not, may be due to conditions occurring in the economy, not associated with the program itself.

Reviews of Wisconsin's innovative programs to move people from welfare to work have produced judgments that it is kind and cruel, successful and a failure. There has been a lessening of welfare rolls and a movement of people to work. Two years after imposing the nation's toughest work requirements as conditions for receiving welfare, Wisconsin cut its welfare rolls more than 90 percent and put about two-thirds of those once on welfare into a job. While some of this change may be due to the requirements of the program, another portion may reflect the program's good luck of beginning during a period of national prosperity and low unemployment.

On the negative side are indications that basic traits of poverty remain. Newspapers report no end of stories about violent neighborhoods, absent fathers, bare cupboards, pathological behaviors, chronic depression, and drugs. After a year in the workforce, only 36 percent of former recipients had more total income than they had on welfare. Only a quarter lifted themselves above the poverty line. Just 4 percent reached incomes more than 150 percent of the poverty line. According to the author of one University of Wisconsin study, "On average, for the middle family here, in terms of their overall economic well-being, W-2 hasn't had a whopping impact."[70]

A review of Minnesota's program found positive results but also included a skeptical note. The number of families living solely on welfare benefits fell about 20 percent. Employment rates among single parents rose by about 35 percent, and income rose 15 percent. Marriage rates among two-parent families increased by 40 percent, and domestic abuse fell 18 percent. Supporters focus on Minnesota's coupling of a work requirement with generous benefits: higher payments than under the old welfare program plus child-care assistance designed to assure that participants who work will come out ahead financially. In other work-welfare programs, clients face the disincentive of welfare payments falling faster than work income increases. As in Wisconsin, however, an explanation for Minnesota's success might lie less with program details than with a booming economy that provided work for almost all who wanted it.[71]

New York City also sought to wean welfare recipients to work. It opened a referral service to connect people with job opportunities. One effort went bad, however, when the *New York Times* publicized referrals to a service that trained welfare recipients to serve as psychics for phone-in clients who paid a per-minute fee for prophecy and advice. The *Times* highlighted the complaints registered with the Federal Trade Commission against the telephone psychics, and within a day the city announced it would no long refer welfare clients to phone-in services seeking people to work as psychics.[72]

Occasionally the successful implementation of one program puts clients into a catch-22 situation where they cannot win. As a result of reforms designed to move people from welfare to work, more than 900,000 low-income parents lost medical coverage. Federal law provides a transition period for allowing people leaving welfare to continue their health insurance under Medicaid, but a number of states have not provided the coverage. The findings vary not only among states but within individual states and seem to depend on how low-level officials interpret different provisions of state and federal laws. Some of the provisions assure continued Medicaid coverage, while other provisions end qualification when an individual's income rises. Perhaps due to the complications, it took more than four years for federal officials to acknowledge that welfare reforms were contributing to an increase in the uninsured.[73]

Food labeling provides another illustration of positive and negative indicators about program success. More and more people are reading labels indicating ingredients, fat content, calories, and other nutritional details, but Americans are also growing more obese. An FDA study found that 56 percent of consumers used the labels "often" to check nutrients and compare brands in 1995, a 13 percent jump over earlier findings; 48 percent said they had changed their minds about buying or using a food because of the new label, which was 18 percent higher than in 1990. However, a Centers for Disease Control and Prevention study classified 17.9 percent of all Americans as obese in 1998. This was a 6 percentage point increase since 1991. A separate study in 1997 said slightly more than half of all Americans needed to lose weight.[74]

The Y2K scare was a passing phenomenon that raised questions about the credibility of dire predictions. Was the scare fabricated to earn employment for computer programmers or hyped out of proportion by the mass media? Governments and industry around the world spent an estimated $500 billion to guard against the bug.

It was not that nothing happened. There were a few glitches but nothing that could not be repaired without great loss. Even poor countries, where it was thought that old computers would be especially vulnerable, managed to enter the year 2000 without drastic consequences. Scaremongers were still predicting disaster as the new century moved through its first weeks. Some accused the media and computer engineers of foul play in order to provide dramatic news (for the media) and employment opportunities (for the engineers). Others were less condemning. Perhaps the scare had provoked enough fixes to prevent inconvenience or catastrophe. The dawning of new centuries has long given rise to millennial fears and hopes. It is appropriate that the concerns associated with our new century focused on computers, which offer threat as well as promise.[75]

A Country Without Snow Shovels

Some problems are so rare as to warrant a policy of indifference. When things go wrong, it may not be a failure of implementation so much as a rare occurrence that just happened to take place.

Countries outside the area of likely snow do not invest in the kind of equipment typical of northern climates. If heavy snow comes once or twice every so many years, it is cheaper to wait for the sun to melt it than to pay for the purchase and maintenance of seldom used machinery. When the snow does come, however, the immediate cost may be heavy.

Jerusalem received a foot of snow during the time I was writing this chapter. The last heavy snow had fallen nine years earlier, so it was not unreasonable for the authorities to be without the tools considered conventional in the northern United States and Europe. The municipality responded with a motley collection of front-end loaders, road graders, and heavy trucks whose function was to use their double tires to splash the snow to the side of the road. The lack of preparation was even more apparent among the city's households. No one owns a snow shovel. There is no word for the tool in Hebrew. Neighbors cleaned their outside steps and sidewalks with brooms, Ping-Pong paddles, and dustpans or kicked it away with their shoes. One person digging out with a garden pitchfork made as much progress as he would by eating soup with a table fork. The buses did not operate. Schools and other public facilities and many stores remained closed. Even two days later, when there was no longer any snow but only wet roads that iced over in the early morning, buses started late and schools opened at 10:00 A.M. The salt-laden Dead Sea was only ten miles away, but the municipality had not stockpiled salt for roads that seldom had ice and had no equipment to spread it.

The city and its neighbors in the Judean mountains (2,500 feet above sea level) were isolated for the better part of twenty-four hours from the rest of the country. When the roads opened they were jammed by sightseers from warmer coastal areas who knew no snow.

What Is Policy?
Where Can Its Implementation Be Influenced?

A problem for someone concerned with policy implementation is knowing the policy. We shall see in the following chapter that some public organizations are designed to keep government officials from meddling in them. One reason for creating organizations in this way is that busy policymakers want to avoid responsibility or even remain oblivious of details that are potentially within their responsibility.

It is also the case that policymakers propose legislation in ways designed to hide changes in policy. One trick used by policymakers wanting to sneak something through the legislative process is to tie a provision onto a popular piece of legislation. If the addition is especially arcane, it might make it into the law books with only a small number of insiders knowing about it. When it becomes law, opponents may have to scramble to learn its implications and try a cumbersome process of passing additional legislation to nullify it. The legislative process is designed to keep new laws at a minimum. Proposals must pass through multiple stages of review by at least one committee, obtain the support of a majority of committee members, and then receive support by at least a majority of voting members in the entire legislative body at least once and often more, depending on the rules. In a legislature with two houses, as in the United States federal government and all but one of the U.S. state governments, the process may have to occur in both houses, with both agreeing about the final wording. Then the chief executive, whether it be the U.S. president or a state governor, has an opportunity to approve or veto the measure. As a result of this complex and typically long process, the advantage goes to those defending an existing provision against subsequent amendments or cancellation, even if the item on the law books was enacted in a sneaky fashion.

What seemed to outsiders a highly technical, somewhat convoluted change in the way lenders would calculate their expenditures on loans to college students was added to a measure concerned primarily with helping disabled individuals return to work. When opponents perceived what Congress had enacted, they calculated that it would mean an extra $1.7 billion in profits for lenders.[76] Provisions offering tax advantages to wealthy individuals—in the form of tax protected deposits for health care and retirement that only the wealthy would be likely to afford— were added to bills concerned primarily with increasing the minimum wage and protecting patients in managed care.[77]

An attractive home for the sneaky add-on is the budget. In a later chapter we shall see that the budget is a bastion of incrementalism, or gradual changes in policy. Because the budget is likely to be a long and highly detailed law, however, it is also likely to attract other long and detailed pieces of legislation, which few if any policymakers will bother to read. Also, when the budget is nearing passage, legislators and the chief executive are unlikely to intervene against it, despite one or more details that they oppose. Lawmakers often consider it better to take some losses in the ongoing political competition than to reject an entire budget.

Congressional culture encourages members to take care of local interests. Members add language to existing bills dealing with other matters having wide support in order to assure work for hometown defense plants, research grants to universities concerned with solving problems of local industries or farmers, and exemptions from environmental control legislation for industrial plants, municipal authorities, and farmers. The *Christian Science Monitor* reported that while corporate profits increased 8.9 percent in the fiscal year ending September 30, 1999, federal corporate tax revenues were down 2.5 percent. It attributed the shortfall to special tax provisions added on to legislation dealing with other issues. Some of these enactments have allowed multinational corporations to shift their claims of expenses and incomes among countries according to which gives the most favored tax treatment. The newspaper reported that some firms increased their expenses for tax purposes by claiming their American operations bought toothbrushes for $171 each and pantyhose for $38 a pair. They minimized reports of income by claiming to have sold missile and rocket launchers for $13 each and radial tires for $5 apiece.[78]

The complexities of corporation taxes lead to name-calling between government and corporate officials. According to former Treasury Secretary Lawrence H. Summers, "Corporate tax shelters are our No. 1 problem." Officials have named Colgate-Palmolive, Compaq Computer, and United Parcel Service as the kind of companies once thought to be concerned about their public image that have involved themselves in tax shams that have not passed muster in the courts. In response to reporters' queries, Compaq did not return calls, Colgate-Palmolive declined to comment, and United Parcel Service said it was "deeply offended" that government officials "would even begin to equate" its tax case with evasion or impropriety.[79] Treasury officials noted that large corporations report larger profits to shareholders than to the Internal Revenue Service (IRS). For corporations with more than $1 billion in assets, there was no gap in 1992, but in 1996 they reported $119 billion more in profits to shareholders than to the IRS.[80]

Court decisions are no less complicated than legislative provisions. They provide another field for contending forces to bend the nature of policy or the details of program implementation in ways to suit their interests. "Splitting hairs" is an epithet used against individuals who quarrel about the meaning of what others see as small details but are essential to the business of lawyers and judges. Different provisions of the U.S. Constitution arguably bring contrary weight to bear on individual issues. The federal character of the government, in the eyes of some interpretations, allows Oregon or any other state to enact laws authorizing physicians to assist in suicide. By other views, however, the interstate commerce clause gives Congress the right to override such laws by virtue of its control over substances that depend on interstate commerce (e.g., the drugs used in assisted suicides). And the Fourteenth Amendment's provision on behalf of protecting life may also give the federal government a say about Oregon's law. What will eventually prevail depends on a lengthy process of suits and countersuits that may work their way to the Supreme Court. Even though a Supreme Court decision may settle a specific case, it may not provide a final resolution of the principle involved. The Court's decisions may change in subsequent cases due to variations in the specifics of a claim and changing personnel on the Court as well as changes in public attitudes about life, suicide, and federalism.

Missions Change with Implementation of New Policies

An organization might try so hard to implement certain of its missions that it employs treatments that are less desirable than the problems they are meant to correct. One example appears in the efforts of the IRS to root out corrupt employees. The program cost the IRS considerable money, and it may have distracted employees and lessened morale out of proportion to the incidence of serious problems actually uprooted. According to one review of the agency, the number of cases brought against agents may equal the number of actions taken by the agency against errant taxpayers. The agency's own plan required the investigation of 5,000 employees, or 1 in 28 (1 in 9 among IRS employees who work as auditors and tax collectors), while in a recent year the IRS initiated only one tax fraud investigation for every 46,000 taxpayers. Moreover, the investigations of employees completed so far do not indicate that the agency has serious problems among staff members. By one report, 68 percent of investigations into allegations of misconduct were found to lack merit; by another report, none of the first 830 complaints of harassment by taxpayers could be substantiated.[81]

A subsequent inquiry into the IRS found that legislation originating with a Republican-dominated Congress had moved the organization from emphasizing tax auditing and collection toward emphasizing service, with a timidity in the face of well-connected taxpayers. The result is that well-to-do taxpayers have less to fear from intrusive audits. High-paid IRS auditors experienced in the technicalities of corporate tax returns have been assigned as low-level customer service workers to answer questions of walk-in or phone-in taxpayers. Furthermore, the entire staff has shrunk by about 14 percent since 1995. According to one report, IRS managers "have concluded that they are supposed to wilt before the rich and powerful, especially those who can get a politician on the telephone." The incidence of auditing is down to one audit in 300 tax returns in 1999, compared to one in 63 in 1981. Together with a reduction in the incidence of auditing is a turn to audits of middle- and lower-income taxpayers. Audits of taxpayers reporting gross incomes of at least $100,000 per year will be even less than the average. And the focus of audits has turned to issues likely to involve middle- and lower-income individuals, such as those failing to file returns or claiming the Earned Income Tax Credit, which is designed to aid the working poor.[82]

The Challenge of New Technology

It takes a while for policymakers to recognize the implications of new technology and to fix the implementation of existing programs accordingly. The Internet allows companies and their customers to act quickly in their best interests, unhindered by political boundaries. However, the Internet challenges the capacity of governments to collect the transaction taxes they feel are due, whether they be value-added or sales taxes or customs duties. The Internet also raises problems for governments that want to limit the information and entertainment individuals can access. Some of this falls under the heading of pornography, some under the heading of material that can incite violence against minorities. Congress considered a measure to prohibit gambling on the Internet. Some 700 websites were said to be collecting $1.2 billion a year in wagers on lotteries, horse racing, and professional and college sports events. The bill had the support of church groups opposed to gambling as well as horse tracks and casinos wanting to eliminate competition. Insofar as a number of the sites came from outside the United States, opponents asked how the wagering could be curtailed.[83]

Yet another problem is the regulation of medicines. State governments have traditionally regulated pharmacies as to which medicines require a physician's prescription and who is entitled to be registered as a pharmacist allowed to sell those products. Numerous websites are selling medicine, with more coming online all the time. No one knows how many consumers are buying medication from them or how many customers have received drugs without a prescription. Neither is it clear how many have received drugs that were contaminated, not approved for use, or imitations of established products. The FDA has proposed itself as the regulator of Internet pharmacies, but state regulatory bodies and the companies to be regulated have not yet signed on to the FDA campaign.[84] A distinct problem is foreign websites that sell drugs not approved for sale in the consumer's country. The U.S. Customs Service seized more than four times the number of packages containing prescription drugs in 1999 as in 1998. Officials assume that many more packages make it through their checkpoints, with some of them designed by foreign shippers to appear as something other than drugs.[85]

Another Internet crime that has eluded authorities takes the form of international hackers based in far-off lands without extradition treaties, who break into the computers of e-commerce firms and steal information such as customers' credit card numbers. They then seek payoff in several ways: demanding payment from the firms for the return of their data; using the credit card numbers to make purchases, crediting themselves with refunds, taking cash from ATMs; and selling the information to others who want to steal from the credit card owners and their banks.[86]

Medical research presents its own problems for policymakers. The more scientists know about hazards, the more issues policymakers face in deciding how, if at all, to take action in a way to assure implementation of policy goals. For some years, the FDA has required labels on food containers to indicate ingredients that have health implications. Now there is a new "dietary demon," an ingredient that has caused concern among researchers because it may pose an even greater threat to health than some of the items already listed on the labels. But part of the policy problem is that with so many ingredients already listed, consumers have trouble distinguishing what is good for them and what is bad. The new ingredient that some want listed, "trans fatty acid," may not register with some consumers, who are already perplexed about the health threats and benefits associated with saturated, polyunsaturated, and mono-unsaturated fat. According to one consumer, "There's a lot of excess information on the labels that I don't understand and if I don't understand it, it's pointless. . . . But if they can make the trans fatty acid labels pithy and explain enough, then it would be very positive."[87] Labels can only include so much information without resorting to type so small as to defeat their purpose. And complexities involving the benefits and dangers of some ingredients may challenge even someone with advanced degrees in nutrition or medicine.[88]

The Challenge of Old Technologies

Old technologies also present problems for policy implementation. An example occurs in the case of what claim to be traditional remedies. The questions that arise include:

- How to measure implementation when the issue is control of medicinal quality of what are formally not medicines.
- How to tell if the FDA is doing its job when congressional action has been explicit in excluding the FDA from its usual concern with medications.

A view that prevailed among medical practitioners was that traditional medicine (including folk and herbal remedies, acupuncture, "alternative care," and homeopathy) is quackery, built on inherited tales and anec-dotes of success but unsupported by serious research. Now FDA permits vendors to sell herbs as dietary supplements without making claims about their medicinal qualities. Critics from inside and outside the FDA worry about the quality of products that pass for remedies, that is, whether they in fact contain what they claim rather than impure herbs or other things that might be dangerous.

Reports are that Americans spent more than $27 billion on providers of alternative health care in 1998. Sales of herbs reached $4.4 billion in 1999, up from $2.5 billion in 1995. One survey found that 46 percent of the population had visited a practitioner of alternative health care in 1997, up from 36 percent in 1990.

A problem with alternative treatments is that a 1994 federal law ex-empts many of them from almost all federal regulation. Unlike conven-tional medicines or food additives, dietary supplements are not pre-screened by the FDA, and they do not have to be proven safe or effective. Rather, the burden of proof is on the FDA to prove that they are harmful before they can be taken off the market. And because there is no requirement of reporting problems associated with supplements, the reports collected are not uniform in their nature and are often anecdotal. While advocates—including the trade associations of supplement manu-facturers—claim that the products have been proven effective by their use over hundreds if not thousands of years, the reality is that products may not be uniform in their ingredients and may cause adverse responses among users. FDA monitoring implicated supplements in more than 2,600 adverse events in the 1993–1998 period, including 184 deaths.[89]

Politicians who themselves felt that they had benefited from alterna-tive medicine pushed budgets and research programs concerned with acupuncture, St. John's wort, ginko, shark cartilage, and other remedies onto the agendas of the National Institutes of Health. Yet the new policy has not proven easy to implement. Critics who identify with conven-tional medicine have referred to the new research as of "incredibly low" quality, "a waste of money," "fraud," and done by investigators who do not "really know much about science." Internal conflict at the NIH led to a string of directors of the new programs who were hired and then left.[90]

*Who Knew—or Who Should Have Known—
About Catastrophes in Time to Stop Them?*

My earlier discussion about a policymaking system as well as this dis-cussion about the elements that affect policy implementation point in the same direction: The success of policy depends on a great number of favorable conditions. Here I present several cases that illustrate the problems in bringing true information to policymakers in time to stop what became catastrophes.

One story concerns a 1998 cruise missile strike against a pharmaceutical plant in Sudan.[91] The attack came in retaliation two weeks after the terrorist bombing of U.S. embassies in Nairobi, Kenya, and Dar es Saalam, Tanzania, that had been linked to the organization of Islamic fundamentalist Osama bin Laden. Intelligence reports connected the pharmaceutical plant to bin Laden and to the manufacture of chemical weaponry.

Immediately after the attack, opponents and skeptics of the U.S. action claimed that the clumsy giant had screwed up again. They said that the factory was a pharmaceutical plant pure and simple, with no connection to nerve gas or any other chemical weapon and no connection with bin Laden. The *New Republic* reported,

> Contrary to government assertions, the plant was indeed manufacturing medicines (about half of Sudan's pharmaceutical needs). There was no heavy security at the facility, and it was not patrolled by the Sudanese military, as was alleged. It was not owned or controlled by the Sudanese government, but by a Saudi banker with *anti*-fundamentalist ties. The chemical EMPTA, which can be used to manufacture VX nerve gas and which was apparently found in a soil sample 60 feet from Al-Shifa's property, does indeed have limited commercial applications. Subsequent testing at the site has found no materials associated with chemical weapons. And no evidence directly linking the factory to Osama Bin Ladin has ever surfaced. Despite all this, it is still possible that Al-Shifa was in some way involved with the production or storage of chemical weapons. But the weight of the evidence suggests it was nothing more than a privately owned pharmaceutical plant.[92]

Among the issues of relevance in this case are conditions of extreme secrecy, the pressure of having to decide quickly, and incomplete evidence used as the basis of a military action. Soil samples taken from a site across the street from the plant revealed traces of a chemical used in the production of nerve gas. Yet fears about leaks to the media kept ranking officials from consulting with government personnel who were experts in the production of chemical weapons.

The bombing of the U.S. embassies in Nairobi and Dar es Saalam occurred while evidence about the pharmaceutical plant/weapons factory, and its possible link to bin Laden, was being evaluated by the CIA and the State Department. The casualties in East Africa put pressure on the United States to strike back against the apparent perpetrator. The fact that terrorists had struck against two U.S. targets simultaneously seemed to prompt administration officials to strike at more than one site used by the alleged terrorist. Targets chosen were bases in Afghanistan and the pharmaceutical plant. Participants in high-level meetings at the White House and the CIA disagree as to whether they raised questions about the suitability of the pharmaceutical plant as a target: either because of uncertainty as to its production of chemical weapons or uncertainty as to its connection with bin Laden.

Articles published more than a year after the missile attack said that Secretary of State Madeleine Albright sought to kill an internal report doubting the justification of the attack and that National Security Adviser Sandy Berger, who seemed to play an important role in planning the strike, claimed he was unaware of any questions about the evidence concerning the pharmaceutical plant.[93] The story of the pharmaceutical plant/weapons factory has had no final resolution. The White House has not admitted to making an error, nor has it apologized or offered compensation. However, the U.S. Treasury Department agreed in the face of a suit to unfreeze the assets of the Sudanese who owned the plant. Those assets had been frozen by the department's Office of Foreign Assets Control after the missile strike.

In the same few days of pressure after the attack on American embassies, another site in Sudan, a tannery, was also put on the target list but then removed. Ranking military personnel reached the White House with their own severe doubts about the relevance of the target for the war against terror and the difficulties of hitting it without significant civilian casualties. Was the strike against one potential target and not another the result of ranking generals noticing problems with one proposed target but not another or the feeling that they might remove one target from a list chosen by the White House but not two?

Intelligence that does not reach the appropriate official or that has been interpreted wrongly has caused its share of national disasters. A controversy still active from World War II concerns whether American officials knew of Japan's intention to bomb Pearl Harbor and did nothing to prevent the attack. By some interpretations, President Roosevelt obstructed peace efforts between Japan and the United States in a calculated way to provoke a Japanese attack. Part of this conspiracy theory is that Roosevelt and his aides blocked the transmission of information about an imminent attack in order to provide them with a good reason for going to war.[94]

The U.S. bombing of the Chinese embassy in Belgrade as part of an extended operation against Serbian forces in May 1999 offers its own tragic series of errors. It began, according to an investigative article published by the *New York Times,* with pressure to provide the military with an expanded list of targets. The purpose of extensive bombing was to force the Serbian leadership to stop the ethnic cleansing of the Kosovo Albanians. However, intelligence officers could not provide enough targets to allow the NATO air forces to keep up the pressure. At one point military commanders demanded 2,000 targets, a figure that was ridiculed by personnel who perceived it as too large a number for a country the size of Ohio. The pressure was so intense that NATO personnel had to draft a cook and a motor pool worker to complete the paperwork involved in the choice of targets. Ultimately a building thought to be a military warehouse was put on the list and cleared through a number of checkpoints that included the president himself. Yet the warehouse identified by maps that did not include street addresses turned out to be the Chinese embassy. Along the way to the actual bombing, at least one person felt that a mistake was about to happen but did not raise objections formally, and his concerns were lost in the bureaucratic tangle. Perhaps fortunately, the bombing killed only three and wounded twenty. Similarly, during the 1991 Gulf War, a facility identified as an intelligence bunker was in fact an air raid shelter for civilians. Its bombing killed a large number of women and children.[95]

An Israeli case concerns the accumulation of information received prior to the attack by Egypt and Syria on Yom Kippur in 1973 and the failure of Israeli intelligence agencies to interpret the data as signaling preparations for war. The chronic problem of military intelligence is not just the availability of information but the mass of information, the problems of sorting the more important from the less important, and interpreting indications as validating one conception of what is likely to happen (e.g., an enemy attack) rather than another (e.g., an enemy training exercise).

Who knew about conditions in Rwanda that were developing toward genocide in 1994? Who cared? Somewhere in the unresolved issues is the suspicion that Western powers cared more about developing crises in Europe than in Africa. Also involved was the skittishness of the White House about getting into another African imbroglio, after having lost eighteen rangers in a humiliating skirmish in Somalia only a year earlier. A United Nations report compiled about Rwanda in 1999 disclosed information about preparations for genocide that resulted in some 800,000 killings in 100 days, mostly of Tutsis by Hutus. Reports from UN military personnel did not reach the highest decisionmaking levels in the international organization, and foreign troops meant for peacekeeping were withdrawn at important points, rather than being re-inforced as the field commanders requested.[96]

What You Do Not See May Not Hurt

"Out of sight, out of mind," "far from the eye, far from the heart," and "lip service" are three epigrams that suggest explanations for the failure of U.S. policy to upgrade the living standards in the far-away islands of Micronesia. Taken from the Japanese during World War II, the islands have passed through the stages of being a U.S.-administered trust terri-tory followed by independence but with a special relationship to the United States that involves continued funding and special access of their residents to the mainland.

Islands with perhaps 200,000 residents, organized as the Marshall Islands and the Federated States of Micronesia, suffered the effects of nuclear weapons testing, then benefited from several generations of Peace Corps volunteers. They also have received U.S. funds that by var-ious measurements amount to more than one-half of their economies. But the image presented is one of being out of sight and out of mind, with bits of money that are significant for the islanders but only lip service for Americans and are not sufficient to make a dent in serious problems. Visitors see shabby housing and dismal public services. Few people in the Marshall Islands speak English, although it is the language of instruction in the public schools. The government has lost millions on failed hotels, expensive aircraft, and other poorly conceived projects. An audit report from the Federated States of Micronesia describes the diversion of millions of dollars budgeted for public projects to private individuals, while the heavily indebted state is unable to provide basic services.[97]

A case involving a Canadian judge illustrates that an insistent indi-vidual can bring to the fore instances of poor implementation that most members of the establishment would like to keep out of sight. Fed up with high levels of alcoholism, drug abuse, and suicide on an Indian reservation, a judge cited tribal leaders for funneling substantial rev-enues from oil and gas reserves to unqualified family members and po-litical supporters rather than to education and other social services.

The judge did not escape without personal cost. Leaders of the tribe called the judge's rulings "inappropriate, false and racist." The Canadian minister of Indian affairs criticized him for airing the Indians' "dirty laundry" in public. The chief judge of the provincial court called the judge's rulings "atrocious" and ordered him transferred to a court where he would have no jurisdiction over the tribe. Yet that decision was overturned as the result of an appeal, and the public controversy it produced led to some results. The Department of Indian Affairs stripped the tribe's leaders of their power. The tribe is reducing its employment roster from 660 to about 400, and forty-seven cases of possible criminal fraud have been referred to the Royal Canadian Mounted Police for further investigation.[98]

Contrary claims as to what happened and who was responsible are common features of inquiries into implementation failures. Some actions are both proper and improper, wise and unwise, depending on who looks at them. In those circumstances, there may be denials and counterdenials about responsibility hedged by the assertion that it really was not the way it looked. Different claims complicate our ability to know what government is doing and what policies it is implementing.

One such case emerged around the U.S. federal government's efforts to fight drug use by shaping the content of television programs and advertising. A law enacted in 1997 authorized the government to spend a billion dollars over five years on antidrug advertising. The law carried provisions for networks to match government spending on antidrug ads. Government officials worked out an arrangement for the networks to benefit financially if they included antidrug messages in program content. Here is the rub: Though many people think it is wise for popular programming to discourage drug use, many people think it is unwise for government officials to influence the content of programming. Participants both affirmed and denied government involvement. Some said that government contacts were "generally with sales executives, not writers and producers." Others confirmed the financial arrangements but said that they knew of no program contents changed as a result. A White House official said that his people reviewed television content "to see if they're on strategy or not." Though some network officials said the White House examined shows after they aired (thus avoiding the delicate issue of censorship), other network officials admitted that they submitted scripts for review in advance.[99]

Personal Foibles and Other Random Noise

Elected leaders are expected to make policy and supervise its implementation. However, we have already seen the long list of conditions likely to weigh heavily on them. Moreover, the person at the peak of government is not necessarily a wise or heroic figure always seeking to do right. Peculiar idiosyncrasies are not absent from those who govern us.

As president, Dwight D. Eisenhower acquired a reputation for indecipherable public utterances that seemed odd in relation to his status as national hero and magnetic personality plus a military career built in part on his capacity to draft incisive and persuasive analyses and to lead a huge multinational force. He admitted to aides that some of his confusing responses to journalists' question were designed to avoid revealing information about intentions he did not want to publicize. Eisenhower did not pride himself in lying but in blurring his actions and plans in reports to the nation.[100]

Richard Nixon is a favorite subject of those who ponder how individuals with great political skills also have the strangest personal traits. Why would he risk having material stolen from his opponents' offices in the Watergate complex when he was way ahead in the polls against a candidate (George McGovern) who began as something of an extremist and was not running a successful campaign? Jews who were close to Nixon, including White House aide Leonard Garment and National Security Adviser then Secretary of State Henry Kissinger, tell of Nixon ranting in their presence about a conspiracy of Jews to bring down his presidency. Kissinger himself is said to have been involved in a complex arrangement designed to lead Air Force crews to bomb Cambodia after they were told they would be bombing positions in Vietnam and then to isolate the crews and explain to them the importance of fudging the truth. The purpose was to support the claim that the United States was not widening the geographic scope of the war.[101]

John Kennedy's mythic sexual prowess may have been his own business except for the woman he shared with a Mafia don. Her own several loyalties may have compromised the president's capacity to make independent decisions about Mafia links to organized labor or a proposed Mafia assassination attempt against Fidel Castro.

There is some question as to whether Ronald Reagan's Alzheimer's disease began while he was still in office or whether it was some other personal quirk that made him seem spacey, unable to recognize his own Cabinet appointees, and fumbling in his discussion of policy details. He either confused or dissembled the legality of selling arms to an Iranian government supposedly the subject of a U.S. embargo and having the Iranians pay the money to opponents of the Sandinista regime in Nicaragua in violation of a congressional ban on U.S. involvement in that country's civil war. A book written by Reagan's authorized biographer describes the president with phrases like "encyclopedic ignorance," "articulation without comprehension," "an apparent airhead," "relentless banality," and "talking nonsense." It quotes Francis Mitterrand, the late president of France, who described Reagan as "a man without ideas and without culture."[102]

Alongside the severe criticisms of Reagan as ill-informed on policy details is widespread admiration of his political skills. Mitterrand asserted that he was not stupid. Reagan's biographer praised him for an ability to "reduce a situation to its simple essence. And simple is not necessarily simplistic."[103] Reagan could speak the language of religious conservatives without sounding so extreme as to offend those whose agenda was not primarily religious; and he could avoid going to church regularly without offending his religious constituency. According to one observer, "Whenever Ronald Reagan spoke about abortion . . . his younger yuppie supporters always thought they saw him wink."[104]

No discussion of high-ranking idiosyncrasies can pass by the well-documented stories of Bill Clinton's sexual adventures and the falsehoods told to official investigators that contributed to his impeachment by the House of Representatives. Could Yassir Arafat have confidence in subsequent messages from Clinton when investigators revealed that the president was having oral sex while speaking with Arafat on the telephone?

Seemingly riding a post-Clinton wave of sentiment in favor of uprightness in high office, an Arizona newspaper found the state's own senator John McCain unfit in his campaign for the presidency on account of what it called a "volcanic temper." According to some accounts, McCain "often insults people and flies off the handle [and can be] sarcastic and condescending."[105] Offenses such as these hardly seemed the equivalent of Clinton's escapades in or near the Oval Office.

The run-up to the 2000 presidential campaign included several exposés of George W. Bush's lack of detailed knowledge, especially in the field of foreign affairs. He referred to Greeks as "Grecians," Kosovars as "Kosovarians," and East Timorese as "East Timorians." He confused the countries of Slovakia and Slovenia and provided a partially correct answer to only one of four questions put to him by a talk-show host who asked him to name the heads of Chechnya, Taiwan, India, and Pakistan, all of which were in the news at the time. A positive spin on Bush's failed test sees it as adding to his appeal as a regular guy:

Bush's lightweight persona has the feel of a deliberate strategy. What Bush understands, and the pundits do not, is that he is a brilliant candidate not despite his anti-intellectualism but because of it. He has stumbled upon a fortuitous moment in which the political culture, tired of wonks and pointy-heads and ideologues, yearns instead for a candidate unburdened by, or even hostile to, ideas. It is a moment made for the chipper governor from Texas, and he is soaring upward, propelled by his own weightlessness.[106]

Ranking officials and entire institutions sometime become embroiled in what seem the most petty of personal quarrels. One such squabble occurred over several months and on the front pages of Israeli newspapers. It found the state comptroller (equivalent to the heads of the U.S. General Accounting Office and Great Britain's National Audit Office) involved in a wrangle between personalities at the summit of the country's policy organs. It began as a quarrel among the chief of the national police, the political minister of police, a key aide of the prime minister, and the legal adviser to the government about a police investigation into activities of the minister of interior.

When the police investigation into the interior minister was well under way, the police chief was dismissed from his position. He claimed that he lost his job because he would not give in to pressure by the police minister to influence the investigation in favor of the interior minister. The police minister denied the charge and made a countercharge that the police chief was dismissed from his position because he initiated a campaign to gain Labor Party support for his candidacy as mayor of Tel Aviv.[107]

The state comptroller accepted the request of Knesset members to investigate the dispute between the police minister and the chief of police. The comptroller's report wandered far from the tradition that state auditors concentrate on issues of financial or program management. It concluded that the police chief had lied about receiving pressure from the police minister and that a prominent aide in the prime minister's office had sought to influence the police investigation. The report led the police chief to initiate a suit against the state comptroller. He charged that his reputation and career had been damaged by being termed a liar and that the state comptroller had not made available to him all the evidence used in judging his behavior. The state comptroller also provoked angry responses from the prime minister's aide and from the legal adviser to the government. Then the state comptroller charged that both of these figures had lied, but later the comptroller corrected herself by indicating that her report may have erred on some details. The storm was not a measured dispute about an official report but conflicting assertions about "who said what to whom."[108] The issue returned to the front pages about a year later when the Supreme Court ruled that the comptroller had not followed proper procedures in refusing the police chief's demands to rebut her conclusions against him. At this point, the police chief exaggerated the support for his position that could be found in the court's decision and claimed that the court had exonerated him from all accusations; the minister of police asserted that the court's decision did not overturn the conclusion that the police chief had lied; and the state comptroller admitted to making some errors in procedure and conclusions.[109]

The president of South Africa, Thabo Mbeki, caused a stir among scientists in his own country and overseas when he challenged the prevailing wisdom about the connection between HIV infection and AIDS. The issue is important insofar as estimates state that between 10 and 20 percent of the South African adult population have acquired HIV. Mbeki fastened onto Internet reports of a minority view among Western scientists and staked out a position against the distribution of medication that could substantially lessen the transmission of HIV infections from women to the newborn. Scientists feared that Mbeki's posturing on behalf of an "African renaissance" and against prevailing views about the disease would fuel a simmering rumor that AIDS does not exist and that safe sex precautions are unnecessary.[110]

What to Believe?

What to believe is a question to ask about what leaders say and what it is said that they intend. Knowing the intentions of leaders seems crucial to anyone concerned with judging the goals of public policy and its implementation. Yet knowing those intentions is often baffling, especially in issues that are controversial.

It is no secret that politicians lie, fib, stretch the truth, or exaggerate their intentions when they are candidates for elective office. And it should be no surprise that such behavior does not cease once they are in office. If they have won high office, like president of the United States or prime minister in a parliamentary system, they will have legions of assistants and hangers-on seeking to embellish their reputation. After they have left office, those who were their aides or supporters may continue the good works on their behalf. Against the chorus of praise will be unceasing criticism from opponents. Involved in the noise will be contrary assertions of what the leaders said, did, or intended. Should historians take an interest in these administrations, there are likely to be succeeding waves of criticism, re-interpretation, and re-re-interpretation about personalities and actions in office.

Clarifying what a politician really meant is a craft practiced by aides, typically after the boss has said something with undesirable echoes. "Gore Clarifies Position on Gays" was the headline three days after the vice president as presidential candidate said he would apply a litmus test to the joint chiefs of staff on the issue of gays serving openly in the military. The complexity of the issue helps to explain why the correction required three days. Gore said, "I did not mean to imply that there should ever be any kind of inquiry into the personal political opinions of officers in the U.S. military, nor would I ever tolerate such inquiries." It took less time for the Republican National Committee to produce a TV ad claiming that two heroes of the 1991 Gulf War, Generals Colin L. Powell and Norman Schwarzkopf, "couldn't pass Al Gore's litmus test."[111]

Contrary interpretations of Lyndon Johnson's intentions in Vietnam illustrate the problems in discerning real meanings. While Johnson's actions showed substantial escalation of U.S. involvement in Vietnam, as well as personal involvement in key decisions about military strategy and tactics, observers have made some changes in their assessments following the release of tapes made of White House conversations.

Among the tapes are bits of conversations among Johnson, Richard Russell, chair of the Senate Armed Services Committee, and McGeorge Bundy, national security adviser. Johnson said, among other things,

> I've got a little old sergeant that works for me over at the house, and he's got six children, and I just put him up there as the United States Army, Air Force and Navy every time I think about making this decision, and think about sending that father of those six kids in there. And what the hell are we going to get out of his doing it? And it just makes the chills run up my back. . . . I don't think it's worth fighting for, and I don't think that we can get out. It just the biggest damn mess I ever saw. . . . It's damned easy to get in a war, but it's gonna be awfully hard to extricate yourself if you get in.

For his critic, former Senator George McGovern, these quotes signal Johnson as a great president severely torn by difficult decisions.[112] But could they not also be the minor chords in a rambling conversation that did not contribute much by way of moderation to the president's substantive policy? Historians earn their reputations by dealing with puzzles of this kind.

Johnson's contemporary and nemesis, Robert F. Kennedy, is also the subject of historical controversy. Was the real Robert F. Kennedy the hard-driving anticommunist who worked for Senator Joseph McCarthy, the antilabor racketeer who pursued Jimmy Hoffa, the ally of civil rights activists who used his power as attorney general to assure the safety of the Reverend Martin Luther King when King was jailed in the South, or the introspective opponent of the war in Vietnam as presidential candidate (i.e., the same war he had helped pursue when he had been in his brother's cabinet)? Competing biographies emphasize different aspects of Kennedy's life, which came to an end before Kennedy had a chance to work out the inconsistencies in his career.[113]

Interpretation of contrary signals is not only a problem for historians. Israelis and others hoping to decipher the intentions of the late Syrian president Hafez al-Assad had the task of gauging mixed signals in real time. Did his demands for major Israeli concessions before beginning negotiations indicate he was a difficult bargainer, or did they signal a posture against negotiations? That is, did he raise the stakes so high as to prevent serious discussion? The latter was the conclusion of one *New York Times* correspondent, who surmised that Assad did not control the Syrian regime securely and thus wanted to squirm out of negotiations with Israel without seeming to be weak.[114]

Guessing the intentions of politicians may be especially difficult in the case of a country like Russia. Its political culture seems undefined or fluid after having disposed of communism but not yet having arrived at norms of transparency, democracy, respect for law, and economic stability. During the campaign for the 2000 presidential election, acting president Vladimir V. Putin seemed to have a lock on the office. Commentators parsed words and actions from both his present and his past positions in an effort to assess what he would do if elected. They found contrary indications toward major issues of international and domestic affairs. As a result, democrats and authoritarians as well as free marketers and those wanting a stronger role for the state drew competing conclusions. "Studious inscrutability" and "forthright in his own vague way" were two descriptions of his style, suggesting an intended vagueness. In response to one questioner, he replied, "I won't tell you." With respect to such an outright refusal to answer the kind of question normal in Western democratic elections, an observer wonders if the candidate knew what he intended or if he was taking advantage of his electoral position and keeping his options open.[115]

The tendency of politicians to stretch the truth, and to promise a great deal, provides material for the comic as well as frustration for the citizen. One story tells about a president who fell out of an airplane over an Iowa cornfield. Rescuers found a farmer but no sign of the president. The farmer said that the president had landed nearby, and that he had buried him. Asked if the president was dead, the farmer said, "He kept saying he wasn't, but everybody knows you can't believe a word he says."[116]

Supporters may be correct in reading a politician's intentions, but they fail when they do not consider the politician's priorities. American Evangelicals expected a lot from Jimmy Carter and Ronald Reagan. Carter described himself as a born-again Christian and was active as a Sunday school teacher who spoke frequently about issues of faith and family. Yet he was also a Democrat; as such he disappointed religious supporters by failing to isolate himself from those who were prochoice or who supported other items on the left-wing agenda.

Ronald Reagan's personal religious credentials were not as clear as those of Jimmy Carter, but his campaign statements in behalf of religiosity and family values, as well as his Republican affiliation, provided him with considerable support from religious Americans, including those disappointed with the Carter administration. With Reagan in charge, religious leaders had access to the Oval Office and won many a photograph with the president but fewer instances of tangible support. Reagan expressed support for religious values, but his immediate priority was economic policy. Also troublesome was the president's appointment of Sandra Day O'Connor to the Supreme Court. He wanted to appoint the first woman to the Court. The one he selected was conservative on numerous issues but had a liberal record on two items of prime importance for religious conservatives: She supported a woman's right to an abortion and the Equal Rights Amendment, which would have enshrined sexual equality in the U.S. Constitution.[117]

It is not only politicians and elected officeholders who mislead. "Disinformation" is the stock-in-trade of senior bureaucrats as well as interest groups and others who participate in policymaking. The targets of misleading information may be other countries or fellow citizens or organizations in relation to whom officials maneuver their political platform. Manufacturing an impression, directing likely opponents away from one's real intentions, and putting the best face on one's actions are workaday elements in policymaking. Labels of "game" and "dance" suggest that maneuver for the sake of the sport is part of policymaking. The *Washington Post* described some maneuvering of the president and congressional leaders in the final stages of budget approval. The reports are not especially clear, but then the tactics being described were themselves designed to confuse. The *Post* described one congressman's approach to his opponents:

> His tactic instead is to propose that the spending be financed by devices like a cigarette tax increase, which he knows they reject. He then attacks them for refusing to approve the spending anyway, and they relent. The caps are breached, but in a way that makes it hard to say that either party did it, a series of fictions that allows them both to have the thing both ways.[118]

Good advice is important to those who make policy or implement programs. Yet it is not easy to speak truth to those in power. Political stories of leaders from ancient kings to the most recent officeholders tell of lives or careers ended when advisers criticized the powerful. The prophet Micaiah is a minor character in the Hebrew Bible, whose short appearance in history involved his critical prophecy about the king's intentions and ended with his imprisonment on a diet of bread and water.[119] Elijah fled to the desert in order to avoid the fate of other prophets killed on the orders of Queen Jezebel.[120] Amos was sent out of the kingdom of Israel on account of his prophecies.[121] King Jehoiakim had Uriah killed for his prophecies.[122] Jeremiah was in and out of trouble during the regimes of Jehoiakim and Zedekiah. One rabbinical tale reports that King Manasseh had the prophet Isaiah sawn in two because of his prophecies.[123] Advisers who provide undesirable opinions to the leaders of modern democracies are not likely to suffer death or imprisonment or be sawn in two. However, they may find themselves ignored, out of work, or moved to offices distant from that of the great leader.

The Problems of Ambiguity and Other Forms of Coping

Among the issues that confuse observers and participants in policymaking is the lack of effort at solving serious problems once and for all. Politicians and policymakers deal with some of their most vexing issues by coping. They seek to take some of the edge from a problem or at least to lessen its costs to themselves and their constituents. They buy time, manage the complaints, and put off a complete treatment. Among the ways they cope is to promise more than they can deliver and hope that claimants will be satisfied with what they receive. Difficult points in discussion are left vague and ambiguous. They may deal with them later or leave them unresolved.[124]

The issue is not simple. Limited resources prevent hiring enough personnel or building enough facilities to respond completely to some problems. Other problems are confounded by sharply contrasting desires. Israelis and Palestinians both want to control Jerusalem. Advocates of prolife or prochoice stances will remain unhappy whatever is decided about abortion. It is likewise difficult to satisfy those who want religious observances in public places and those who stand firm in opposition.

I shall return to the topic of ambiguity and other modes of coping in Chapter 4, when I discuss them in the context of ways that policymakers simplify their actions. The extensive use of ambiguity and other forms of coping in policymaking testifies to their utility. Here I emphasize that coping leaves issues unresolved, thereby adding to the complexity of politics. Though some policymakers may feel that coping by means of an ambiguous statement is the best they can do, others may focus on the dark side of ambiguity and protest its lack of clarity. Unresolved demands fester. Their frustration, together with the complaints of program clients, fuels political opposition, animosity toward all politicians, and widespread feelings of alienation.

Faith and Politics

Religion has a great deal to do with the lack of obvious solutions to public problems. It also contributes to the convoluted ways in which policymakers operate. For Karl Marx, religion was the opiate of the masses. A little boy at Sunday School once defined "faith" as "believing firmly what you know isn't true."[125] In our terms, religion might be considered one of the factors that gets in the way of a comprehensive assessment of which public policies are appropriate to which jurisdictions. Policymakers are likely to consider or reject some proposals according to whether they follow the tenets of certain religions, no matter what support these proposals receive from the public or what economic costs they would incur.

Much of the research about religion, politics, and public policy is set in the United States. The topic is especially fascinating in the context of technological and economic traits that would seem to push the society toward secularism.[126] Surveys find that over 90 percent of Americans profess a belief in God, almost 80 percent say that religion is important to them, more than 60 percent are likely to have attended a religious service within the past week, and about the same number say they pray daily. Between one-third and two-thirds report that they have witnessed a miracle, felt the direct presence of God, or had one of their prayers answered.[127] Harold Bloom uses the terms *religion-soaked* and *religion-mad* for American society.[128] Mormon leaders in Utah and Protestant clerics in other states oppose legalized gambling and liberalized liquor regulations. Catholic clerics, Orthodox Jews, Mormons, and conservative Protestants lead the crusade against abortion. Although the same groups are less unified on homosexual rights and capital punishment, these issues draw much of their importance from religious doctrine.

Attacks against the teaching of evolution and the promotion of "creationism" in the classroom are not dusty relics of U.S. history. A wave of state legislation and administrative actions against the teaching of evolution occurred in the 1920s, especially in the South. One Kentucky school teacher was charged and convicted in 1922 for giving instruction that the earth was round.[129] After several decades of dormancy following the "monkey trial" of John T. Scopes in a small Tennessee town during 1925, the issue has returned to the political agenda. The considerable movement of "home teaching" draws some of its strength from parents who want to teach creation as it appears in the Book of Genesis as well as praying along with school lessons. Science teachers in numerous locales have suffered pressure that they discuss the "theoretical" nature of evolution and its lack of firm proof, plus demands that they teach creationism as a viable alternative to evolution. The Kansas Board of Education decided in 1999, for instance, that students would no longer be examined on the issue of evolution in state tests of their competency. Education authorities in Oklahoma and Alabama have required the insertion of statements or the application of stickers on approved textbooks stating that evolution is a "controversial theory" that refers to the "unproven belief that random, undirected forces produced a world of living things."[130] A survey released in 2000 found a large majority of Americans favor the teaching of both evolution and creationism. One commentator concluded that the results reflect "a pluralistic society and public [that demand there be] a place for both." He also noted a postmodern feeling that no single view can provide complete understanding of most issues, revealed in one survey response, "Well, you never know."[131]

Ahead of the decision of the Kansas Board of Education, a high school science teacher answered a student's question about creationism with a comment about "non-scientific crap." Eventually the 64-year-old instructor was pressured into retirement. Local observers differ as to whether the retirement was due to the power of the religious right or more simply a move against a teacher who had long provoked anger for his crusty style.[132]

The decision of the Kansas Board of Education had implications for local elections in 2000. Board members who identified with the anti-evolution posture lost in the balloting.[133] A subsequent vote rescinded the ban on testing about evolution.

A remnant of religious bias appeared to surface when the first Catholic candidate for chaplain of the U.S. House of Representatives failed to win nomination. The Republican Speaker of the House selected a Presbyterian minister instead, despite strong support for the Catholic candidate in the committee chosen to make a recommendation. The disappointed candidate and some House members were quoted as saying that religious preference was involved. One member reported that a colleague asked the Catholic priest what his collar represented and whether he planned to wear it in the Capitol.[134] Three months later, after Republicans had suffered from charges of anti-Catholic bias associated with George W. Bush's campaign stop at Bob Jones University, the Republican leadership of the House found a way to appoint its first Catholic chaplain.[135]

Stretching the truth, even outright lying, is no less a problem in dealing with religious leaders than with secular politicians. Critics caught the Reverend Jerry Falwell, the founder of Moral Majority, in a fabrication concerning his claim that he had asked Jimmy Carter why he had homosexuals on his presidential staff. According to Falwell, the president replied that since he wanted to represent everyone, he had to hire some homosexuals. However, White House staff had a transcript of the alleged conversation that demonstrated the interchange had never occurred. Falwell excused himself by calling his statement a parable or allegory. This, in turn, led one of Falwell's fellow preachers to call those words "a new name for a lie."[136]

It should be no surprise that religion figures prominently in Israel's politics. The country declared itself a Jewish state in its 1948 Declaration of Independence. What makes religion controversial in Israel is not only the presence of assertive minorities of Muslims and Christians but varieties of Jews. For someone born a Jew, there is no obligation to accept doctrine or observe ritual. Jewish agnostics and atheists, as well as those who are overtly secular or antireligious, make up their parts of Israel's majority.[137] Religious issues crowd the political agenda that is already burdened by problems of security and delicate postures that involve both talking and fighting. Emotions mask what may be the real desires of activists and complicate the tasks of those who would see to orderly policymaking and program implementation.

The agenda of continuing dispute among Jews includes:

• The significance of the biblical Land of Israel and how much of that imprecise landscape should be insisted on, or bargained away, for the sake of peace. Not the least of the issues in this cluster is Jerusalem, with its Jewish, Christian, and Muslim neighborhoods and holy places.

• Which aspects of religious law should be enforced by state authorities, and which bodies should have the final say in determining the nature of religious law and its application to individual cases? This cluster of issues concerns activities permitted on the Sabbath and religious holidays; the sale of nonkosher food; rules of modesty and decency; abortions, organ transplants, and other medical practices; the treatment of ancient Jewish graves uncovered in construction projects; who should be considered a Jew; and who should be given the designation and authority of "rabbi" to perform marriages, divorces, and conversions to Judaism.

• What should be the rights and privileges of various categories of Jews? Religious and secular Jews, and ultra-Orthodox and non-Orthodox Jews, as well as Jews from North Africa, Ethiopia, and Asia, feel they have been treated unfairly by other Jews.

Several controversies involving non-Jews were prominent at the approach to the millennium. For example, when the Christian mayor of Nazareth sought to fix up a rough plaza alongside the Basilica of the Ascension, religious leaders of the city's Muslim majority demanded the right to erect a new mosque on the site in order to commemorate the nearby grave of a Muslim who fought against Christian Crusaders. They staked out their claim by setting up a temporary prayer site under a cloth sun shield. Locals quarreled as to which religious group owned the site, while the Israeli government sought to move forward with improving the city's infrastructure with an eye toward a flood of pilgrims marking the millennium and threats from the Vatican that the Pope's own visit might be canceled if the government sided with the Muslims.

In Jerusalem, meanwhile, the nerves of secular authorities focused on security precautions at the Church of the Holy Sepulcher. Planners thought about increasing thousands of pilgrims squeezing through a limited doorway, together with lots of candles and an occasional commotion caused by frenzied religious experience. While some voices urged reliance on the Lord to assure safety, technocrats wanted to open another exit in case of fire or some other emergency. While leaders of the several congregations claiming ownership and rights in the holy site agreed with the need for emergency provisions, there were quarrels as to who would have the right to decide about and execute the renovations and who would own the key to the new door. It had taken twenty-seven years for clerics associated with different churches to plan and execute the restoration of four arches in the Church of the Holy Sepulcher; arguments about the painting of the cupola required three decades.[138]

For some Jewish observers, both the Nazareth and the Jerusalem disputes reflected the efforts of hostile religious groups to embarrass the Jewish state. The Vatican, for its part, accused the Israeli government of fomenting dispute between Christians and Muslims.[139] With respect to the controversy in Nazareth, the Vatican said, "The decision of the Israeli government seems to lay the basis for future contrasts and tension between the two religious communities, Christian and Muslim. . . . The political authorities have a great responsibility in this case, because rather than favoring unity they are creating the foundations to foment division." The Israeli Foreign Ministry "utterly rejected" the Vatican's criticism. In what could be seen as recalling Church-sponsored anti-Semitism, the ministry said the Vatican statement "unfortunately recalls the ancient practice of pointing the finger at the wrong cause."[140]

The Latin Patriarch (the head of the Roman Catholic Church in Israel), the Orthodox Patriarch, and the Armenian Patriarch declared a closure of their churches as an act of protest against the prospect of the Nazareth mosque. The front page of a leading Israeli newspaper carried a photo of Christian pilgrims burdened under a large cross unable to enter the Church of the Holy Sepulcher, and the front page of the *Washington Post* described Christians who had saved for years to visit the holy places and now found themselves locked out.[141]

The two events were linked. As a result of tensions between the churches and the Israeli government over the mosque in Nazareth, it seemed unlikely that the involved groups would make any progress over the emergency exit at the Church of the Holy Sepulcher.[142]

Jerusalem also provided the site for officials concerned that extremist sects would see the millennium as the time for mass suicide or other violence designed to bring forward an "end of time" scenario based on the Book of Revelation. Relying on information supplied by the U.S. Federal Bureau of Investigation (FBI) as well as its own undercover activities, the Israeli police expelled two American groups in 1999. Christian critics said that Israeli actions were heavy handed.

In spite of these controversies, January 1, 2000, passed without much ado. The Israeli police took some strange-acting figures into custody and transferred them for observation to mental hospitals. The police also prevented the efforts of an Israeli comic, who would have appeared at one of the gates to the Old City of Jerusalem dressed as Jesus. According to the *Times* of London,

> In the end, Jerusalem escaped The End, and the hundreds of pilgrims, sightseers and hooligans who thronged the Mount of Olives for a grandstand view of apocalyptic fireworks were obliged to settle for a few damp squibs. . . . The Golden Gate in the temple walls of the Old City failed to open for a new messiah; the doomsday cultists whose visions of impending Armageddon had been bothering the Israeli government for weeks went quietly home to bed. . . . The Mount of Olives . . . looked more like a football stadium as hymn-singing pilgrims . . . struggled to make themselves heard above the secular chants of exuberant German tourists and the howls of fundamentalist preachers.

The *Times* also noted that one believer felt that the crowds expecting a miracle on January 1 had it all wrong. According to this believer's reading of biblical text, the second coming was to happen on April 6, 2000.[143]

Since the millennium, the Palestinian Authority has continued to face problems associated with religion. A controversy dating back to the Russian revolution—and concerned with competing claims for ownership between "Red" and "White" Russian Orthodox Churches (one based in Moscow and the other in New York)—has not disappeared with the end of communism. A spat over a Russian Orthodox monastery in Jericho found an American nun staking a claim inside the facility on behalf of the White Church, while the Palestinian Authority had decided that the Red Church should have ownership rights. The case was made more interesting insofar as the nun was the sister of former White House aide George Stephanopoulos, who managed to involve U.S. officials in the controversy even while denying that he was trying to use his influence.[144]

I return to the minefields of Jewish, Christian, and Muslim relations in the Holy Land in Chapter 4 in connection with the power of symbolic statements and actions.

What Is a Country?

Some disturbances of policymaking and program implementation are so profound as to stand outside the comprehension of people fortunate enough to live in orderly and democratic societies. Reports from the ill-defined border between Angola and Namibia illustrate the opposite of order, to the extent that concepts like state, government, and policy have no meaning. Angola's civil war is bad enough: It has been going on since 1974 when the country gained its independence from Portugal. Originally the war was an element in the Cold War rivalries with Russia and Cuba supporting one side and the United States and South Africa supporting the other. Yet even after global politics changed, the Angolan war continued, with rival sides aspiring to control areas rich in oil and diamonds. The misery of a potentially rich country is only one consequence of the fighting. The war has spread over what purport to be national boundaries. Governments in the neighboring countries of Zambia and Namibia are not strong enough to keep out armed Angolans who raid villages for food and people, whom they force into their own cadres.[145]

On the other side of Angola, over its northeastern border, is another shell of a country, the Democratic Republic of Congo (formerly Zaire). The fighting here has been perpetuated with the aid of outsiders from Uganda, Rwanda, Burundi, Congo-Brazzaville, the Central African Republic, Sudan, Kenya, Tanzania, Zimbabwe, Angola, and Namibia. Uganda and Rwanda began as allies in the Congo, then began fighting each other as each supported rival Congolese groups. Provoking the rivalries were the prospects of picking up some of the Congo's wealth of diamonds and gold.[146] The suffering caused by these wars may touch Westerners occasionally via pictures of miserable refugees, starving children, and piles of bones.

* * *

This chapter has dealt with some of the unsolved—and perhaps unsolvable—questions of political science: What causes politicians to act as they do? Why do governments offer the policies that they do and fail to offer others? and Why are some programs implemented only partially—or in ways said to be different from the intentions of policymakers—while others are not implemented at all?

My way of wrestling with these questions was to begin describing the prominent complexities in politics and policymaking. I started by portraying a policymaking system, a schematic meant to simplify the portrayal of reality by providing a place for each element that has some influence on policy. As we saw, however, researchers employing the scheme have filled and overfilled it, with additional components and further lines depicting streams of influence. There is no end of individuals, institutions, and activities that can influence the chances of an issue to reach the agenda of policymakers or interfere in the implementation of a policy formally enacted.

I shifted from relatively abstract discussions of elements, factors, and phenomena that affect policies to the particulars of individual cases. The common thread that links all of these discussions is their addition of complexity, confusion, and uncertainties to policymaking. Together, these traits limit the prospects of officials pursuing comprehensive assessments of cause and effect or making strictly rational calculations about the most suitable ways for dealing with public problems. The case of the missile attack on a Sudan pharmaceutical plant thought to be manufacturing chemical weapons illustrates the uncertainties that can attend a military operation conceived with high concerns for both secrecy and speed of execution. In other cases we saw that when religious doctrine is involved in the choice or rejection of particular policy options, no amount of argument may alter the postures deemed acceptable.

Among the elements I found important in choosing policy options, and later the actual operation of programs, are the multiple interests affected by a topic and the pressures they bring to elevate its importance or to bury it. Involved here are the perspectives of individual politicians, key members of the bureaucracy, the traditions of states and administrative units, and the decisions of courts. Participants in policymaking do not always play fair with one another. Or perhaps the informal rules of the game permit exaggeration or even gross distortion in reports, along with the manipulation of statistical findings to strengthen one's case. The idiosyncrasies of political leaders come into play, as do religious doctrines that elevate some policy options to the level of holy writ while consigning others to the work of the devil. When problems are too complex to solve once and for all time, officials cope. They pursue partial solutions. Ambiguity may help in a political campaign by suggesting different outcomes to constituents with different interests. However, it also adds to the lack of clarity for people wanting to know what the government will offer.

There are no recommendations that assure success in dealing with these complexities, confusions, and disturbances of coherent policymaking. However, there are ways of meeting one's needs despite the complexities. In Chapter 4 we see the working of several devices that individual citizens and policymakers use to simplify their choices and avoid the maze of uncertainties. First, however, I devote another chapter to the complexities: public organizations designed to minimize control by officials with responsibility for the provision of public services.

Notes

1. Richard I. Hofferbert, *The Study of Public Policy* (Indianapolis: Bobbs-Merrill, 1974).

2. Charles Duhigg, "Means of Dissent," *New Republic,* December 20, 1999. Internet edition. For a criticism of international financial institutions that justifies some of the protesters' assertions, see Joseph Stiglitz, "The Insider: What I Learned at the World Economic Crisis," *New Republic,* April 17, 2000. Internet edition.

3. Thomas L. Friedman, "Senseless in Seattle II," *New York Times,* December 8, 1999. Internet edition. See also Friedman, "1 Davos, 3 Seattles," *New York Times,* February 1, 2000. Internet edition.

4. John W. Kingdon, *Agendas, Alternatives, and Public Policies* (Boston: Little, Brown & Company, 1984). See also Thomas A. Birkland, *After Disaster: Agenda Setting, Public Policy, and Focusing Events* (Washington, DC: Georgetown University Press, 1997); Larry N. Gerston, *Public Policy Making: Process and Principles* (Armonk, N.Y.: M. E. Sharpe, 1997), chapter 3; and James W. Dearing and Everett M. Rogers, *Agenda-Setting* (Thousand Oaks, Calif.: Sage Publications, 1996).

5. *Congressional Record,* Daily Digest, January 19, 1999, p. D29.

6. Amy Argetsinger and Tracey A. Reeves, "In Maryland, Lawmakers Try to Cover All the Bases," *Washington Post,* January 22, 2000, p. A1. Internet edition. Carey Goldberg, "For Many States, Health Care Bills Are Top Priority," *New York Times,* January 22, 2000. Internet edition.

7. Kingdon, p. 216.

8. Kingdon, pp. 90–91.

9. Tamar Lewin, "Calls for Slavery Restitution Getting Louder," *New York Times,* June 4, 2001. Internet edition.

10. Kevin Merida, "Slavery: America's Unattended Wound," *Washington Post,* November 23, 1999, p. C1. Internet edition.

11. Ruth Gledhill and Roland Watson, "Archbishop Calls for Split from State," *Times of London,* December 27, 1999. Internet edition.

12. Frank Swoboda and Kirstin Downey Grimsley, "OSHA Covers At-Home Workers," *Washington Post,* January 4, 2000, p. A1. Internet edition.

13. Frank Swoboda, "Labor Chief Retreats on Home Offices," *Washington Post,* January 6, 2000, p. A01. Internet edition.

14. Frank Swoboda, "OSHA Exempts White-Collar Telecommuters," *Washington Post,* January 27, 2000, p. A01. Internet edition.

15. Roberto Cespedes, "The Mystical Power of Elian," *New York Times,* April 4, 2000. Internet edition.

16. Lizette Alvarez, "In 2 Countries, 6-Year-Old Cuban Is Political Symbol," *New York Times,* January 9, 2000. Internet edition.

17. Anthony Lewis, "Elian and the Law," *New York Times,* April 1, 2000. Internet edition.

18. John F. Harris, "Gore Stand on Elian Stirs Up Democrats," *Washington Post,* April 1, 2000, p. A01. Internet edition. Peter T. Kilborn, "Miami Area's Mayors Ride a Volatile Political Wave," *New York Times,* April 17, 2000. Internet edition.

19. Rick Bragg, "Haitian Families in U.S. Face a Tough Choice," *New York Times,* March 29, 2000. Internet edition.

20. Laurence H. Tribe, "Justice Taken Too Far," *New York Times,* April 25, 2000. Internet edition.

21. "Reno for President," Thomas L. Friedman, *New York Times,* April 25, 2000. Internet edition.

22. Published by the University of California Press (Berkeley).

23. Daniel A. Mazmanian and Paul A. Sabatier, *Implementation and Public Policy* (Glenview, Ill.: Scott, Foresman and Company, 1983), p. 40.

24. Mazmanian and Sabatier, pp. 41–42.

25. Robert Pear, "President Admits 'Don't Ask' Policy Has Been a Failure," *New York Times,* December 12, 1999. Internet edition.

26. Roberto Suro, "Military Not Uniform in Training on Gays," *Washington Post,* March 4, 2000, p. A1. Internet edition.

27. Steven Lee Myers, "Survey of Troops Finds Antigay Bias Common in Service," *New York Times,* March 25, 2000. Internet edition.

28. Robert Pear, "Many Employers Found to Violate Law Requiring Parity for Mental Health Coverage," *New York Times,* May 18, 2000. Internet edition.

29. David Firestone, "Suburban Comforts Thwart Atlanta's Plans to Limit Sprawl," *New York Times,* November 21, 1999. Internet edition.

30. R. Jeffrey Smith, "Outside Efforts Do Little to Mend Fractured Bosnia," *Washington Post,* January 23, 2000, p. A25. Internet edition.

31. David M. Herszenhorn, "HUD Takes Control of Aid to New York City Homeless," *New York Times,* December 22, 1999. Internet edition.

32. Jodi Wilgoren, "Seeking a Superhero: Can Anyone Handle Schools' Chief Job?" *New York Times,* December 26, 1999. Internet edition.

33. Gina Kolata, "'Single Use' Medical Devices Are Often Used Several Times," *New York Times,* November 10, 1999. Internet edition.

34. Louis Uchitelle, "I.N.S. Looks the Other Way on Illegal Immigrant Labor," *New York Times,* March 9, 2000. Internet edition.

35. Howard Margolis, *Dealing with Risk: Why the Public and the Experts Disagree on Environmental Issues* (Chicago: University of Chicago Press, 1996).

80   Politics and Policymaking

36. Craig Whitlock, "When Victims of Abuse Are Left Unprotected," *Washington Post,* November 14, 1999, p. C1. Internet edition.

37. Cheryl W. Thompson, "Police Cars Uninspected, Unregistered," *Washington Post,* November 17, 1999, p. A1. Internet edition.

38. Arthur Leathley, "2 Trains a Day Go Through Red Lights," *Times,* November 15, 1999. Internet edition.

39. Thomas L. Friedman, "Next, It's E-ducation," *New York Times,* November 17, 1999. Internet edition.

40. Deborah Nelson and Rick Weiss, "Hasty Decisions in Race to a Cure?" *Washington Post,* November 21, 1999, p. A1. Internet edition.

41. Deborah Nelson and Rick Weiss, "Gene Researchers Defend Test on Teen," *Washington Post,* December 9, 1999, p. A06. Internet edition.

42. Sheryl Gay Stolberg, "Agency Failed to Monitor Patients in Gene Research," *New York Times,* February 2, 2000. Internet edition.

43. Rick Weiss and Deborah Nelson, "FDA Halts Gene Experiments at University," *Washington Post,* January 22, 2000, p. A1. Internet edition.

44. Rick Weiss, "Monitoring Tightened for Genetic Research," *Washington Post,* March 8, 2000, p. A03. Internet edition.

45. M. D. Cabana, C. S. Rand, N. R. Powe, A. W. Wu, M. H. Wilson, P. A. Abboud, C. Rubin, and H. R. Rubin, "Why Don't Physicians Follow Clinical Practice Guidelines? A Framework for Improvement," *JAMA (Journal of the American Medical Association)* 282, 1999, 1458–1465.

46. Richard Neustadt, *Presidential Power: The Politics of Leadership* (New York: Wiley, 1976).

47. Stephen Barr and Rajiv Chandrasekaran, "For Y2K, Americans Staying Firmly on the Ground," *Washington Post,* November 17, 1999, p. E1. Internet edition.

48. Anemona Hartocollis, "Red Tape Snags Principals' Outserts; Superintendent Says He Was Blamed," *New York Times,* January 25, 2000. Internet edition.

49. Allen R. Myerson, "Big Trouble for Tiny New York Oil Industry," *New York Times,* January 10, 2000. Internet edition.

50. James Risen, "C.I.A. Inquiry of Its Ex-Director Was Stalled at Top, Report Says," *New York Times,* February 1, 2000. Internet edition.

51. "Bail for Wen Ho Lee," *New York Times,* August 23, 2000. Internet edition.

52. "An Overview: The Wen Ho Lee Case," *New York Times,* September 28, 2000. Internet edition.

53. Rene Sanchez, "Police Scandal Shakes Los Angeles," *International Herald Tribune,* February 14, 2000, p. 3.

54. William Claiborne, "Illinois Order on Executions Lauded," *Washington Post,* February 1, 2000, p. A2. Internet edition.

55. Kineret Rubin-Shostack, "Corruption in Israeli Local Authorities," M.A. thesis submitted to the Department of Political Science, Hebrew University of Jerusalem, 1998. Hebrew.

56. See, for example, Graham K. Wilson, *Interest Groups* (Oxford: Blackwell, 1990).

57. John M. Broder, "Pharmaceutical Industry Steps Up Efforts to Kill Medicare Drug Plan," *New York Times,* June 28, 2000. Internet edition.

58. Carey Goldberg, "Spouse Abuse Crackdown, Surprisingly, Nets Many Women," *New York Times,* November 23, 1999. Internet edition.

59. David A. Vise and Lorraine Adams, "Despite Rhetoric, Violent Crime Climbs," *Washington Post,* December 5, 1999, p. A03. Internet edition.

60. Fox Blutterfield, "Cities Reduce Crime and Conflict Without New York–Style Hardball," *New York Times,* March 4, 2000. Internet edition.

61. Abby Goodnough, "Answers Allegedly Supplied in Effort to Raise Test Scores," *New York Times,* December 8, 1999. Internet edition.

62. Brigid Schulte, "Principal Resigns Amid Reports of Cheating," *Washington Post,* June 1, 2000, p. A1. Internet edition.

63. Jonathan Weisman, "Only a Test: The Texas Education Myth," *New Republic,* April 10, 2000. Internet edition.

64. Gretchen Morgenson, "Forecasts Made Rosy for Investors, but Results Are Sometimes Paler," *New York Times,* December 21, 1999. Internet edition.

65. Caroline E. Mayer, "3 Companies Settle Rebate, Coupon Cases: FTC Calls Promotions Misleading, Too Slow," *Washington Post,* January 11, 2000, p. E03. Internet edition.

66. Juliet Eilperin, "House Votes to Restrict EPA Use of Smog Data," *Washington Post,* June 22, 2000, p. A01. Internet edition.

67. "E-xaggeration," *Economist,* October 30–November 5, 1999. Internet edition.

68. Lee Hockstader, "New Statistics on Poor Jar Israeli Complacency," *Washington Post,* December 21, 1999, p. A25. Internet edition.

69. Timothy M. Sneeding, Michael O'Higgins, and Lee Rainwater, eds., *Poverty, Inequality and Income Distribution in Comparative Perspective: The Luxembourg Income Study (LIS)* (New York: Harvester Wheatsheaf, 1993).

70. Jason DeParle, "Bold Effort Leaves Much Unchanged for the Poor," *New York Times,* December 30, 1999. Internet edition.

71. "Welfare Success in Minnesota," *New York Times,* June 14, 2000. Internet edition.

72. Nina Bernstein, "New York Drops Psychic Training Program," *New York Times,* January 29, 2000. Internet edition.

73. Robert Pear, "A Million Parents Lost Medicaid, Study Says," *New York Times,* June 20, 2000. Internet edition.

74. Guy Gugliotta, "Food Labels: By Some Measures, a Well-Read Success," *Washington Post,* January 3, 2000, p. A03. Internet edition.

75. Stephen Barr and Rajiv Chandrasekaran, p. E1. Chandrasekaran, "Y2K Bug Has No Bite So Far," *Washington Post,* December 31, 1999. Internet editions. David Kentenbaum, "Why the Press Didn't Understand Y2K," *New Republic,* January 17, 2000. Internet edition.

76. Juliet Eilperin, "Quietly, House Gives Sallie Mae a Potentially Huge Break," *Washington Post,* October 28, 1999, p. A16. Internet edition.

77. "Bad Tax Cuts Inside Good Bills," *New York Times,* April 12, 2000. Internet edition.

78. David R. Francis, "Bye-Bye Corporate Tax Revenues," *Christian Science Monitor,* November 3, 1999. Internet edition.

79. David Cay Johnston, "Corporate Taxes Fall, but Citizens Are Paying More," *New York Times,* February 19, 2000. Internet edition.

80. Glenn Kessler, "Treasury Aims to Shutter Tax Shelters," *Washington Post*, February 29, 2000, p. A01. Internet edition.

81. David Cay Johnston, "I.R.S. Employees Face More Investigations by Treasury Agents," *New York Times*, November 18, 1999; and "Phantom Rogues at the I.R.S.," *New York Times*, August 19, 2000. Internet editions.

82. David Cay Johnston, "Reducing Audits of the Wealthy, I.R.S. Turns Eye on Working Poor," *New York Times*, December 15, 1999. Internet edition.

83. John M. Broder, "Bill to Ban Most Forms of Internet Gambling Gains in House," *New York Times*, July 14, 2000. Internet edition.

84. Amy Goldstein, "FDA Moves to Control Online Drug Sales," *Washington Post*, December 27, 1999. Internet edition.

85. Robert Pear, "Online Sales Spur Illegal Importing of Medicine," *New York Times*, January 10, 2000. Internet edition.

86. John Markoff, "An Online Extortion Plot Results in Release of Credit Card Data," *New York Times*, January 10, 2000. Internet edition.

87. Sally Squires, "The Case of the 'Phantom Fat,'" *Washington Post*, January 11, 2000, p. H14. Internet edition.

88. Sally Squires, "High Irony: New Labels Are Short on Facts," *Washington Post*, March 7, 2000, p. H14. Internet edition.

89. Guy Gugliotta, "Herbal Products Boom Takes Human Toll," *Washington Post*, March 19, 2000, p. A01. Internet edition.

90. Sheryl Gay Stolberg, "Folk Cures on Trial: Alternative Care Gains a Foothold," *New York Times*, January 31, 2000. Internet edition.

91. James Risen, "To Bomb Sudan Plant, or Not: A Year Later, Debates Rankle," *New York Times*, October 27, 1999. Internet edition.

92. "Apologize," *New Republic*, November 6, 1999. Internet edition.

93. Risen, "To Bomb Sudan Plant, or Not."

94. Robert B. Stinnett, *Day of Deceit: The Truth About F.D.R. and Pearl Harbor* (New York: Free Press, 1999), as reviewed by Richard Bernstein, "'Day of Deceit': On Dec. 7, Did We Know We Knew?" *New York Times*, December 15, 1999. Internet edition.

95. Steven Lee Myers, "Chinese Embassy Bombing: A Wide Net of Blame," *New York Times*, April 17, 2000. Internet edition.

96. Barbara Crossette, "Inquiry Faults U.S. Inaction in '94 Rwanda Genocide," *New York Times*, December 17, 1999. Internet edition.

97. Colin Woodard, "America's Half-Forgotten Islands," *Christian Science Monitor*, December 27, 1999. Internet edition.

98. Steven Pearlstein, "A Death Moves Canada to Examine Indians' Lives," *Washington Post*, December 27, 1999, p. A17. Internet edition.

99. Howard Kurtz and Sharon Waxman, "White House, Networks, Cut Anti-Drug Deal," *Washington Post*, January 14, 2000, p. A1. Internet edition.

100. Fred Greenstein, *The Hidden Hand Presidency: Eisenhower as Leader* (New York: Basic Books, 1982).

101. Leonard Garment, "Richard Nixon, Unedited," *New York Times*, October 19, 1999. Internet edition; and Seymour M. Hersh, *The Price of Power: Kissinger in the Nixon White House* (New York: Summit Books, 1983), pp. 60–61.

102. Edmund Morris, *Dutch: A Memoir of Ronald Reagan* (New York: Random House, 1999). Passages quoted or paraphrased come from pages 241, 414, 443, 579, 636.

103. Morris, p. 238.

104. William Martin, *With God on Our Side: The Rise of the Religious Right in America* (New York: Broadway Books, 1996), p. 310.

105. Howard Kurtz, "McCain Tries to Temper Reports of Outbursts," *Washington Post,* November 2, 1999, p. A3. Internet edition.

106. Jonathan Chait, "Race to the Bottom," *New Republic,* December 20, 1999. Internet edition.

107. *The Jerusalem Post,* September 5, 1994, p. 3.

108. *The Jerusalem Post,* November 28, 1994, p. 1.

109. *Ha'aretz,* October 31, 1995, p. 1. Hebrew.

110. Jon Jeter, "Mbeki vs. the AIDS Experts," *Washington Post,* May 16, 2000, p. A1. Internet edition. On national leaders who act against the best interests of their countries, see Yehezkel Dror, *Crazy States: A Counterconventional Strategic Problem* (Lexington, Mass.: D. C. Heath, 1971).

111. John F. Harris, "Gore Clarifies Position on Gays: No 'Litmus Test' for Joint Chiefs," *New York Times,* January 9, 2000. Internet edition.

112. George McGovern, "Discovering Greatness in Lyndon Johnson," *New York Times,* December 5, 1999. Internet edition.

113. See Sean Wilentz's review of Ronald Steel, *In Love with Night: The American Romance with Robert Kennedy* (New York: Simon & Schuster, 1999), *New York Times,* January 8, 2000. Internet edition.

114. Thomas L. Friedman, "Frozen in Damascus," *New York Times,* December 5, 1999. Internet edition.

115. Michael Wines, "Putin Is Russia's Front-Runner, but His Plans Are a Mystery," *New York Times,* March 22, 2000. Internet edition.

116. Charles McCarry, "Candidates Can Be Too Candid," *New York Times,* December 13, 1999. Internet edition.

117. Martin, chapter 9.

118. "The Art of Budget Leaks," *Washington Post,* December 30, 1999, p. A30. Internet edition.

119. I Kings 22.

120. I Kings 18, 19.

121. Amos 7:10–17.

122. Jeremiah 26:20–23.

123. Ephraim E. Urbach, *The Sages: Their Concepts and Belief,* translated by Israel Abrahams (Cambridge: Harvard University Press, 1987), p. 559.

124. See Ira Sharkansky, *Ambiguity, Coping, and Governance: Israeli Experiences in Politics, Religion, and Policymaking* (Westport, Conn.: Praeger Publishers, 1999).

125. Tim Chappell, "Rationally Deciding What to Believe," *Religious Studies* 33, no. 1, March 1997, 105–109.

126. David C. Leege and Lyman A. Kellstedt, eds., *Rediscovering the Religious Factor in American Politics* (Armonk, N.Y.: M. E. Sharpe, 1993); Kenneth D. Wald, *Religion and Politics in the United States* (Washington, DC: CQ Press, 1992); Stephen D. Johnson and Joseph B. Tamney, eds., *The Political Role of Religion in the United States* (Boulder, Colo.: Westview Press, 1986); Robert Wuthnow, *The Restructuring of American Religion* (Princeton: Princeton University Press, 1988); R. Laurence Moore, *Selling God: American Religion in the Marketplace of Culture* (New York: Oxford University Press, 1994);

and Michael J. Lacey, ed., *Religion and Twentieth-Century American Intellectual Life* (New York: Cambridge University Press, 1989).

127. *Time,* February 6, 1995, p. 48; and Wald, p. 12.

128. Harold Bloom, *The American Religion: The Emergence of the Post-Christian Nation* (New York: Simon & Schuster, 1992).

129. William Martin, *With God on Our Side: The Rise of the Religious Right in America* (New York: Broadway Books, 1996), p. 14.

130. Lois Romano, "Oklahoma's Divisive Disclaimer on Evolution," *Washington Post,* December 1, 1999, p. A3. Internet edition.

131. James Glanz, "Poll Finds That Support Is Strong for Teaching 2 Origin Theories," *New York Times,* March 11, 2000. Internet edition.

132. Annie Gowen, "In Kansas, a Creationist Casualty?" *Washington Post,* November 4, 1999, p. A1. Internet edition.

133. Pam Belluck, "Evolution Foes Dealt a Defeat in Kansas Vote," *New York Times,* August 3, 2000. Internet edition.

134. Juliet Eilperin, "Appointment of Chaplain Splits House," *Washington Post,* December 3, 1999. Internet edition.

135. Matthew Vita, "House Gets 1st Catholic Chaplain," *Washington Post,* March 24, 2000, p. A01. Internet edition.

136. Martin, p. 211.

137. Ira Sharkansky, *The Politics of Religion and the Religion of Politics: Looking at Israel* (Lanham, Md.: Lexington Books, 2000).

138. Deborah Sontag, "At Riven Holy Sepulcher, Anxiety as Crowds Loom," *New York Times,* December 1, 1999. Internet edition.

139. *Ha'aretz,* November 24, 1999, p. 1. Hebrew.

140. Sarah Delaney, "Vatican Criticizes Israeli for Mosque Plans," *Washington Post,* November 23, 1999, p. A17. Internet edition.

141. *Ha'aretz,* November 22, 1999, p. 1. Hebrew. Lee Hockstader, "Holy Land Churches Close to Protest Mosque," *Washington Post,* November 22, 1999, p. A1. Internet edition.

142. Sontag, "At Riven Holy Sepulcher."

143. Tony Allen-Mills, "Israeli Relief as Doomsday Is Postponed," *Times,* January 2, 2000. Internet edition.

144. Lee Hockstader, "Nun Sounds Trumpet at Jericho: Sister of Ex-Clinton Aide Takes On Rival Russian Church," *Washington Post,* January 28, 2000, p. A17. Internet edition.

145. Jon Jeter, "Namibia's Soldiers Without a Cause: Angola Lures Villagers into Bloody Civil War," *Washington Post,* January 27, 2000, p. A21. Internet edition.

146. "Kigali and Kampala: Congo's Hidden War," *Economist,* June 17–23, 2000. Internet edition.

3

Organizations Designed Not to Be Governed

In the previous chapter we saw laws designed not to be noticed and a variety of other conditions that get in the way of knowing what will be policy or how existing policy will be implemented. In this chapter, I will examine public service organizations designed not to be governed. Or to be more exact, these groups are not held accountable to the governments that fund them in customary ways.

A common image of governmental organization is the hierarchy of departments under the apparent control of the chief executive. It is expected that heads of units will control the activities of subordinates and report in turn to superiors who will hold them responsible for the orderly operation of their organizations. A chief executive—such as the U.S. president or a prime minister in a parliamentary government—will answer to the electorate for the operation of the entire government.

The organizational chart of the U.S. government displays fourteen cabinet-level departments reporting to the president (Agriculture, Commerce, Defense, Education, Energy, Health and Human Services, Housing and Urban Development, Interior, Justice, Labor, State, Transportation, Treasury, and Veterans Affairs) plus fifty-seven "independent establishments and government corporations" that range alphabetically from the African Development Foundation and the Central Intelligence Agency to the U.S. International Trade Commission and the U.S. Postal Service.

The first hint of a problem in the coherence of the U.S. government is that different official publications offer different lists of independent agencies. The *Statistical Abstract* published by the Census Bureau includes agencies (e.g., American Battle Monuments Commission and the

Smithsonian Institution) that do not make it to the organizational chart in the *U.S. Government Manual* published by the National Archives.

Public Organizations That Are Not Governmental

Further problems appear in a large and growing segment of public organizations that go by several labels: quasi-governmental, government corporations, government contractors, commissions, authorities, districts, consultants, not-for-profit, tax-exempt, units on the margins of government, and the "third sector," that is, neither purely public nor private. The labels are not precise and may be affixed without consistency to organizations that differ or resemble one another. As political scientist Jameson Doig points out,

> Confusion over names and characteristics is a not infrequent response of those who first enter this corner of the governmental zoo. "Authority," "corporation," "special district" and "commission" are titles used to identify governmental agencies of unusual shape and temperament; but the zoo keeper seems to have affixed labels almost at random, so that a "public authority" in one cage may be a very close cousin to a "government corporation" pawing the ground in another enclosure, while yet another "corporation" flies from tree to tree, sharing little in common with the first two inhabitants.[1]

What is common among these organizations is that they provide public services, often with the financial aid and, ostensibly, the program direction of government units. But they do all of this outside the hierarchy by which elected officials can supervise their work.

It is possible to gauge the growth of these bodies in several ways. In the United States, the financial outlays of the national government grew by a multiple of 8.2 times between 1970 and 1990, although the number of federal civilian employees actually declined from 3 to 2.8 million. The explanation is that more and more federal outlays represent programs implemented not by U.S. government agencies and employees but by money transferred by those agencies and employees to other organizations. Some of these "other" organizations are the agencies of state and local governments. But many are nongovernmental or quasi-governmental organizations that receive moneys directly from the federal government in exchange for providing services. There is also a lot of money that flows from state and local governments (some of which comes initially to them from the federal government) to nongovernmental and quasi-governmental organizations.

The activities performed by nongovernmental and quasi-governmental organizations parallel those of government. They include prisons and security agencies that incarcerate convicts and guard governmental installations; social service agencies that provide health, training, and other educational services outside the framework of government clinics or schools and that send homemakers to help the elderly and disabled; companies that provide low-cost housing to clients who meet criteria acceptable to government agencies; and consultants who review government activities and provide detailed planning for policy changes.

One reason for the prominence of these bodies is the continued growth in demand for public services, along with economic expansion that provides the financial wherewithal. Growth in activities supported by policymakers has exceeded the capacities and desires of government officials to control every phase of policy design and service delivery.

"Privatization" has been prominent since the 1980s. It involves turning things over to the private sector and making clients pay more of the real cost of services. There has been a decline in accountability to the public; elected representatives and professional government personnel no longer keep close track of many of these activities. Advocates of privatization believe that the private sector, with its elements of competition and a concern for financial gain, would provide better services at a lower price than a purely government operation. For some scholars and political activists, however, this is a matter of debate. Nonetheless, those on the side of privatization are winning the votes in Congress and state legislatures as well as the national parliaments of numerous other countries.

Privatization and other ways of shedding the responsibilities of government owe something to the permanent urge to simplify. Insofar as government itself becomes difficult to manage, its tasks can be made more manageable by being made smaller. Yet the process is partly an illusion. Transferring programs and whole organizations from government, per se, may not shrink government except in a formal sense that is misleading. Despite privatization, the government often retains a role in financing and managing new bodies, perhaps at a distance and with official claims to avoiding involvement in the details of administration. The entirety of what the government does directly and indirectly continues to grow, becomes more complicated, and provides additional reasons for those affected to pursue other ways of simplifying their lives.

Under the heading of privatization, governments sell companies that they own to the private sector, or they sell some of their shares in those companies. Typically the government does not rid itself entirely of influence over the entity that is "privatized." A formerly government-owned airline, electric utility, water line, railroad, or telephone company may remain subject to government supervision and regulation in the name of safety, quality of service, or pricing. The result is more bodies somewhere in the interstices between sectors: not entirely public and not entirely private. To complicate the matter, residual government ownership or control differs from one entity to another. Degrees of enforcement also vary, so that the formal rules may not reveal who controls hiring, the selection of key officials, programming, and pricing.

The transfer of activities from government authorities to some other bodies that are linked to government—but not exactly part of government—is not new. Officials have long organized some activities under the rubric of government-owned corporations, or statutory authorities. Organizations with these formats manage utilities, railroads, telecommunications, airlines, banks, and agricultural and industrial activities. The universal and long-standing phenomenon of local governments also indicates that central government officials admit they cannot do everything and that some degree of regional variation and flexibility is appropriate in administering public policies. The United States counts more than 50,000 municipalities, towns, counties, and school districts. There are another 35,000 "special districts," which are responsible for water and sewage, libraries, parks, air- and water ports, police and fire protection, mosquito control, and numerous other functions. These bodies benefit from various financial lines between them and local, state, and national governments. Some possess their own authority to collect taxes or borrow money. Some are governed by their own officials elected by the voters, and others are nominally responsible to municipal or state government officials. They differ greatly in the formal or informal elements of self-rule, with partial, complete, or no effective supervision from other governmental bodies.

Several authors have identified the problems of holding accountable organizations that fit on the margins of government or in the third sector somewhere between the public and private sectors. One observer notes a "thickening of government," or the proliferation of service agencies and units to manage them, that produces a diffusion of power and responsibility and blurred lines of accountability.[2] Among the problems are:

• The nongovernmental status of service providers makes it difficult for government administrators to hold them accountable despite the fact that these services are partly paid for by government.

• The autonomy of nongovernmental firms that work for government under contract enables politicians to avoid blame when programs sour.

• Each of the multiple providers of government funds has formal responsibilities for the oversight of quasi-governmental entities. However, each provider may rely on others to perform oversight, with the result that little oversight occurs.

• Government agencies and private sector donors may support organizations partly because of the worthiness of the causes they serve and the voluntary nature of some staff members. Charities and faith-based organizations enjoy the prestige associated with voluntarism and religion. Those who provide funds may feel uncomfortable about holding committed staff and volunteers to account. In other words, the prestige of being a donor to a valued cause gets in the way of looking closely at the activities being supported.

• Some providers of funds have an incentive not to look too closely at bodies that receive their largesse. Politicians have been found to profit personally, or through their families, from quasi-governmental organizations that provide them with favors or "kickbacks" of one form or another.[3]

The General Accounting Office has reported about the huge number of third sector organizations in the United States, and the incapacity of accountability mechanisms to review systematically even the relatively simple issue of whether they merit tax-exempt status. The Internal Revenue Code allows tax exemption under twenty-five categories, including labor unions, social clubs, and credit unions. There are 650,000 registered charities, among more than a million organizations that have been approved for tax-exempt status.[4]

Charitable organizations are not necessarily saints. Some call themselves by names similar to those of well-established organizations, seemingly for the purpose of fooling donors into sending money to them rather than to the better-known rival. In the field of doing something nice for a child with a serious illness, one journalist finds the Make-A-Wish Foundation, Grant-A-Wish Foundation, Grant-A-Wish Network, Children's Wish Foundation International, Fulfill a Wish Foundation, and Wishing Well Foundation USA. One hundred fifty charities registered with the Internal Revenue Service (IRS) include "breast cancer" in their name.[5]

For some politicians, faith-based organizations have particular appeal. George W. Bush perceived their usefulness when he was governor of Texas and has, since becoming president, sought to expand their role in providing social services throughout the United States by facilitating government funding of their activities. Supporters see the personnel of these organizations motivated by caring values not found in secular bureaucracies. Organizations dealing with drug dependency, the training of welfare recipients, or the rehabilitation of individuals with criminal records may use their religious norms to instill feelings of self-worth and responsibility in their clients. Moreover, money raised by religious organizations can supplement government funds.

As with secular charities, however, the reputation of faith-based organizations can get in the way of accountability. Formal procedures to test claims of success and track expenditures may be in place, but the aura of faith may keep government officials from looking too closely. As discussed in a later chapter, some claims about faith-based counseling programs for prison inmates have not clearly stood up to systematic tests.

A number of media exposés have focused on the problematic behavior of charities; tax-exempt organizations; government contractors that provide social services, including faith-based organizations; and the government bodies that are supposed to be supervising them. A number of charges surface time and again:

• Organizations spend inordinate sums on fund-raising and the salaries of key administrators.

• Organizations compete with each other to provide similar services, and they resist coordination, either among themselves or by government agencies.

• Individuals who have become prominent on account of major government positions (e.g., Chairman of the Joint Chiefs of Staff General Colin L. Powell and Surgeon General Dr. Everett C. Koop) have lent their name to organizations claiming to provide public service, but the service either is not provided as claimed, or the prominent figure mixes public service with profit-making activities.[6]

• Privately run prisons abuse the inmates or otherwise fail to provide the services included within their contractual obligations.

• Well-regarded medical insurers, including affiliates of Blue Cross, have been found guilty of mismanagement and fraud in their role as government contractors responsible for approving payments to health care providers.[7]

• Operation Smile, a program to send plastic surgeons to poor countries in order to repair children with cleft palates and lips, was accused of putting speed and numbers above caution and safety, with the result of unduly high incidences of post-operation complications and death. The problems became public with the resignation of distinguished members of the organization's board of directors and the decision of some prominent corporate donors to cease their support.[8]

• Research organizations, set up as nonprofit think tanks, have been found receiving substantial grants from corporations that stand to benefit from the nature of the organizations' reports. The issue becomes especially problematic when there is no mention by the organization of the source of its funding and its reports present a veneer of scientific objectivity. Major sugar producers, as well as Exxon, Hertz, Philip Morris, U.S. West, Microsoft, the insurance company AIG, and labor unions have funded studies that end up endorsing their positions on public issues.[9]

• Several organizations appealing to Muslim communities in North America and Europe as providers of humanitarian services have been associated with terrorist activities. Money said to be meant for food, clothing, education, health services, and other humanitarian activity has been used for weapons and the training of fighters and linked to deadly incidents such as the attacks on the World Trade Center and the Pentagon on September 11, 2001, and the earlier bombing of American embassies in Nairobi and Dar es Salaam. American officials have begun to scrutinize some thirty organizations (out of some 6,000 Islamic groups operating worldwide), but they concede that the issue is highly sensitive due to both domestic politics and diplomatic pressures. While organization personnel cite expenditures for humanitarian activities, officials focus on individuals associated with the organizations who have also affiliated with organizations known to be involved in violence.[10]

Israel relies on its Law of Associations to provide some oversight with respect to its third sector. The law requires associations to register with the Ministry of Interior, specify their objectives, submit annual audited financial statements, establish a board of directors and an audit committee, and inform the ministry about the membership of those bodies. The law also requires all associations to convene annual meetings and maintain proper bookkeeping practices. Finally, the law grants the registrar of associations the power to conduct investigations of an association's management and operations and to recommend to a court that an association in violation be dismantled.[11]

While the Law of Associations appears to provide for extensive accountability of associations, the state comptroller has found severe shortcomings in its implementation:

• Many associations submit financial reports beyond the deadline or do not submit them at all.
• The registrar of associations has limited means for analyzing the financial reports of the associations.
• There is no systematic updating of information about the associations' boards of directors.
• The registrar of associations has conducted few investigations of associations, and despite findings that seem to warrant dismantling, the registrar has never recommended that this step be taken.[12]

The various kinds of bodies on the margins of the state put a premium on *maze smartness,* both for policymakers who would influence what they do and for citizens who would find the correct source for the services they desire. Which body provides what service in each locale? This question is asked time and again when there is a confusing mixture of governmental, quasi-governmental, and seemingly private organizations, offering competing or overlapping services. Yet another issue requiring maze smartness is knowing where to complain when services seem to be inadequate. Accountability is not only a principle of good government. It is a way for officials and clients to know which buttons can be pressed to acquire appropriate information as well as whom to pressure in order to correct problems.

The first step in becoming maze smart consists of knowing that a service exists somewhere in the collection of public and other organizations. Subsequent steps involve knowing the criteria for accepting clients and providing services, who funds what, and which organizations can intervene to change practices.

For example, home care for the elderly may come from a different organization than home care for the disabled who are not aged. One organization's home care may provide hot meals but not shopping while another provides shopping and only cold meals. Catholics may get a better deal from the organization that serves them than Jews, or the reverse, despite the fact that both get part of their money from the local authority, a state or federal agency, and a regional charity like United

Way. Programs may be similar from one organization to another, but the individual clients may feel better cared for by one or another's volunteers.

Quasi-governmental organizations tend to share a trait that adds to problems of control: Many of them provide services that depend heavily on professional personnel who insist on using their discretion in dealing with individual cases. Physicians, attorneys, social workers, and other highly trained individuals feel they must have a certain degree of latitude in treating their organization's clients. Many of them also feel qualified to have a role in deciding what their organizations should provide by way of services or how they should divide the budgets available to them. The general rule is that professionals raise problems for administrators and political overseers. Even priests and military officers—supposedly working in the most rigid of hierarchies—argue that the realities of their tasks require some room for maneuver amidst the dictates of superiors.

Who But a Person with Illusions
Would Seek to Administer a Major University?

For university students and teachers of political science, the problems of unmanageable establishments appear close to home. Higher education is a prime example of organizations that resist government. This is especially true of institutions that enjoy high prestige. Creativity is more important than orderly administration. Personnel are skilled in rhetoric, analysis, and criticism. Programs vary in concept and are dynamic in the face of scientific discoveries and shifting perspectives. Prestigious state universities are buffered from public control by boards of governors or regents. Politicians may appoint the members of these bodies, but their terms may be long and overlapping so that no one political incumbent can dominate the board. Private universities also have multimember boards of governors to protect them from the influence of individual donors or alumni. All of this makes problems for anyone who would describe policymaking or implementation in higher education.

Universities vary perhaps only in degree from other organizations staffed by highly trained professionals in the problems presented to those who would control them. The distinctions of universities may reflect the traditions of academic freedom—which may stretch to faculty insistence on controlling organizational details distant from what they teach—as well as academics' feelings that they are the brightest stars in the universe and cannot heed directions from individuals who lack their intelligence and sensitivity.

Writing about academics ranges from the incisive literary portraits by David Lodge[13] and C. P. Snow[14] to the systematic analyses in the *Journal of Higher Education* as well as commentaries that criticize the status quo and propose reform.[15] For someone seeking to describe higher education, it is no easy task to sort the general pattern from nuance, formal structures from the informal. It is also difficult to phrase the description and analysis in a way to satisfy academic colleagues who are familiar with contrary cases and who are practiced in the ways of critical peer review.

Higher education deserves extended treatment here not only because it is a topic likely to touch the personal concerns of readers but also because of its inherent significance. Higher education is important for the resources it absorbs as well as for its promised impact on society. Financial outlays are difficult to summarize, given the reliance on numerous sources of governmental and nongovernmental funds, but they are likely to place this field of service among the most heavily financed, along with health and primary and secondary education. Upwards of 50 percent of relevant age groups study in higher education in well-to-do societies (90 percent in Canada).[16] Students and their parents see higher education as an entry to desirable occupations, incomes, and lifestyles. Empirical studies leave no doubt that graduates will be more prosperous than others and reach higher levels in public and private sector employment.

Challenges to Weberian Aspirations

Those who learn about management in university may aspire to organizations that follow the models described by Max Weber that emphasize management, regimentation, control, hierarchy, and accountability. However, those who would manage universities come up against traditions that emphasize the intelligence and creativity of key staff members, their talents for the criticism of what is, and their inclination to reform, revise, and create anew.[17]

What Weber wrote about bureaucracy in the first quarter of the twentieth century is no longer the final word. Contemporary organizational theorists distinguish between numerous organizational shapes, from the highly pyramidal to the nearly flat, and describe no end of behaviors associated with one class or another of bureaucracy.[18] Yet the key features that Weber identified remain dominant in the literature, at least as the model from which others distinguish their own traits.

Even Weber, in newspaper articles published between 1908 and 1919, commented on the lack of fit between the formal rules and actual practice in universities.[19] Weber's norms of bureaucracy encounter academics' insistence of collegial governance. Standardization according to formal rules with a minimum of exceptions falls to the principle of academic freedom, wide variation among units with different missions and quality, multiple sources of funding, and the presence of prima donnas among the academics who are to be controlled. In the words of one official with responsibility for managing some programs at Columbia University, "The faculty are independent spirits, and we can't make them do anything."[20] There is also the problem of earmarked funds, or resources limited to specific purposes, that remain outside the control of central administrators. Insistence on quality control falls to the multiplicity and fuzziness of purposes and standards in academia. Concerns for systematic evaluation fall to the artful dodging of skilled academics and the principle of academic freedom.

There are, to be sure, segments of tertiary education that do lend themselves to uniformity and regimentation. They are more likely to be found in the large number of teaching-oriented institutions rather than those that prize creative research. The most prestigious institutions seek to recruit intellectually aggressive academics, who are likely to resist regimentation. The boundaries are blurred between one type of institution and another. Variations appear not only among free-standing institutions but within individual systems having multiple campuses, like that of California, and national systems seemingly under the control of a coordinating committee, like Israel. Even within individual institutions, units as small as faculties and departments may have their own traditions. Allan Bloom summarized the situation by noting that the university does not "project a coherent image."[21]

There is a connection between the first and second segments of this chapter. It is fitting to think of prestigious universities—and the problems involved with holding them accountable—in the context of third sector organizations. Great universities are part of the third sector insofar as they operate with a mixture of governmental and nongovernmental funds and administrative procedures. They are extreme models of the third sector, however, on account of the internal creativity—and lack of organizational discipline—that they foster. The heads of great universities may be able to guide their operation, but to do so they have to persuade a large number of independent-minded individuals who think of themselves as the colleagues of administrators and not their subordinates. "Control" is more elusive in the university than elsewhere.

Higher Education in Israel

I received all my formal education in the United States and spent more than twenty years as regular and visiting faculty at several U.S. universities. Since 1975, I have been at the Hebrew University of Jerusalem. Visits for brief or extended periods at universities in several other countries have taught me that all universities are not the same, but they share traits that confound administration. The details below come from the Hebrew University. Some of them reflect features of national politics and culture, but the prominent elements of obtuse structure and the frustrations of administrators are apparent elsewhere.

In many ways, Israeli universities resemble organizations of higher education in other countries. [22] Especially in the case of institutions that aspire to intellectual leadership, there is likely to be a large role for faculty participation in university governance. This entails decentralization and a role for a senate or other faculty body that seems to prize extended discussions over quick decisions. Insofar as the heart of a distinguished university lies dispersed in numerous academic departments and research institutes, policy decisions are likely to respect the differences in disciplinary norms between these units. Academics' concern for careful deliberation is associated with the importance of committees, representative of the university's various units, which are assigned the task of preparing issues for a policy decision. Other committees deal with the application of policy to individual cases, whether it be deciding on which applicants are admitted to the student body, who qualifies for financial aid, or whether a master's or doctoral thesis qualifies for acceptance. University faculty not only do the work of teaching and research but also have a major role in funding themselves and their institution. Prestigious universities rely heavily on grants received from governments and foundations concerned with advancing research. Universities have rules about the expenditure of research grants, but researchers, who raised the money and presumably know how best to spend it, are likely to have considerable discretion.

The multiple sources of university funding—from government, research grants, student tuition, donations from alumni or other patrons, and the earnings of an endowment—also get in the way of centralized control. Among the simple rules heard in universities and other organizations are "Money talks," and "The person who pays the piper selects the tune." Academics who want to control their own work can apply for a grant or approach a donor. University administrators who want independence from certain dictates (whether it be government or a prominent alumnus) can look for money elsewhere.

The details of such structures and procedures vary from one university to another and from one country to another. The larger picture, however, is one of complex institutions that respect the skills of faculty and researchers. Governing structures tend to grant them considerable leeway, which is another way of saying that central controls are loose, whether by central university officials or the governments that provide much of their money.

Israeli universities rely on the government for close to 90 percent of their operating funds, although none are formally defined as government institutions. In exchange for support, they must accept the decisions of the Finance Ministry and the Coordinating Committee for Higher Education for the key issues of staff salary, student fees, and new programs and staff positions.

Academic self-governance includes deans elected for fixed terms by tenured academics in each faculty and a rector (i.e., the chief academic administrator) elected for a fixed term by all-faculty senates dominated by tenured professors. These terms for academic administrators are short, typically in the range of three to five years, and get in the way of long-range planning. University presidents have responsibility for overall institutional management and fund-raising and are chosen by boards of governors composed of distinguished citizens and overseas donors as well as some faculty members. Israeli universities resemble others in depending on committees of faculty members, sometimes with student representatives, to render advice or final decisions on issues of faculty hiring, promotion, and discipline; student discipline; and curriculum.

Israel's modest population (6,000,000) and the Hebrew language of instruction produces a small intellectual community limited in its capacity to recruit overseas personnel. It is common for academic departments to hire their own graduates, with some senior professors acquiring a reputation for squiring a stable of acolytes through graduate training and then from junior to senior ranks on the staff. Patronage breeds antagonisms. In order to protect the hiring and promotion process from favoritism, universities have instituted cumbersome procedures involving distinguished referees from overseas as well as secret membership for committees charged with approving appointments and promotions. Because of the several stages in each process and dependence on the cooperation of busy professors from outside the country, tenure procedures lasting less than a year are unusual; those taking more than two years are not uncommon.

Acquiring tenure and advancement in academic rank appears to demand similar achievements as in the better universities of the United States. The principal Israeli ranks are lecturer, senior lecturer (typically associated with tenure), associate professor, and full professor. Promotion criteria emphasize publication, with less credit given for teaching quality and service in university administration and other venues. Although there are some variations among and within the universities, the demands with respect to publication emphasize international (i.e., non-Israeli) journals subject to peer review or prominent university presses in the case of books. A document making the rounds of Israeli academics proclaims that God himself could not receive tenure at an Israeli university, for the following reasons:

- He had only one major publication.
- And it was in Hebrew.
- And it had no references.
- And it wasn't published in a refereed journal.
- And some even doubt He wrote it Himself.
- It may be true that He created the world but what has He published/done since then?
- His cooperative efforts have been limited.
- The scientific community has not been able to repeat His results.

It is no easier to govern a university in Israel than it is anywhere else. From a local perspective, it does not seem possible that there is anything less orderly than the way we do our academic business. Israeli universities display numerous gaps between formal rules and actual practice, often evading formal policy by counting themselves as exceptions to that policy. Several examples appear in the realm of faculty compensation.

On the one hand, public sector salaries figure prominently in public discussion and media coverage as does the norm that it is not wise to change the "salary," per se, for individual groups of workers. This principle stems from a cumbersome history of labor relations in which salaries for various groups of workers have been linked formally to other similar groups. The result is that one group (e.g., university faculty members) could not win a salary increase without triggering increases throughout the economy. Insofar as the Finance Ministry has a hand in the negotiations for all public sector salaries and is usually set against wide-ranging increases, each sector has learned to demand special *fringe benefit payments* in place of an increase in salary. The claim is that the payments are justified on account of features unique to the occupation in question. Some of the most bizarre payments made to various groups have been a "height allowance" paid to telephone and electric workers who must climb poles, a "shame allowance" to tax auditors who claim that the nature of their work inhibits social contacts, and an "effort allowance" to laboratory technicians. Some years ago military officers and health personnel received a special payment for being "on call" all hours of the day and night. University academics latched onto the idea and won a payment on the claim that students and colleagues call for help after normal working hours. The point is that these special allowances are fictions meant to compensate workers in one field without spreading the benefit to workers in other fields whose "salaries" are linked to the group at issue. The pathos is that tricks learned by one group tend to spread through the economy. Workers in numerous fields, including university teachers, receive off-salary payments for personal automobiles (whether or not they have cars or driving licenses), home telephones, clothing appropriate to their work, and annual vacations. Currently a professor's total monthly compensation comprises roughly 50 percent salary and seniority payments and 50 percent other payments.

One of the prominent other payments offers another illustration of how a subset of formal rules more or less cancels another set of rules said to define an important principle. Some years ago government negotiators agreed to the principle of paying faculty members for devoting full time to one's principal university duties of teaching and research. This is a substantial part of compensation, accounting for roughly 8 percent of annual pretax pay. The argument that won the day was that such a payment would elevate the quality of faculty teaching and research by encouraging teachers to forgo part-time jobs and contracting, which they had taken in order to supplement their incomes. Alongside the primary idea, however, have come a number of exceptions. Individuals can continue to receive the "full time" supplement if their extra work falls below certain monthly levels varying by academic rank, if it occurs within a number of favored activities (e.g., administering a university program or teaching in programs for overseas students, military personnel, or university preparatory programs), or if the university rector has signed off on one's application for an extra job in another institution.

Beyond defining subsets of rules to evade the principles included in other rules, Israeli universities are not above simply evading the rules that stand in their way. In this, they reflect the rough-and-tumble that has been described as the nation's public sector generally. Cynical Israelis speak of their country as a "voluntary state," where officials as well as citizens accept only the rules that are convenient.

The state comptroller has access to the universities on account of state funding. Just as other state auditors tend to focus on university management rather than academic programs,[23] Israel's state comptroller has concentrated on financial reporting. A series of audits published in 1999 sharply criticized departures from formal regulations and more general principles of good management. It noted that universities paid senior administrative staff in ways that violated rules laid down by government bodies and that the universities—with the encouragement of the Coordinating Committee for Higher Education—published financial reports that were incomplete. Among the items left out were future obligations, mostly for staff pensions, that amounted to some U.S.$2.85 billion.[24]

The Hebrew University of Jerusalem

The Hebrew University is a problematic organization due to blurred public and private lines of authority and a multinational character in structure, programming, and personnel. It prides itself on being "the university of the Jewish people." There is not only extensive fund-raising among Diaspora communities but a governing board with a heavy representation of Diaspora figures. Prominent in its programs of teaching, research, and publication are activities dealing with the history and current affairs of Jewish communities abroad as well as Jewish texts in their numerous languages.

Though the benefits of overseas donations and other international contacts are undeniable, they carry problems for university financial officials. The success of annual fund-raising among donors remains unclear until the end of the year. The value of proceeds depend on exchange rates between Israeli currency and those of the several countries where moneys are collected. And the value of investments made for the sake of the university in Israel and foreign countries depends on the changing performance of different national economies, government bonds, and stock exchanges. Even overseas Jewish donors with unlimited emotional feelings for the preeminent Jewish university encounter competitive fund-raising from other Israeli universities as well as from Israeli hospitals, local authorities, and religious institutions, not to mention worthy claimants from Jewish and Gentile organizations in their own countries. Government regulations in the countries of donors impose a substantial degree of organizational autonomy on the overseas units of the universities that recruit donations. Added to this is some Israeli Diaspora tension between Jerusalem and overseas personnel associated with the university as to who knows best the interests of the university and the inclinations of prospective donors.

Overseas fund-raising entails competition not only with other Israeli and Jewish organizations but also among units and individuals of the Hebrew University. University officials are torn between turning faculty members loose on donors and seeking to control the process from the center. There may be no better stimulus of a generous donation than an academic intent on funds for a heartfelt project that holds the key to peace in the Middle East; understanding the past, present, and future of the Jewish people; or finding a solution to medical, social, or economic calamities. Yet it is embarrassing, and counterproductive to fund-raising, when different faculty members stumble over the same potential donor and create the impression that the university is unlimited in its appetites and unclear as to its priorities. For the creative faculty member, the ideal priorities for the university are his or her own good ideas. For the institution's managers, however, the appetites of its teachers and researchers are only one more indication that Max Weber was not thinking of universities when he conceived his ideal types of bureaucratic organizations.

There is no shortage of tension and controversy among creative staff members and institutional managers intent on maintaining some control. One administrative response to creative staff is to accept more proposals than resources permit and to rely on the future generosity of others to balance the books. Like many universities, the Hebrew University owes much to both public and private donors. Despite the donors, however, Hebrew University's appetite exceeds its resources. It has the largest debt of any Israeli university.

In a perpetual scramble to keep the deficit from growing, university finance personnel strive to maintain close control over resources, including those meant to fund teaching and research in academic units. In order to boost government funds provided on a per-student basis, the administration has pressured departments to lower standards for admitting students, despite policies that the Hebrew University is to be the quality center of Israeli higher education. Administrative officers do not release detailed budgetary figures in order to frustrate comparisons by department heads as to how much each has received from the central administration. Administrators demand detailed justifications for funding requests, defer response, require additional detail when asked again for a response, and defer once more when they receive additional details. Official expressions with respect to funding programs are likely to be amorphous and may be followed by postponement, revision, or cancellation of commitments thought to be in hand. Financial arrangements include oral agreements that the central administration does not commit to writing and may alter without advance notice. Expenditures from research funds may be held up in the central administration. Equipment suppliers occasionally refuse to release an order, or insist on adding a surcharge, because the university has imposed a delay on paying its bills. Donors who gave their money to support certain programs may find some of the funds siphoned off for general university purposes. Faculty members who accept administrative responsibilities learn they must press hard for resources. Whether for tactical reasons or in earnest, department chairs and college deans often assert that it is their own sacrifice that allows other programs to flourish.

* * *

In this chapter I have continued the discussion of the complexities of politics and policymaking in order to further illustrate why so many participants pursue simplicity. Here the concern has been with organizations that are important parts of the public sector but that are designed in a way to frustrate control by elected officials.

Initially I described quasi-governmental, or third sector, organizations. Receiving much or most of their money from government, they offer services that in the past were provided directly by governmental departments. Indeed these groups may be shaped by contracts originating in government. However, the quasi-governmental bodies are insulated from direct control by government. There may be formal lines of reporting and responsibilities defined in contracts, but genuine supervision tends to be loose if it exists at all. For the most part, these organizations run themselves.

Great universities are quasi-governmental and members of the third sector but have traits that are even more problematic for those who would hold them responsible to elected officials than other organizations in those categories. There is more freedom given to the professional staff and fewer lines of discipline available to administrators. Largely because of the weight of "academic freedom," government officials refrain from looking too closely at what occurs in universities. Where there is auditing, it tends to focus on issues of management and the operation of physical facilities rather than having anything to do with teaching or research.

The approach to university governance varies with the perspective, stakes, and personal inclinations of participants. Most students and faculty spend their time oblivious to issues of policy setting or management. They go about their own activities, with students expecting courses to be offered as advertised and teachers preparing their lessons, moving forward with plans for research, writing, and vacation. More likely to be concerned on a continuing basis are faculty members with administrative roles, ranking members of the permanent administrative staff, members of the board of governors, and government officials whose responsibilities touch on university finance.

Who governs? How? and Who gets what? are classic questions of politics having relevance to institutions of higher education. These institutions use considerable public resources and in return provide services of great importance to individual students and to society. Collegial structure, multiple sources of funds, and academic freedom all create ambiguity in the issues of who governs and how. Weberian norms of hierarchy, explicit formal rules, standardization, and clear lines of accountability fade in the face of dispersed sources of funds, decentralized decisionmaking, a mixture of peer control and public accountability, and individual faculty members who expect to govern their own work.

What is it that we learn from the large and amorphous segment of public service under the heading of "higher education"? Prominent among its lessons for political science are the problems of government officials and citizens who would assure themselves control over the nature of public policy and its implementation. These problems are severe in the case of organizations that are quasi-governmental and especially severe in the case of universities.

In the following chapter I discuss how the complexities of policymaking and program implementation described in Chapters 2 and 3 spur administrators and elected officials to simplify operations. It is important to remember that simplifications do not assure control for these policymakers. Some efforts only add to complexity. But simplification is a widespread response to what I have described to this point.

Notes

1. Jameson W. Doig, "If I See a Murderous Fellow Sharpening a Knife Cleverly . . . The Wilsonian Dichotomy and the Public Authority Tradition," *Public Administration Review* 43, 1983, 292–304. See also B. Gideron, R. Kramer, and L. M. Salamon, eds., *Government and the Third Sector* (San Francisco: Jossey Bass, 1992); L. M. Salamon, *Partners in Public Service: Government–Non-Profit Relations in the Modern Welfare State* (Baltimore: John Hopkins University Press, 1995); and Rathgreb Smith and Michael Lipsky, *Nonprofits for Hire: The Welfare State in an Age of Contracting* (Cambridge: Harvard University Press, 1993).

2. Paul C. Light, *Thickening Government: Federal Hierarchy and the Diffusion of Accountability* (Washington, DC: Brookings Institution, 1995).

3. Smith and Lipsky; Marilyn Taylor, "Between Public and Private: Accountability and Voluntary Organizations," *Policy and Politics* 24, no. 1, January 1996, 57–72; Kevin Kearns, "The Strategic Management of Accountability in Nonprofit Organizations: An Analytical Framework," *Public Administration Review* 54, no. 2, March/April 1994, 185–192.

4. "Tax Exempt Organizations: Activities and IRS Oversight" (Washington: General Accounting Office, June 13, 1995).

5. Reed Abelson, "Some Charities Cash In by Playing the Name Game," *New York Times,* December 30, 1999. Internet edition.

6. Holcomb B. Noble, "Hailed as a Surgeon General, Koop Criticized on Ethics," *New York Times,* September 4, 1999. Internet edition. Reed Abelson, "Charity Led by General Powell Comes Under Heavy Fire, Accused of Inflating Results," *New York Times,* October 8, 1999. Internet edition.

7. Robert Pear, "Fraud in Medicare Increasingly Tied to Claims Payers," *New York Times,* September 20, 1999. Internet edition.

8. Reed Abelson with Elisabeth Rosenthal, "Charges of Shoddy Practices Taint Gifts of Plastic Surgery," *New York Times,* November 24, 1999. Internet edition.

9. Dan Morgan, "Nonprofits as Tools in Corporate Arsenal," *Washington Post,* January 29, 2000, p. A1. Internet edition.

10. Judith Miller, "Some Charities Suspected of Terrorist Role," *New York Times,* February 19, 2000. Internet edition.

11. Yael Yishai, "State and Welfare Groups: Competition or Cooperation? Some Observations on the Israeli Scene," *Nonprofit and Voluntary Sector Quarterly* 19, no. 3 (Fall), 1990, pp. 215–236.

12. *Annual Report #47* (Jerusalem: State Comptroller, 1997), pp. 590–603. Hebrew.

13. David Lodge, *Small World: An Academic Romance* (New York: Warner Books, 1991); *Changing Places: A Tale of Two Campuses* (New York: Penguin Books, 1978).

14. C. P. Snow, *The Masters* (Harmondsworth: Penguin Books, 1956).

15. See, for example, Charles W. Anderson, *Prescribing the Life of the Mind: An Essay on the Purpose of the University, the Aims of Liberal Education, the Competence of Citizens, and the Cultivation of Practical Reason* (Madison: University of Wisconsin Press, 1993); Allan Bloom, *The Closing of the American Mind* (New York: Simon and Schuster, 1987); and Clark Kerr, *The Uses of the University* (Cambridge: Harvard University Press, 1982).

16. World Development Indicators, 1999 (Washington: World Bank, 1999). Available online at www.worldbank.org.

17. See, for example, Paul R. Trowler, *Academics Responding to Change: New Higher Education Frameworks and Academic Cultures* (Buckingham: The Society for Research into Higher Education & Open University Press, 1998); John Radford, Kjell Raaheim, Peter de Vries, and Ruth Williams, *Quantity and Quality in Higher Education* (London: Jessica Kingsley Publishers, 1997); James S. Coleman with David Court, *University Development in the Third World: The Rockefeller Foundation Experience* (Oxford: Pergamon Press, 1993); Leon D. Epstein, *Governing the University: The Campus and the Public Interest* (San Francisco: Jossey-Bass Publishers, 1974); Henry D. R. Miller, *The Management of Change in Universities: Universities, State and Economy in Australia, Canada and the United Kingdom* (Buckingham, UK: Society for Research into Higher Education & Open University Press, 1995); Jan De Groof, Guy Neave, and Juraj Svec, *Democracy and Governance in Higher Education* (The Hague: Kluwer Law International, 1998); Gordon M. Marsden and Bradley J. Longfield, eds., *The Secularization of the Academy* (New York: Oxford University Press, 1992); Michael D. Cohen and James G. March, *Leadership and Ambiguity: The American College President* (New York: McGraw-Hill, 1974).

18. See, for example, J. L. Gibson, J. M. Ivancevich, and J. H. Donnelly Jr., *Organizations: Behavior, Structure, Process* (Homewood, Ill.: Irwin, 1991); and J. Pfeffer, *New Directions for Organizational Theory: Problems and Prospects* (New York: Oxford University Press, 1997).

19. Max Weber, *Max Weber on Universities: The Power of the State and the Dignity of the Academic Calling in Imperial Germany*, translated and edited by Edward Shils (Chicago: University of Chicago Press, 1973).

20. Karen W. Arenson, "Columbia Sets Pace in Profiting off Research," *New York Times*, August 2, 2000. Internet edition.

21. Alan Bloom, p. 380.

22. For a more complete report of what is described here, see Ira Sharkansky, "Governing a Hybrid: The Hebrew University of Jerusalem," *International Journal of Public Administration* 24, no. 11, 2001, 1189–1210.

23. Ira Sharkansky and James J. Gosling, "The Limits of Government Auditing: The Case of Higher Education," *Politeia: Journal for the Political Sciences* 11, no. 1, 1992, 2–15.

24. *Reports on the Audit of Institutions of Higher Education* (Jerusalem: State Comptroller, 1999), p. 33. Hebrew.

4

Choosing Simple Solutions for the Problems of Politics and Policymaking

This chapter stands against Chapters 2 and 3. In those chapters we saw the conditions in politics, policymaking, and program implementation that get in the way of knowing what to do, with certainty that one's actions will produce the desired results. I described budget add-ons and the burgeoning of quasi-governmental units and noted that these conditions reflect the efforts of some players to hide what occurs or to limit their accountability to the public or the government that provides funds. In universities, decisionmakers can elude control by politicians and policymakers as well as by ranking academics, students, and other administrators.

Despite all the lack of clarity and the uncertainty of cause and effect, we should not see government as out of control. Democratic regimes operate with reasonable degrees of service delivery, economic growth, and citizen satisfaction. Citizens may protest and vote against the incumbents, but political violence is marginal in democratic countries. Threats of revolutions are limited to the proclamations of extremists. In some arenas, as in the case of elections to the U.S. House of Representatives and Senate, there is no clearer measure of citizen satisfaction than voters returning incumbents to office. From 1968 to 1990, the success of incumbents ranged between 88 and 99 percent for the House of Representatives and between 55 and 97 percent for the Senate.[1]

This is the key chapter of the book, and the question at its center is, How do citizens and policymakers manage amidst complexity and uncertainty? One simple answer is, Imperfectly. The more satisfying answers are that they simplify their reality and learn routine ways that allow them to make decisions—decisions that are imperfect but reasonable in light of constraints.

The topics to be covered here represent several devices that ordinary citizens as well as political activists and policymakers use to simplify their choices. They are not ideal, and this chapter does not advocate their use. Rather, it describes their use. The underlying message is that these methods are used because they are simpler than profound inquiries and carefully designed responses.

Much of the material to be covered here is already familiar to readers of political science texts and is likely to have been viewed in other contexts. We all know about political parties. They provide part of our identity and offer simple guidance that helps us choose candidates and define our positions on policy questions. We all practice incrementalism, although we may not think of it as such. Incrementalism is a subtle but ever present feature of how policymakers make most of their choices. We all use—and are the targets of—slogans that simplify communications. We postpone deciding about unpleasant issues, sometimes to the point of never deciding. We cope in a variety of ways with pressures. We respond ambiguously to problematic situations, often without pondering the implications of our actions. These are some of the simplifying devices that we examine here. They are all around us. Perhaps until now, readers will not have recognized their importance in simplifying political complexity.

Parties, incrementalism, slogans, and ambiguity are generic devices to simplify political complexities that are widely present in all polities. Along with them are numerous tactics that we also learn from textbooks or mentors. They may not be as pervasive in their presence or weighty in their impacts as these generic devices, but they are important nonetheless. I describe briefly several of the tactics apparent in the daily activities of political activists and policymakers that facilitate, annoy, or even enrage, depending on whether we are on the giving or receiving end and depending on how the tactics are employed.

Political Parties

Political parties are cornerstones of democratic politics and policymaking. They provide leadership and instruction to citizens and elected officials. They simplify options and help individuals, legislators, and chief executives to define their political identity and choose candidates, allies, and policy options.

This is not to say that citizens and officials in democratic polities are automatons fixed in party loyalties. Adherence is impressive but not automatic. Individuals depart from established loyalties under the influ-ence of candidates' personalities, economic conditions, or changes in their own sense of personal well-being. Numerous citizens will vote against the party candidate if they feel their economic status has deteri-orated during a period of that party's rule. Lots of voters live without a clear party identity and either float from one party to another or abstain altogether from voting. At significant points in the legislative calendar, individual representatives may waver with respect to staying with their party colleagues, and the chief executive must shop for support in the opposition party.

A great deal of political science written about public opinion, elec-toral politics, and the policy choices of legislators and chief executives addresses cases when parties do not dominate the scene, when a party is losing power, or when there are widespread shifts in party affiliation. To appreciate the general impact of political parties, however, it is impor-tant to recognize the unstated assumption in this science: Parties are the most prominent feature of democratic politics, and most of the time they provide the clearest guidance and the most certain predictors of how citizens and elected officials will behave. The wholesale reelection of incumbents, which is a feature of most congressional elections, sug-gests that party loyalty is a prominent feature of the process that selects members of Congress. The legislators themselves are more likely to vote with their parties than according to any other category. A fair amount of the time, congressional votes come down to a majority of one party voting against a majority of the other party. From 1963 to 1987, this occurred in the Senate for between 33 and 51 percent of the votes, depending on the year, and in the House for between 29 and 64 percent of the votes.[2]

For the congressional party whose colleague sits in the White House, the president's leadership and party loyalty provide a strong combina-tion. From the administration of Dwight D. Eisenhower to that of Bill Clinton, the president's party members voted with the president between 64 and 87 percent of the time, depending on the year, when the presi-dent took a position with respect to pending legislation. Presidential leadership was not absent in the case of congressional members of the nonpresidential party. However, congressional members of the nonpres-idential party voted with the president only 31 to 52 percent of the time, again depending on the year.[3]

The influence of party begins at home. Research in Great Britain, the United States, and West Germany (prior to the merger with East Germany) found just over 50 percent, and in some cases as high as 70 percent, of major party affiliations passed on from parents to children. Children who do not adopt their parents' party ties do not adopt another party in mass but divide in small proportions among other parties and a lack of party affiliation. In one study of Republican families in the United States, for example, 54 percent of the children identified as Republican, 25 percent as Democrats, and 21 percent as Independents. In the case of Democratic families, 70 percent of the children identified as Democrats, 10 percent as Republicans, and 20 percent as Independents.[4]

The process of party socialization may begin with children perceiving generalized images of good and bad associated with the major parties. Party loyalties transmitted at home are likely to find reinforcement in school and the neighborhood. Party allegiances correspond roughly with socioeconomic characteristics, and people of similar income levels and ethnicity cluster in the same neighborhoods and send their children to the local school. Eventually individuals come to acquire policy postures consistent with their party identity. One study found 86 percent of Democrats and 71 percent of Republicans expressing policy attitudes consistent with their party identities. Comparable figures elsewhere were 89 percent of British Conservatives and 84 percent of British Laborites, and 93 percent of West German Christian Democrats/Christian Socialists and 55 percent of West German Social Democrats.[5]

Party attachment tends to increase with age. Young individuals in both Great Britain and the United States (i.e., those between 15 and 24 years of age) have responded to surveys indicating strong party attachments at the rate of 40 percent, while 60 percent and more of those 65 and older show strong attachments.[6] In both countries, studies have found that party identification is more stable than affinities for a variety of policy positions on issues like legalizing marijuana, abortion, racial integration, and gender equality in the United States and the role of the royal family, trade union influence, industrial nationalization, and affiliation with Europe in Britain. The findings suggest that while the salience of particular issues comes and goes, voters' party affiliations tend to remain and may contribute to the process by which they decide where they stand on particular issues.[7]

Voting is the focus of political party activities, and we should realize that voting is one archetypal way of simplifying difficult choices. Ideally it occurs after a period when competitors seeking office, or seeking to formulate policy, try to persuade the undecided and their opponents. When there is no consensus—and that is typical in election contests and in the case of difficult policy problems—the way to peaceful resolution is by voting. Rules employed in each forum—whether a popular election, a legislative chamber, a court, or an administrative committee—define what percentage of the entire body, or what percentage of those present and voting, is required for victory.

Political parties do not offer salvation for political uncertainties. In some cases, the medicine is worse than the problem. Favoritism and patronage go along with parties. Parties traditionally have provided material inducements to gain voter support, and few citizens are self-denying philosophers or saints interested in the general good. Many want to support candidates who will favor their interests and implement them in ways that provide direct benefits. Some want government investments to develop the local economy, or they desire better facilities at the local school or hospital. Others want more direct and immediate goodies: a job, a favorable decision on their request to a government program for aid with their business, or a cash payment for voting correctly.[8]

Party corruption (including direct payments or other personal inducements for political cooperation) is more a matter of the third world and the lesser-developed corners of well-to-do democracies. However, corruption is not absent from idealized locales. Some would argue that the support provided along party lines for the impeachment of President Bill Clinton (i.e., the Republican position) or his defense by Democrats represented a kind of party corruption.

Corruption is a slippery concept. What to some may be legitimate responses by officials to the interests of their electoral supporters or help with shortcuts through the bureaucratic formalities is to others an obvious case of corruption. It is conventional to consider corruption not as simple illegality but as violations of conventional morality or the informal rules of the game.[9] In other words, what is conventional in Illinois may be corruption in neighboring Wisconsin.

There is a recent Israeli case of party patronage that is testing the capacity of the country's judicial system to deal with actions that are ostensibly illegal, but which have provided service to a substantial sector of the population. SHAS is the Hebrew acronym of a political party that has developed since the mid-1980s to serve ultra-Orthodox Jews tracing their origins to North Africa. The community has considered itself disadvantaged both in the distribution of opportunities at large, and at the hands of the Jews of European origin who dominated the older ultra-Orthodox parties. SHAS has grown to the point where it elected 17 members of the 120-member Knesset in 1999. This made it the third largest party, only two seats behind the second largest party and nine seats behind the largest party. Important in the party's growth is its network of schools ranging from kindergartens for three-year olds through religious academies for adults. The money for these schools has come from deals struck with prime ministers and finance ministers by SHAS party leaders willing to participate in governing coalitions. One such leader was Ariyeh Deri, who served initially as the senior administrator of the Interior Ministry and then as interior minister. These positions gave him control over the government's financial aid to municipalities. "Affair Deri" began in 1991, when the country's newspapers and then the state comptroller detailed the ways in which he provided special funding to local governments on condition that municipal officials transmit substantial portions of the money to SHAS schools.

At this writing, Deri has been found guilty of exploiting his government positions for personal gain, and has been sentenced to three years in prison. Pending is a second trial concerned with his funneling of moneys to the SHAS schools as well as what may become third and fourth trials on other charges.

Despite the substantial charges levied against Ariyeh Deri, he remained the effective leader of the country's third largest party through the election campaign of 1999. Soon after the campaign, and under pressure from the prime minister–elect, SHAS named another of its parliamentarians as party leader. Yet somewhere was Ariyeh Deri, perhaps pulling on the strings or setting himself up as a figure the party could not repudiate.

A few months into Deri's prison term, the Knesset passed what was called "Deri's law." It provided that a prison inmate may be released for good behavior after serving one-half of the sentence imposed, rather than after two-thirds as had been the law.

Mexico is another country with traditions of party patronage that—to many observers—cross over the boundaries into corruption. The Institutional Revolutionary Party (PRI) proclaimed several waves of reform for the sake of attaching Mexico more firmly to the community of democratic nations, but it had trouble ridding itself of established practices. In the presidential primary campaign of 1999 (which itself was a step toward democratization), local officials beholden to the dominant party faction placed bulldozers on the road to an opposition rally, causing those wanting to participate to get off their buses and walk more than a mile to the rally site. Radio personalities who dared interview opposition leaders within the PRI have lost their air time. Meanwhile, citizens who support the establishment candidate received their usual allotments of preelection groceries and building supplies.[10] For the first time in seventy years, the PRI lost the national election, held in 2000. Observers are waiting to see if the non-PRI president can root out corruption established over the course of several generations.

Incrementalism: If It Was Good Enough Yesterday, It's Good Enough for Tomorrow

Equal to political parties in its prominence as a provider of simplified guidance to activists in politics and policymaking is the routine that goes by the name of incrementalism. It is a pervasive circumstance of the human condition that, most of the time, things change gradually. Transformations come in *increments*.

Some of what we have to say under the heading of incrementalism will strike readers as pedestrian. Continuity is the theme. The child who was four feet seven inches tall yesterday will be very close to that height today. With somewhat less certainty, we can say that the offspring of short parents are likely to be shorter than average. Countries and regions that were poorer than average a decade ago are still likely to be poorer than average, even if they have shown signs of economic development. However, some few of those poor places may have jumped beyond their prior ranking due to discoveries of natural resources, the ability to take advantage of new economic conditions, or creative leadership. A few other places will have slipped below prior economic rankings on account of bad experiences.

Incrementalism is built into social relationships via the strength of social class to perpetuate itself. Individuals from established families are more likely than the poor to have the money, the connections, and the awareness of how to do things in order to achieve higher quality education, career success, reasonable wealth, and the passing on of opportunity to the next generation of their own children. The tendency of individuals to select spouses from their own social groups adds to the process of intergenerational continuity. There is the occasional Eliza Doolittle, the character of George Bernard Shaw who gets a chance at a dramatic leap forward. More common is incremental change: the child of a blue-collar family who makes it to a modest professional position as schoolteacher, accountant, nurse, or pharmacist, and whose own children move higher. There are also cases of slippage, as in the epigram "shirt sleeves to shirt sleeves in three generations."

We have already seen some indications of incrementalism in the discussion of political parties. Individuals tend to maintain their attachments from one election to the next and pass on their loyalties to children. Insofar as party loyalties tend to become stronger with age, it appears that continuity, which is an important component of incrementalism, grows incrementally with age.

There are several explicit manifestations of incrementalism in policymaking. Administrators and judges spend most of their time extending precedents to the ongoing flow of new cases and claims. The essence of precedent is consistency in decisions. What was good for client x should also hold for other clients showing similar traits. It is possible to distinguish cases. A client who wants something different from the conventional service may get it by persuading officials that his or her special traits justify something different from the conventional award. Judges and administrators may see the imperfections in the precedent and either change the rules outright or declare a justified exception or departure from established precedents.

Government budgets are explicit in focusing policymaking on increments. Typically, the documents that pass between operating units and the central budget office and between the budget office and the legislature list the allocations for the previous and current years as well as the allocations being proposed for the coming year. In this way, officials who request funding can justify the increment requested by virtue of changing workloads or other considerations, and those who decide on the budget can parcel out increments according to their view of the greatest need or the greatest political support.

The important component in incremental budgeting is the "base," or the figure allocated in past and present years. It provides the starting point for calculating the next year's budget. Researchers who study the budget process provide explanations and justifications for incrementalism, as well as reservations about its utility, that carry over to other fields of public policy. The base of existing spending has a certain sacredness as the support of current programs. The assumption is that programs are justified by virtue of their existence and age and cannot be cut back significantly without engendering severe opposition from staff and clients.

Incremental changes are likely to be positive but can also be negative. Some call negative increments *decrements.* Insofar as they are small, increments and decrements are subject to correction in later years with a minimum of damage. A program that grew too fast can be slowed down or halted in its development to allow administrative corrections. A program that was cut back too much can be given an infusion of additional resources in order to overcome some of the problems caused.

In budgeting as elsewhere, incrementalism is not an iron law. It only occurs most of the time. On occasion there are great leaps forward, or severe cutbacks. Moreover, the concept of an increment is flexible. Is it 1 percent or 10 percent? Even the continued addition of small increments will add up to significant change over the course of several years. When is a large increment or an unbroken series of small increments in effect a significant, nonincremental change? The literature provides no clear answer.

Insofar as there is incrementalism in budgeting, there is also incrementalism in the programming that the budget supports. Most details carry over from one year to the next. Additions or deletions of client services and changes in regulations are likely to come piecemeal. The reasons are similar to those in budgeting. Policymakers do not wish to create disturbances by too many sweeping changes. They may not be sure of the effects to be gained and so they do not want to risk going too far in any direction when the results are uncertain. And perhaps most of all, policymakers lack the time and resources to examine everything every year. They can look closely only at small pieces of the whole or at proposed increments beyond what exists. In other words, they simplify their tasks by considering only incremental changes.

Students learn about incrementalism in their academic courses and absorb it in training programs concerned with budget practices. Incrementalism received praise in a review of an expensive and problematic program of research and development concerned with antimissile missiles. A government panel commended the military and its prime contractor for having "formulated a sensible, phased, incremental approach to the development and deployment decision—while managing the risk."[11] Vermont's governor praised the strategy of incrementalism for helping him enact one provision after another in what has become one of the most generous state programs of health coverage. An earlier effort to provide health coverage to everyone in the state failed in the legislature. In response, he began enacting his plan gradually, increasing it in steps to cover low-income adults, drug coverage for the elderly, and expanded coverage for children. "I now realize that the only way you can do this is incrementally. . . . You do it piece by piece and bit by bit because you can't take on every special interest all at once."[12] Hillary Rodham Clinton made a similar observation. It reflected the prominent failure at the beginning of her husband's presidency, when she headed a task force to prepare a comprehensive program of health reform. She admitted that she once had "an idea or two about how to improve health care in our country" but had learned "the wisdom of taking small steps to get a big job done."[13]

Incrementalism has its opponents. They label it a bulwark of conservatism, a sell-out to the establishment, and a an easy way to avoid hard decisions. In defense, supporters of incrementalism may plead guilty in part but assert that incrementalism only reflects a conservative streak in human nature, that is, an inability to examine many problematic issues all at the same time.

Just because incrementalism is easy for policymakers does not make it fair or just. It can cause puzzling unfairness when policy moves forward one step at a time. Some benefit, while others, seemingly similar in their needs, do not. On account of publicity given to the videos rented by Supreme Court nominee Robert H. Bork, Congress passed a law prohibiting the disclosure of video rental lists. That was a small increment in policy change. The law does not protect library patrons or book store customers from having their reading habits publicized.[14] Likewise, when a school district increases incrementally the services to one group of handicapped students, the parents of children with a different handicap may charge that the program is unfair. If officials provide enough resources in the future to provide services for an additional kind of disability, it will be too late for the children who lost out earlier.[15]

The weight of incrementalism is apparent in major policies with respect to the great issues. Governments are unlikely to change dramatically their lines of action with respect to neighbors, allies, or antagonists in international relations. Postures concerning environmental protection; abortion; the legalization of drug use; rights of the disabled, ethnic minorities, homosexuals, and women; universal provision of medical coverage; gun control; and other sensitive issues are likely to change occasionally, perhaps after years of pressure, and then only in stages, or incrementally.

Again, the reservations noted above apply here. Significant changes have occurred in each of these fields. There are no rigid laws in politics or policymaking, but there are tendencies. Incrementalism is one of the strongest. Seldom are there simultaneous changes in several prominent fields. Even more rare are revolutions that in dramatic ways change policies across the range of public services. Revolutions are likely to be violent and to depart from the control of those who began them. Death and destruction are likely to be widespread and random in their incidence. It is not necessarily the evil who suffer when revolutions occur. Incrementalism is better.

Slogans

Slogans deserve mention along with political parties and incrementalism. Like them, slogans simplify politics and policymaking in that they simplify communication. Without slogans, advertising could not exist, and religion would be in trouble. Slogans provide some meaning to those incapable of or uninterested in understanding what is complex. They also express more than they say. They reinforce or trigger existing sentiments. They can soothe or provoke, bring out what is attractive or ugly, in their audience.

As such, the term *slogan* has some negative connotations associated with politics: manipulative, self-serving, superficial, evasive, demagoguery, and corruption. Yet slogans are also tools that facilitate the more attractive face of politics: a concern to recruit supporters in order to facilitate coalition building, and the persuasion of adversaries. These features of politics render it a civilized way of dealing with disputes.

Slogans are short expressions associated with commercial or political advertising meant to express ideas, aims, or the nature of an individual or organization in ways that are simple and easy to remember and communicate. Dictionaries employ terms that hint at the problems as well as the nature of slogans: epigrams, cries, mottoes, propaganda, hyperbole, ambiguity, parables, and half-truths. Slogans distort as well as communicate. Their impact can be harmless, as when persuading consumers to buy one soap rather than another ("It floats," a slogan in behalf of Ivory from the 1940s) or leading voters to find something attractive in a candidate's personality ("I like Ike," in support of Dwight D. Eisenhower). Slogans can hurt or be dangerous when they distinguish "us" from "them," "friends" from "enemies," and promote the hatred of ethnic, racial, or religious communities.

Slogans are part of the routines and standard operating procedures (SOPs) that simplify politics and policymaking. They allow activities to go forward with a minimum of thought and planning. Slogans convey images. They reinforce existing attitudes and behaviors as well as seek to spread those attitudes and behaviors more widely in the audience. Like other routines and SOPs, slogans indicate how individuals should respond to situations that resemble those encountered previously.

The attractions of slogans are apparent in their wide use, although some uncertainty remains as to the utility of individual slogans. This issue is part of the larger puzzle concerned with the questions What do politicians mean by what they say? What affects public opinion? and Who leads whom?[16] Nonetheless, commercial and political managers spend great sums to identify the slogans that will advance their campaigns. The definition of a slogan that works is one that garners support for a candidate or a line of action, even if the candidate does not define his or her program clearly or the line of action at issue does not indicate all the important steps and their implications.

The problems with slogans come when they promote oversimplification or demagoguery, encourage lies, discourage nuance and the pursuit of explanation, lead individuals to actions that are harmful to them directly ("Light up a Lucky" in behalf of Lucky Strike cigarettes), or add to social problems by inciting animosity and violence. Slogans can be too successful, creating a climate of opinion that discourages changes in policy when existing programs do not work as believed or when conditions shift. Slogans become policy when they keep elites from abandoning the status quo. The harm can be great, as we shall see when considering slogans that have become popular enough to retard changes in policies. That is the time when slogans become so dominant that they are, in effect, policies.

The following sections will illustrate several varieties of slogans with relevance for politics and policymaking, with an emphasis on the advantages and disadvantages of these simplifying mechanisms. Most examples will come from the United States and Israel. These are not the only countries where slogans play important roles in public affairs, but they are those that the author knows best. In order to understand the nuances in political language, it is essential to know the cultural landscape.

Dangerous Versus Benign Slogans

Slogans range from the harmless to the hazardous. At the latter extreme are those used in behalf of tobacco and alcohol as well as political incitement against racial, ethnic, or religious groups. It is forbidden to place in certain media slogans that boast the pleasures of alcohol or tobacco. Several countries ban propaganda meant to incite against minorities. Slogans in behalf of fast cars may be legal but cause some observers to grit their teeth.

Political slogans can skirt the boundaries of good taste or spill over to the realm where they reinforce animosities and threaten violence. An ultra-Orthodox congregation sponsored the slogan "Netanyahu is good for the Jews" in the 1996 Israeli election campaign. Its subtext was that Shimon Peres was not sufficiently supportive of Jewish religious issues and was too inclined to make concessions in the peace process to the Palestinians and other Arabs. Only a few months earlier, Prime Minister Yitzhak Rabin had been killed by a religious Jew who felt that Rabin was bargaining away the Land of Israel. Some time later, the group that promoted the slogan about Netanyahu and the Jews changed its mind. Netanyahu, who was prime minister at the time, had made concessions to the Palestinians in the city of Hebron, and he was not good enough for the Jews.

Political candidates and their supporters use campaign slogans. When Franklin D. Roosevelt pledged himself "to a new deal for the American people" as part of his speech accepting the Democratic Party's nomination in 1932, he provided a label that helped with several years' worth of legislative proposals as well as four electoral victories.

"States' rights" served the American South over a long period from the struggle about slavery to that about racial integration. Despite the tarnish applied to it by the Civil War and numerous decisions of the U.S. Supreme Court, "states' rights" still surfaces, in the South and else-where, when state or local authorities find themselves limited by deci-sions of the national government. However, "states' rights" has not been strong enough to overcome the support rendered "one man, one vote," "equal opportunity," or "affirmative action."

"Separate but equal" served for more than half a century to justify separate and manifestly unequal services for African Americans. Re-cently the spirit, if not the words, of "separate but equal" has enjoyed a reprieve by African American parents dissatisfied with policies of trans-porting their children for the sake of integration. They prefer neighbor-hood schools. Some want schools that are mostly or entirely African American. "Separate but equal" still carries a stain in the history books. However, equality now has a chance to coexist with separation on ac-count of strong support for African American political goals.

Slogans do not assure success in political disputes. Skills of slogan creation and propagation are available to all sides. "Right to life" and "freedom of choice" are closely paired for public support and intensity on each side of the debate about abortion, and neither assures success in specific confrontations. The dominant actors remain the U.S. Supreme Court and lower judiciary bodies as well as Congress and state legislatures. Meanwhile, the affection associated with "small business" and "care givers" adds flavor to a group's economic demands, but does not assure success against competitors. Both slogans figured in the efforts to amend or kill the Clinton administration's comprehensive health care bill. Organizations of small businesses objected to the mandated provision of health insurance, and various groups of physicians and other care givers objected to one or another provision that threatened to limit their actions or their incomes.

Slogans in behalf of racial, ethnic, or religious groups help to bestow self-respect on minorities not well esteemed by the majority. They provide one component of individual and group development, even if they do not assure any political success in the short term. The expression "chosen people," along with the beliefs associated with it, has bolstered Jewish pride since it was included in the Hebrew Bible. "Black is beautiful" won its place in the 1960s during a time when African Americans were gaining civil rights, higher-quality education, and middle- and upper-income jobs. For some individuals, "black is beautiful" may compensate, at least in part, for the suspicions that "affirmative action," rather than individual merit, has been responsible for one's success.[17]

Subtle slogans can reinforce ethnic, religious, and racial animosities without being so blatant as to fall afoul of laws against incitement. Billboards referring to "them" in U.S. elections during the 1970s hinted at the welfare and crime associated with nonwhites. "Cosmopolitan" in the Soviet Union was a negative code word meaning Jew.

Some slogans truly are war cries. "Remember the *Maine*, to hell with Spain" was the work of inflammatory journalism in the run-up to the 1898 war with Spain after an explosion sank the battleship *Maine* in Havana Harbor with more than 200 U.S. deaths. Inquiries never did establish a connection between the explosion and Spaniards, but the war was over before the investigations began.

"A land without people for a people without a land" distorted reality while it served the Zionists who brought Jewish settlers to Palestine in the latter part of the nineteenth century. It is now one of the items targeted by "post-Zionist" revisionist Israeli historians as well as Palestinian activists.

Some Slogans Are More Attractive
than the Policies They Promote

It may be easier to craft an attractive slogan than to assure successful policymaking and program implementation. "Affirmative action" and "comparable worth" developed in the environment of equality that has prevailed in the United States from the late 1960s. Affirmative action promised to undo or compensate for a history of discrimination against African Americans and other selected minorities. Comparable worth sought to compensate for the gross differences in wages paid to occupations filled largely by women compared to those filled predominantly by men.

Both slogans began with inherent problems. Affirmative action benefited only groups officially recognized as deserving aid. It did not promise equity and has not delivered it. It provided considerable benefits to individuals identified as African Americans, Hispanics, Native Americans, Asian Americans, and women. Left out from most programs were poor whites, many of whom have suffered from histories of family disadvantage no less serious than those of preferred minorities. Also problematic was the gross category of "Asians." Some jurisdictions ignored distinctions and grouped Chinese Americans and Japanese Americans, who tend to score well on educational and economic measures, with Asian groups more clearly in need of aid. The terminology confused my Israeli wife, who registered as an "Asian" when she studied at the University of Utah while I was a visiting professor.

In order to forestall claims of discrimination, policymakers and administrators insisted that affirmative action did not require quotas that, in effect, limited the chances of unfavored groups to be accepted for schooling or work. Nonetheless, affirmative action provoked legal challenges from individuals who claimed that they were losing opportunities for education, employment, or contracts because of their race, ethnicity, or gender. Chinese Americans, who did not benefit from affirmative action in California, as well as whites brought suit against state and local bodies in that state. State and federal courts limited or banned practices associated with affirmative action, and the policy found itself outlawed as a result of referendum initiatives placed on state ballots. The incidence of African Americans enrolled in Texas and California universities plummeted as a result of restrictions against affirmative action. Some well-known opponents of affirmative action began to have second thoughts. Nathan Glazer, for example, wrote that ending affirmative action would cause so much damage for the aspirations and advancement of African Americans that opponents should rethink their position.[18] The ethnic Chinese American who served as chair of the ethnic studies program at the University of California at Berkeley predicted that within three years, the outlawing of affirmative action would allow Asians to make up more than 50 percent of total undergraduate enrollment on the eight University of California campuses. He looked ahead to yet another round of political tinkering: "If that happens, there is going to be a backlash."[19]

Comparable worth is, if anything, even more complex and problematic than affirmative action. It not only concerns the relatively simple task of recruiting students, employees, or contractors of a given race, ethnicity, or gender but also seeks to replace market decisions about the salaries paid to all individuals working in entire occupations. Comparable worth goes beyond "equal pay for equal work." That slogan would not increase salaries for women in low-paid occupations where the vast majority of employees are women. Comparable worth wrestles with conditions where a number of occupations in which women dominate provide lower wages than a number of occupations in which men dominate. Like affirmative action, comparable worth is susceptible to political manipulation. Groups with power use the slogans to advance their agenda. The techniques of comparable worth involve the designation of occupational components (educational requirements, skill, effort, responsibility, physical demands, social contribution, danger, social appeal, or stigma) and the appointment of boards of people thought to be skilled in such things to decide what clusters of components should be of equal worth. Outcomes characteristically equate heavily female and lower-paid occupations to heavily male and higher-paid occupations.

Campaigns in behalf of comparable worth have won enactments in Connecticut, Iowa, Minnesota, Montana, New York, Oregon, Washington, and Wisconsin. Authorities in St. Paul decided that librarians have the same worth as firefighters. A judge in the state of Washington ruled that clerk-typists should be paid the same as warehouse workers. Nurses in Denver claimed the same pay as tree trimmers. Despite its appeal to certain circles, comparable worth has not been able to overcome economic forces in what remains a market-oriented economy. Supply and demand continues to drive wages up in occupations that enjoy high demands and limited supply, like computer programming, and keep wages low in those with high supply, like office workers, no matter what the gender profiles. Recognizing the antagonism to "comparable worth" that had built up over a decade of criticism, the AFL-CIO introduced a new initiative in February 1999: "equal pay."[20]

Attractive Slogans that Exaggerate Opportunities

There are slogans that serve a purpose but also produce expectations that are not realized fully. Examples are "participation," "transparency," "power to the people," and "freedom of information." These have made their appearance in numerous settings, often coupled with themes of political renewal, openness, and democracy. "Participation" has been used as a motto and theme by nongovernmental organizations to justify their existence. Yet we should recall the insight of Roberto Michels that nongovernmental as well as governmental organizations are likely to be oligarchies.[21] Their leaders and professional staffs prize some degree of autonomy from the membership and set limits on the penetration of member concerns to their agenda.[22] In some cases, the limits become cruelly authoritarian even while the slogans in behalf of participation remain. The U.S. government claimed to take a great step forward with "freedom of information" but included in the regulations opportunities for governmental agencies to exempt numerous categories of documents from public access and to take their time about providing other documents.

International Slogans

"Privatization" has spread through much of the world since being adopted as policy by Margaret Thatcher in the United Kingdom and Ronald Reagan in the United States. It conveys promises of efficiency and improved quality as well as reductions in the heavy hand of government bureaucracies. However, the meaning of "privatization" varies widely. The word has been used for campaigns to sell all of a government's holdings in an enterprise or to sell only part of the government's holdings. It appears in efforts to reduce government subsidies for basic foods, public transportation, and health insurance and to reorganize government ministries into government-owned companies.

"Liberal" has acquired left-of-center, progressive meanings in U.S. politics, but "liberalization" appears along with privatization to signify a freer economy, without government controls and without the social welfare implications of "liberal."

Agencies from wealthy countries and international organizations have imposed privatization on aid-seekers as a condition of receiving financial assistance. However, the slogan does not assure first world benefits to third world countries that lack substantial resources in the private sector. In some cases, "privatization" has meant selling public assets to foreign investors or to local cronies of the current rulers. Corruption occurs as national governments provide loans to favored individuals in order to buy government assets. The loans may begin with terms more generous than conventional bank loans and improve exponentially as authorities do not demand repayment from well-connected borrowers.

"Three strikes and you're out" means, at the extreme, a life sentence for individuals convicted of three serious crimes. It has figured in numerous state government campaigns and the Clinton White House efforts against crime. Opponents say it is too simple. Individuals convicted of crimes close to the boundary of serious, such as acting as couriers, perhaps unknowingly, in the sale of drugs, have found themselves sentenced to long terms. Advocates of "three strikes" claim that it permits discretion and that prosecutors and judges use its harshest sanctions only against individuals who deserve them. Opponents and advocates each present stories to bolster their claims.[23]

The general idea to become tough on crime also figures in Tony Blair's activities to revitalize the Labor Party. The association of "three strikes" with baseball loses its meaning across the Atlantic. Blair uses "zero tolerance" for his anticrime theme as well as other efforts to improve British society. There is to be zero tolerance for poor schools, domestic violence, and homelessness. The crime element of the theme is directed more broadly at all crime than the American counterpart concerned with serious crime. It has led left-wing opponents of the prime minister to charge that he was producing a police state and to embark on their own campaign to promote zero tolerance of police brutality.

Efforts to end welfare dependence and encourage work also have traveled between countries. The U.S. effort to promote "From Welfare to Workfare" became "From Welfare to Work" in Britain. Yet an examination of efforts in both countries indicates that similarities in themes and slogans do not ensure an identity of programs. In this case, each country's history of welfare activities had created a multitude of conceptions, programs, and entitlements whose existence shaped the alterations being made. In the United States, for example, federalism has retained its influence: State governments differ in the extent to which they have taken advantage of federal innovations in behalf of workfare. Moreover, studies have shown considerable variation in administrative application of regulations meant to encourage or force welfare recipients to work.[24]

When a Slogan Becomes Policy

Usually slogans are tools for the accomplishment of commercial or political goals. Occasionally they fuse with the goals and prove to be stumbling blocks on the way to constructive change. It is not easy to decide if a slogan is secondary or primary, disposable or indispensable. Two extreme examples to be examined here are the slogan-policy of "war against drugs," which has been pursued in the United States since the Nixon administration, and "Jerusalem must remain united under Israeli control," which has been Israeli policy since 1967. The judgments made about both slogans may be subject to dispute and of course to change. Politics is dynamic, although these cases appear to be, at least for the time being, suffering from less than the usual flexibility. In both cases, some activists have moved to free themselves from the most conservative postures associated with the slogans, but their road has proved difficult. In both countries, policymakers seem to be held prisoner by slogans that have proved too successful with the voters. Policymakers who might want to change policies, that is, to try something new or to recognize changes in relevant conditions, have been reluctant to depart from what the public has accepted.

The American war against drugs: harm without benefit. United States policy on illicit drugs provides an extreme example of a slogan-driven policy continuing to prevail, despite considerable evidence of its shortcomings or actual harm. The slogan of a "war on drugs" is directed against those who produce, transport, sell, or use illicit substances.[25] Relatively little attention is allocated to the treatment of habitual users and even less to the possibility of mitigating self-destruction, as in providing sterile needles against the spread of AIDS. Marijuana is arguably less harmful than tobacco or alcohol, but its status as an illicit substance has kept federal authorities from authorizing its use as a palliative even for the most painful illnesses. A U.S. government–sponsored study concluded that the active ingredients in marijuana appear to be useful for treating pain, nausea, and the severe weight loss associated with AIDS. In response, the director of the Office of National Drug Control Policy said there was "enormous confusion in law enforcement" about how to handle the issue and added, "We've got people with mischievous agendas at work." A spokesperson for America Cares, a parents' antidrug group said, "I'm concerned about the message we are sending. . . . Kids interpret things differently than adults. What they're going to hear is, 'Marijuana is good for something.'"[26]

Among the skirmishes in the war on drugs is the question of whether to include alcohol in the antidrug propaganda. To date, the generals in charge of the war have resisted demands from Mothers Against Drunk Driving and scientists who claim that teenage use of alcohol is a "gateway" associated with later use of other drugs. The ostensible reason for not including antialcohol messages is not to dilute the primary message against other substances. Skeptics point to large campaign contributions from the beer and liquor industries to members of the House and Senate who sit on key committees.[27]

The results of the war on drugs include great increases in the incidence of incarcerated Americans and the expenditures allocated to their imprisonment, serious charges about violations of civil rights, distortions in foreign policy toward countries that grow the raw material or through which the drugs pass, and little if any demonstrable impact on the availability or use of drugs.

Commentaries on U.S. efforts to halt drug production or trafficking in Latin America describe the failure to overcome government corruption, hypocrisy with respect to civil rights, and denials of reality among U.S. officials who claim success. Senator Kay Bailey Hutchison, a Republican from Texas, quoted the director of the Drug Enforcement Administration as saying that corruption in Mexico is "unparalleled to anything I've seen in thirty years of law enforcement." The senator went on to explain that connection between corruption and the flow of drugs:

> Record levels of illegal drugs are entering the United States from Mexico. . . . Clearly, certification and decertification [of Mexico's cooperation] have no meaning against a backdrop of rampant corruption and trafficking in Mexico and the drug epidemic on America's streets. The current certification process has become a finger-pointing exercise in mutual deception, while too little progress is being made in the drug war.[28]

The *New York Times* linked the Mexican minister of defense with drug dealing and money laundering. The report concluded that U.S. officials would rather do the safe thing of arresting a number of middle-level law-breakers than face the foreign policy risks involved in Mexican corruption at the highest levels.[29] A later article detailed problems of corruption, drug trafficking, and violent crime in the state of Baja California, despite the coming to power of an opposition party that was ostensibly committed to reform.[30]

Corruption is not only something attached to the drug producing countries of the third world. The wife of the former commander of the U.S. army's antidrug operation in Colombia pleaded guilty to smuggling drugs into the United States, and the commander himself admitted helping his wife launder the money earned from her activities.[31] The officer was sentenced to five months in prison and five months of home detention for concealing knowledge about his wife's activities while they lived in Bogota.[32]

The incidence of inmates in state and federal prisons increased from 93 per 100,000 population in 1972 to 427 per 100,000 in 1996. The estimated prison population reached 2,000,000 in February 2000. It was an occasion for expressions of doubt as to the efficacy and costs of incarceration as well as the racial bias in the U.S. judicial system.[33] Most of the increase was linked to harsher punishment of drug offenders, and it placed the United States outside the range of other Western democracies. Spain and the United Kingdom incarcerate at about one-sixth the U.S. rate, Holland and Scandinavia at about one-tenth.

It is not apparent that tough treatment of dealers or users has any significant impact on the commerce or the consumption of drugs. Moreover, punishments do not fall equally upon different groups. Rates of incarceration are eight times higher for African American than for white males. One-third of young African American men (and more than one-half in some locales) have been caught up in the criminal justice system. They are in jail or prison, on probation or parole, or under pretrial release.[34] Critics speak in terms of an undeclared civil war that contributes more to antigovernmental cynicism than to any reasonable goals of lessening drug consumption.

Part of the racial differential results from especially harsh mandatory penalties enacted against drugs favored by minority populations. Possessing five grams of crack is a felony in some jurisdictions with an automatic five-year prison term, while having five grams of cocaine in powder form is a misdemeanor that may carry no jail sentence. Media accounts tell about individuals jailed for long periods, with their families disrupted or destroyed, for what may have been the innocent carrying of a package for a friend that included forbidden substances. Uncounted numbers have suffered injuries, property damage, violations of civil rights, and death as a result of overly zealous policing.

The equipping of local police departments with war-ready firearms reflects the end of the Cold War and the availability of surplus military hardware as well as policies that enable the taking and selling of valuable property from suspected drug dealers, sometimes without proving their guilt. A member of the Fresno, California, SWAT team has a semi-automatic Beretta pistol as well as a Heckler & Koch MP5 submachine gun, plus a twelve-round shotgun called the Street Sweeper. The thirty-four-member unit has at its disposal two helicopters equipped with night-vision goggles and people-detecting heat sensors, an armored personnel carrier with a turret, and an armored van. Civil liberties activists document a narrowing of individual protections involving mandatory drug testing, expanded police powers of stopping and searching, and wiretapping. Some of the more bizarre expressions of the war include:

• The national drug czar endorsed the idea of beheading drug dealers while being interviewed on the Larry King show.
• The Senate voted authority to shoot down suspected drug planes.
• A congressman proposed an Arctic Penitentiary Act that would establish remote prison camps (what one critic called "an American Gulag") for drug offenders.
• The military invaded Panama in order to seize the head of its government, General Manuel Noriega, for drug trafficking.

Ranking politicians sense the public's support for a war against drugs. During his 1992 campaign, Bob Dole said, "We will make drug interdiction a priority for our intelligence services, beefing up not just technical operations but also human intelligence operations." He promised to "expand our use of military technology, including reconnaissance and satellites and area surveillance and listening posts to track drug movements toward our borders." As part of her campaigning for the 2000 presidential election, Elizabeth Dole said she would renew and strengthen the war on drugs. At times President Bill Clinton and members of his administration expressed support for greater emphasis on the prevention and treatment of addiction, but at other times their emphasis was on war, more money for police and prisons, and severe punishment. According to the *New York Times,* the "Words Are Different; Policy Is Unchanged."[35] The Clinton budget submitted in 1999 included $12 billion for law enforcement, interdiction, and other efforts to attack narcotics supply. That was a 30 percent increase since 1996 and nearly a doubling of such funding over the most recent decade. In early 2000, President Clinton announced plans to provide Colombia with more than $1 billion in military and development aid over the next two years in order to combat narcotics cultivation and trafficking and to prop up its democracy. Critics worried that the money would bolster a government with a record of civil rights abuses in its campaign against left-wing rebels. Supporters of the aid noted that the rebels control drug-producing areas and encourage production as a way of financing their campaigns.[36] A skeptical report about increased U.S. aid to Colombia in the *Economist* concluded that "Americans will have to look not just at the supply but also at the demand for drugs. That means they will have to consider alternative policies at home, even at decriminalization. This is a war that will not be won with helicopters."[37]

Funds for treatment continue to lag. Across the nation, treatment centers could accommodate only about one-half of hard-core users. Funding for treatment in Washington, D.C., fell by 37 percent between 1993 and 1998.[38] In May 1999, the National Institute on Drug Abuse loosened its regulations against medical marijuana. The move seemed a tactical retreat, while still maintaining opposition to state governments that would legalize the use of marijuana for treatment. The ruling came only after two separate government studies had found potential for medical benefits in marijuana. One critic of the government said, "It's an implicit acknowledgement that the government has blocked research into medical marijuana for explicitly political reasons for the last two decades."[39]

Early signs from the Bush administration suggest that the war on drugs will continue. About the individual mentioned as likely to be appointed the drug "czar," the *Economist* commented, "Mr Walters is to the drugs war what first world war generals were to trench warfare. . . . His basic reaction to the heavy losses sustained so far seems to be merely to increase the size of the attack." At the same time, the magazine provided one more pessimistic assessment:

> By any reasonable measure, America's "war on drugs" is a disaster. At home, ferocious "mandatory sentencing" laws are the main reason for the country's huge prison population. Almost one in four of the country's 2m prisoners are there for drug offences, with only a limited chance of becoming productive members of society when they are released. Abroad, America is being sucked into domestic conflicts, notably in Colombia; and recently its forces shot down a "drugs" plane

in Peru that turned out to be carrying missionaries. Meanwhile, drugs have never been easier to get in the United States, with prices lower, purity higher and experimentation among schoolchildren as rampant as ever.[40]

The war on drugs provides opportunities for politicians and others to fabricate victories out of murky statistics. The mayor and the police commission of New York City claimed credit for reducing the incidence of crack use when a major reason behind a decline may only have been changing fashions in drug use and the shift of former crack users to other substances.[41]

"Sound and fury signifying nothing" is an appropriate summary for the war on drugs. According to *New York Times* columnist Anthony Lewis, "Drugs are a subject that has paralyzed American political leadership for a generation and more. The war on drugs fills our prisons without reducing drug use. But only a few politicians have been brave enough to say that the emperor has no clothes."[42]

Despite great sums spent on a war against transportation and sale and the punishment of users, plus incalculable collateral damage, the tangible results are not apparent. Clinton's general in the war on drugs said that about one-third of the cocaine shipped to the United States had been seized, but enough was getting through so that drugs on the street had "never been cheaper."[43] Surveys indicate that one-third of Americans over the age of twelve have experimented with marijuana or other illegal substances.[44] The National Household Survey on Drug Abuse estimated that about 14 million people had used an illegal drug in the past month during 1997, a number barely changed since 1988. A report of the Office of National Drug Control Policy found that drug use is not uniquely a problem of the inner city and that corruption is not limited to Latin American sources or routes of supply to the United States. Marijuana has become the number one cash crop in poor areas of Kentucky, Tennessee, and West Virginia, and the production and use of methamphetamines, or speed, is prominent in parts of Missouri, Kansas, Iowa, and the Northwest. Drug and alcohol abuse in some Northern Virginia high schools is worse than in some high schools of inner Washington, D.C. And a number of sheriffs in Kentucky are facing drug-related charges.[45]

"War on drugs" is a powerful slogan that survives considerable testimony that the campaign against drug use has not been successful. As we see in the following section, it is not the only slogan that limits the flexibility of policymakers.

Problematic Israeli Slogans

Expressions of "chosen people" and "Promised Land" as well as Jewish claims over Jerusalem have biblical authority and carry weight with much of the Israeli Jewish population. The traumas of the Holocaust, mass migration of Jews to Palestine and Israel, and Israel's success in several wars and economic development reinforce those who see God's hand in Israel. The modern slogan of "no choice," used to explain Israel's policy of preemptive strikes against Egypt and Syria in 1967 and against the Iraqi nuclear program in 1981, together with several incursions into Lebanon, also limits policy flexibility. Despite a slogan heard occasionally, it was never the case that "Every Arab is a terrorist." Substantial numbers of Palestinian Arabs from Israel or elsewhere, as well as leaders from the surrounding countries, seem committed to negotiating reasonable accommodations. Yet it remains the case that some Arabs remain committed to terror as a way to achieve their own uncompromising solutions to the "Israeli problem." Some Israeli Jews have also proven to be terrorists in pursuing their answer for the "Arab problem." The situation is delicate. To date, "Give peace a chance" proved for a while to be capable of competing with older slogans. Israeli officials who gave up parts of the Promised Land have enjoyed the support of a Jewish majority in the population. However, the struggle has not been easy and the ultimate outcome is not certain. As this book is being prepared for press, a wave of violence that has killed several hundred Arabs and Jews has put the peace process on hold.

The weight of Israeli slogans on policy is especially heavy with respect to Jerusalem. The problems with the slogan "Jerusalem must remain united under Israeli control" cannot be summarized so readily by quantitative measures as in the case of the U.S. "war on drugs." Several issues exist under the rubric of "Jerusalem." I will address the most prominent. It concerns sovereignty, or *who rules the city.* The issue of who gets what among the various religious and ethnic groups is also important but is arguably secondary to the issue of sovereignty and closer to the normal range of disputes about the distribution of policy benefits in heterogeneous localities.

One feature of the Jerusalem problem is the fixation of elected officials on symbolic conflict while seeming to overlook coping mechanisms that they have already used with success. These coping mechanisms have, in effect, accepted the notion of a Jerusalem that is divided de facto. However, because of the slogan that Jerusalem must remain united under Israeli control, Israeli officials have been hampered in claiming some measure of policy success for shared rule and in moving further in the direction already taken.

I do not intend to trivialize the city's problems by calling them symbolic. Jerusalem's name carries profound emotional impact. It was for Jerusalem that the term "crusade" was coined. Disputes between Roman Catholic and Greek Orthodox clerics about the management of holy places in the nineteenth century figured in the run-up to the Crimean War.[46] Calls by religious and political figures for uprising, revenge, blood, and plunder still come from near and far.

The problems focused on Jerusalem are widely thought to be the most difficult on the agenda of the Israeli-Arab peace process. Individuals of different ethnic and religious communities are suspicious of one another. They have limited economic contacts, even fewer social connections, almost no intermarriages, and contrary views as to Jewish and Arab rights in the city.[47] They have different mass media and schools and bus and taxi lines, and they live in their own neighborhoods. However, the neighborhoods are scattered and interspersed in ways that defy clear physical separation of the city into areas to be associated with Jewish and Palestinian countries.

While the key Israeli slogan-policies speak ritually about a united city under Israeli control, the reality has been more flexible. Although Israel insists on sovereignty, it has been a complex sovereignty with substantial de facto autonomy. Despite the formal annexation of Arab neighborhoods to Israel soon after the 1967 war, officials allowed businesses and professionals to practice under Jordanian licenses and the supervision of Arab associations, rather than force them to accept Israeli licensing and the rules of an Israeli Chamber of Commerce or professional societies. They permitted Arabs to deal in Jordanian dinars and other foreign currency against the regulations of the Bank of Israel that applied to other Israeli residents. Israel's tax authorities imposed their rates and standards of administration gradually on East Jerusalem, which had been accustomed to much lower rates and the uneven quality of Jordanian enforcement. It is part of continuing suspicion and stereotyping that Jewish Jerusalemites claim that their country is lax in taxing East Jerusalemites, while Arabs living there claim that their taxes are higher than those on the Jews. Municipal and national educational authorities retreated from an effort to impose Israeli supervision on the curricula of East Jerusalem schools. They provide financial support to schools that teach according to Jordanian or Palestinian curricula and prepare their graduates for Arab universities. Despite the formal hostilities between Israel and Jordan from 1967 to 1992, the two countries cooperated tacitly on a number of projects. There was an informal Jordanian consulate operating in the East Jerusalem Chamber of Commerce. Arabs living under Israeli rule could maintain themselves as Jordanians by keeping their official papers up to date and registering newborn children as Jordanian citizens.[48]

Most far reaching with respect to sensitive religious issues has been Israel's acceptance of de facto Muslim control over Haram Esh Sharif, with its Al Aqsa Mosque and the Dome of the Rock. Jews call the same place the Temple Mount, on account of the temples constructed by Solomon, returnees from exile in Babylon, and Herod. In order to accommodate Muslim sensitivities, Israeli authorities have refused permission for Jewish activists to pray on the Temple Mount.

The ambiguities in Israeli policy continued after the signing of the Oslo accords with the Palestinians in 1993. Israeli negotiators insisted on an absence of official Palestinian institutions in Jerusalem. Yet they agreed subsequently that Palestinian residents of the city could vote in elections for the Palestinian Authority. Although Israeli officials deny that it occurs, it is clear to all who read the Israeli press that Palestinian authorities are involved in the operation of schools and hospitals in Arab neighborhoods, members of the Palestinian elected assembly deal with constituent problems in Jerusalem, and that Palestinian security forces operate in the city. An article in the prestigious Israeli newspaper *Ha'aretz* cited an Israeli government report that Palestinian security forces "kidnapped" thirty-nine individuals from Jerusalem in 1997 and twenty-one in 1998, and that they "arrested" eighty-nine persons in Jerusalem during 1997 and fifty in 1998.[49]

Israeli responses in the period of violence that began in the autumn of 2000 have not been less ambiguous. Periodic proclamations to seal the borders between Israeli and Palestinian areas have caused Palestinians to be stopped at blockades on the main roads but not on side roads, dirt trails, and footpaths leading from the West Bank to Arab neighborhoods of Jerusalem. Israeli warnings of massive retaliation to Palestinian violence have sometimes meant nothing and at other times have been followed by warning shots into empty fields or destructive and deadly shelling.

Alongside the willingness of Israeli officials to blur the concept of sovereignty are indications that Israeli and Palestinian officials stumble amidst the ambiguities. They testify to the emotions associated with

Jerusalem and the difficulties of politicians in admitting to their own actions. The Likud party ran its 1996 election campaign with slogans that accused Prime Minister Shimon Peres of being willing to divide the city and permitting the Palestinians to take part of it as a national capital. Peres's response was to deny any such intention. He committed himself to maintaining a united city under Israeli rule. What was missing from the Labor Party response was an effort to educate the Israeli public as to the ambiguities of the issues concerned with Jerusalem and the possibilities inherent in de facto modes of autonomy for East Jerusalem.

Why the shrill and stubborn response from the Labor Party? Perhaps its leadership wanted to maintain a strong posture on the city in preparation for bargaining with the Palestinians, whose own leadership stood behind slogans that demanded a national capital in Jerusalem. If this was the thinking of the Labor leadership, it was weakened by comments made by its own parliamentarians and its partners in the parliamentary coalition. Peres's political colleagues cited reasons of equity and pragmatism as requiring compromise with the Palestinians on the issue of Jerusalem.

More persuasive is another explanation for the Labor Party's formal posture on Jerusalem: its fear of the Jewish electorate's concern for the city. A media flap in May 1998 showed that the Palestinians as well as the Israelis have trouble with the ambiguities of Jerusalem. Israeli television broadcast pictures of a large structure being built alongside the boundary of the Jerusalem municipality. It took some days before Israeli authorities could agree that it was entirely outside of their municipality.

According to initial reports, the building was to be the parliament of the as yet undeclared Palestinian state. For some Israeli officials, the situation was ideal. The Palestinians could say that they had a capital in Jerusalem. Israel could accept the fact but would not have to concede the point. It was not in Israel's Jerusalem. Right-wing activists boiled. The building proved the duplicity of Prime Minister Netanyahu. He had promised continued Israeli control over all of Jerusalem, yet he was permitting the construction of the Palestinian capital closer to the Western Wall than the Israeli Knesset. Ardent nationalists among the Palestinians also saw the building as betrayal. Palestinians have their own strong slogan, that they must have an independent state with Jerusalem as its capital. Yassir Arafat was agreeing to put his capital only in the suburbs of Jerusalem and not in the city itself. Arafat waffled. His aides first said that the building was not the parliament. It was a public facility, perhaps a university. Then it was said to be for Arafat's offices.

In events surrounding the Camp David meetings of July 2000, both Israeli and Palestinian leaders came up against the problem of Jerusalem. The leaks from negotiators mentioned shared sovereignty over parts of the city, along with Israeli transfer of some neighborhoods to Palestinian rule and Palestinian acceptance of Israeli sovereignty over Jewish neighborhoods built on what the Palestinians had claimed was their land. When the meetings ended without agreement, however, the Israeli leadership returned home to severe criticism for offering too much to the Palestinians, and the Palestinians seemed intent on their own insistence on full control over Arab sections of the city. Moreover, the Palestinians seemed unwilling to abandon another of their own honored slogans, concerned with the right of Palestinian refugees to return to the homes they abandoned during the wars of 1948 and 1967.

More than any other leading Israeli politician, Ehud Barak campaigned in 2001 in behalf of dividing Jerusalem between Israeli and Palestinian cities, as part of the concessions that he felt were necessary for achieving peace. Ariel Sharon and his supporters hammered against Barak the charge that he was threatening Jewish heritage and Israeli safety with the concessions he had offered, or would likely offer if he won another opportunity to be prime minister. Barak persisted in the campaign to explain the merits in dividing Jerusalem. A week prior to the election, the media detailed recommendations of a committee that he appointed, which included dividing the Israeli municipality in two. One of the cities would be named Al Quds (Holy City) and would be the capital of a Palestinian state.[50] However, Barak himself backtracked from what seemed to be a concession of partial or full sovereignty to the Palestinians with respect to Temple Mount, or Haram Esh Sharif. The election results went heavily against Barak: 63 to 37 percent. In twentieth-century U.S. history, only Franklin Roosevelt's victory over Alf Landon was similar to the Sharon landslide in a contest for national leadership. The day after his victory, Sharon prayed at the Western Wall and reiterated his commitment to maintaining a united Jerusalem under Israeli control.[51]

This is not the place to sort out all the options that face Israeli and Palestinian negotiators, much less those representing the Vatican, the Greek Orthodox Church, Jordan, and other players that have claimed a stake in Jerusalem. Nor is it the place to assert that the issue of Jerusalem, per se, was entirely responsible for the defeat of Ehud Barak. The concept of Jerusalem is sufficiently complex to allow achievements for both Israeli and Palestinian authorities. Most of the city is not holy to any of the major faiths. Much of metropolitan Jerusalem to the north, east, and south of the Israeli municipality is heavily Palestinian, and a considerable part of it has already been handed over to the Palestinian Authority. A binational metropolitan area that straddles national boundaries can share the magic of the name *Jerusalem* between Palestinian and Israeli authorities. Nevertheless, the Israeli election of 2001 suggests the dangers in challenging a well-entrenched slogan.[52]

When Policymakers Are Hoisted on Their Own Petard

"Hoisted on one's own petard" is a fitting aphorism for situations when slogans come to dominate policymaking and contribute to inflexibility and failure. A slogan may dominate when it taps deep roots with ethnic or religious symbolism, when prominent leaders from a wide range of the political spectrum have given it unconditional endorsement, and when it has proved useful over a considerable period of time.

In the cases considered here, neither U.S. nor Israeli critics have been able to challenge intense or well-organized defenders of the status quo, who benefit from established and powerful slogans. Supporters of a war on drugs and a united Jerusalem completely under Israeli control occupy the symbolic high ground. Most candidates for elected office either identify with the slogans or accuse their opponents of abandoning the policies associated with them.

Politics and public policy are dynamic, even when the status quo seems to be bolstered by powerful slogans. A number of policy activists and judges in the United States have moved to introduce flexibility into the treatment of addicts. Even the national drug czar has called the criminal-justice system a "disaster" and lent his support to a treatment strategy. Some states provide their courts with discretion with respect to sentencing individuals convicted of drug-related charges to prison or treatment. Some treatments have been found to be promising with respect to certain kinds of addicts. They are more effective and much less costly than prison. Yet these movements face strong opposition from those who promote drug seizures and punishment. The general picture is that a war against drugs continues.[53]

Israeli critics have expressed their reservations about the merits of the status quo with respect to Jerusalem for some time now.[54] They received no encouragement from officials in the Rabin-Peres or Netanyahu governments. Prime Minister Barak showed flexibility to the extent of moving beyond the Israeli slogan concerned with the control of a united Jerusalem. After the Camp David meetings of July 2000, though, he found himself roasted at home for daring to depart from the conventional posture. And he did not have the good fortune of meeting parallel flexibility among the Palestinians. As this is being written, violence prevails, and Israel's prime minister has signaled his opposition to concessions on Jerusalem.

This material should not be read as a diatribe against slogans. They are inevitable in politics as in other activities involving mass persuasion. They are prominent among the ways that activists pursue simplicity among the cacophony of actors, demands, and policy options clogging the media. Innovation in politics may be impossible without them, as the public may be unwilling or unable to absorb the detailed pros and cons involved in complex issues. Opponents have access to their own slogan-makers as well as to detailed arguments. Even the slogans identified here as especially powerful have not precluded challenges that some day might find their way to bringing about significant change in policy. For the time being, however, the U.S. slogan about drugs and Israeli and Palestinian slogans about Jerusalem have the upper hand.

Cope: Do Not Cross All the T's and Dot All the I's

Coping is a mode of simplifying policy choices that abjures the pursuit of a fulsome solution to the problems at hand. The synonyms of coping show that is does not seek to solve problems once and for all time: *contend, deal with, endure, fight successfully or on equal terms, handle, hold one's own, manage, struggle, subsist, survive, negotiate, bargain, barter, weather, adapt,* and *satisfice.*[55] These imply decisions that are "good enough," even if they are not what any of the participants really want. Coping need not be simplistic, but it is more simple than seeking to solve once and for all time a problem that has defied solution time and again. In this sense, coping qualifies as one of the ways that political activists and policymakers use in order to work in the context of too many demands and uncertainties as to what might happen if choices are made clearly in behalf of one course of action.

Prominent among the stresses of politics are contradictory demands, as when one group demands increased spending for services while another group complains about taxes or government debt and urges cutbacks. There are seldom enough resources to pay for everything that people want. Among groups willing to innovate there are further complications among those wishing to pursue specific programs in different ways. There is also likely to be competition between those who want the same prized appointment or contract.

Uncertainty is the bane of public life. Policymakers are not sure that a proposal will accomplish what its advocates promise. They do not know how rival countries, political parties, or individual politicians will respond to an initiative. Well-laid plans go astray if there is an unexpected increase in the cost-of-living index or the exchange rate of the national currency, the death of a political ally who was expected to provide important support, or a major act of violence.

Ambiguity as a Way of Coping

As a strategy for dealing with problems, coping is associated with a variety of tactics. Or to put it more simply, there are several ways to cope, and ambiguity is prominent among them. It is a lubricant of politics that appears in many settings.[56] It serves politicians who make numerous promises that are far reaching in their implications without specifying just what will be delivered. The appeal of ambiguity for a policymaker is the opportunity to skip over especially contentious issues in the hopes that an "understanding" will facilitate accommodations. Adversaries can reach agreement on the main outline of a program without bogging down in all the messy details. Legislators enact laws that describe general lines of action. They do not spell out all the implications but leave actual rule-making and implementation to administrative bodies. University administrators are vague in committing themselves to support the proposals of faculty members. They are also vague when they approach funding bodies to pay for university activities. And academics may believe their unspecified promises to pursue excellence and prepare the next generation for rewarding lives. Among the reasons for making such promises, however, is the inability to be much more specific about the payoffs from higher education.

The ambiguity in the treatment of religious disputes among Israeli Jews is apparent when both religious and antireligious activists claim losses in what seems like an ongoing tug-of-war. Both can also claim gains, but they tend to avoid boasting in order to play the downtrodden at the next encounter. On some occasions, each can claim *both* victory and defeat, as when authorities enact measures that seem to favor one side but then fail to implement them.

• In the case of the construction of roads and a new stadium that were opposed by religious activists on account of their causing violation of the Sabbath, the outcomes were delay or alteration in the implementation of policy rather than total reversal. One road project was delayed and its roadbed shifted slightly to avoid uncovering ancient graves excavations. The project then went forward despite additional graves located along the line of the new plans. A long-running conflict over a road through a religious neighborhood in Jerusalem currently stands with the closure of the road during certain hours on the Sabbath and religious holidays. This resolution is under appeal in the Supreme Court. Religious activists want to close the road entirely on the Sabbath and religious holidays. Secular activists want the road open at all times.

• Laws prohibiting the sale of nonkosher food are enacted but generally not enforced. A newspaper report indicated a significant increase in the shops selling pork in response to immigration from the former Soviet Union.[57]

• The contrasts between religious law, the rules followed by state authorities, and actual practices are especially muddied in the fields of marriage and divorce. Israeli couples who cannot be married by the Orthodox rabbinate on account of one or another provision of religious law, or who do not wish to be married in an Orthodox ceremony, can marry overseas. Couples wishing to separate can similarly go through legal procedures outside of Israel, sometimes arranged by mail without leaving Israel. The Israeli Interior Ministry and Israeli courts accept foreign documents concerned with marriage and divorce and register individuals accordingly.

Israel's practice of ambiguity has not been free of problems in religion as in other issues. The government warns that this is no magic potion capable of dealing with all problems in a satisfactory manner. While neither religious nor antireligious activists have been able to dominate, neither is satisfied. Some Jews suffer because the state does not enforce religious law strictly enough. Others suffer because the state is too Jewish. The intensity of hatred appears on the faces and in the screams of religious and antireligious Israelis when they demonstrate against one another. Still others suffer because they cannot tolerate a situation where there are no clear outcomes to the chronic disputes.

When Doing Nothing Is the Simplest, and Maybe the Best, Policy

We saw in the discussion of implementation in Chapter 2 that officials do not always carry out their formal responsibilities as expected. Here we see that a failure to act, or a nondecision, may actually be a useful device when there is a controversy about policy. The failure to decide may be the simplest, and perhaps the best, decision.

A widely cited study of nondecisions explained how they serve established interests not wanting to expand public policies and thereby deprive the powerless of benefits.[58] Israeli nondecision in the case of legal casinos is more clearly a case of avoiding a decision at the confluence of conflicting pressures when there are no great losers as a result of the nondecision.

A proposal to legalize casino gambling in Israel has languished on the political agenda for several years, with occasional blips of interest by ranking policymakers. Their failure to decide—or even bring the matter to prolonged public debate—illustrates a way of dealing with dispute. It is not a case of high drama but thereby seems representative of much activity in policymaking arenas when officials ignore troublesome demands.[59]

Israelis have access to lots of gambling, both legal and illegal, but not to a legal casino within their own country. It is also a country practiced in the art of coping with serious problems.[60] The government that came to office in 1999 was preoccupied with contentious issues of negotiations with the Syrians and Palestinians, a pullout of Israeli troops after occupying parts of Lebanon for eighteen years, and occasional turmoil with religious parties about Sabbath observance and the funding of religious schools.

The question of a casino enjoyed the support of the prime minister and finance minister. While these officials are at the top of the national pecking order, their advocacy of an issue does not assure adoption. In this case, their proposal encountered a rejection but no formal action. While no analyst can claim to have identified a case of final nondecision, this instance qualifies, at least for the time being. It illustrates nondecision as a simple response to an issue by overburdened policymakers.

The previous government had appointed a committee of inquiry to consider a legal casino in 1995. The committee surveyed the legal and illegal options facing Israeli gamblers, considered problem gambling as well as economic issues, and proposed the development of legal casino gambling with appropriate safeguards with respect to problem gamblers. The report generated a bit of controversy, most prominently from political parties identified with the religious community (Orthodox and ultra-Orthodox). The issue briefly moved higher on the political agenda three years later against the background of a new Palestinian casino, operated by an Austrian concern in the city of Jericho, that had attracted a nightly flow of tour buses and private cars from Israeli cities. Israeli policymakers, especially the prime minister and minister of finance, asked why they should allow some of the nation's money to flow to the Palestinians when they might be able to funnel it to an Israeli casino, take some of the proceeds in taxes, and help the economy of a depressed town.

Israelis' legal gambling focuses on the kiosks in every urban neighborhood and small town that sell tickets for the weekly lottery, sport pools, and a variety of games offering instant winnings. Government agencies operate the games; skim sizable sums for the support of education, sport, and other favored activities; and advertise heavily in print and electronic media. Top prizes have reached the equivalent of U.S.$7.5 million, and the government sweetens the pot by forgoing taxes on the winnings. For those interested in casino games, no one in the small country is more than a ride of an hour or two from a casino over the border (in Jericho thirty minutes by road from Jerusalem and an hour and a half from Tel Aviv; in Taba a few minutes from Eilat) or the gambling boats that sail from Eilat and Haifa. The *New York Times* described the Jericho casino as the largest and most lucrative investment of the Palestinian Investment Fund.[61] Advertisements in Israeli newspapers tout the features of the floating casinos, which offer kosher food and international entertainment. One company operating a casino boat offered a bond issue on the Israeli stock exchange and indicated revenues of $5.4 million during a recent three-month period. According to the commission appointed to consider casino gambling, a sizable number of the Israelis who travel abroad each year cite gambling as a primary or secondary reason for their trips.[62] Illegal casinos operate in various Israeli locations and receive only occasional attention from the police.

Opposition to gambling came from a variety of sources. Newspaper accounts reported religious and secular, Jewish and Arab members of the Knesset who usually compete with one another on issues of national security and social and economic policy who shared stories about individuals led to personal disaster on account of gambling. A day after the prime minister and finance minister proposed a casino for a poor town in the southern desert, thirteen government ministers indicated their opposition and only seven supported it. The floor leader of the prime minister's party in the Knesset said he would cut off his right hand before raising it in support of a casino.

With regard to U.S. social policy, Peter Bachrach and Morton S. Baratz describe occasions when policymakers' failures to make decisions harm the poor or those without political clout. In the case of the Israeli casino, a failure to decide seems to hurt no one. This inertia seems less an act that rewards political power than an evasion of action where politicians are divided, none of the advocates seem intense, and many are busy with more pressing matters. There is no political drama but the avoidance of conflict. To date, officials have resolved the issue negatively, without a formal vote. This kind of nondecision may be widespread in policymaking. It represents an efficient use of time and energy. It weeds issues from the agenda with a minimum of effort. The action appears reasonable and cost free. In the case of a legal Israeli casino, the variety of opponents and the number of existing options to serve Israeli gamblers have made nondecision the simplest option.

Other Rules of Simplicity

Party loyalty, incrementalism, the use of simplifying slogans, the artful use of ambiguity, and convenient nondecisions do not exhaust the neat devices, tricks, or coping mechanisms that activists use to simplify their choices in policymaking. There are many others, some of which are presented briefly here. The details of each case are less important than the general point: Activists use these and other simplifications in order to avoid pondering endlessly the options that lie before them. Some of the rules have found their way into textbooks of politics and policymaking, and some pass informally from mentors to newcomers.

I have no intention to provide an authoritative definition of how political activists and policymakers deal with their tensions and opportunities or to identify all the problematic implications that might flow from individual devices. Furthermore, I would reiterate that I do not intend to endorse any of the devices described. The point is to provide a sample of how individuals simplify the complexities of politics and policymaking. As we shall see, some of the rules involve difficult choices. They may be "simple" only for individuals skilled in their use. Some of them are harmful, at least to some who want to benefit from public policy. I return to the problems involved in simplifications, and will discuss intelligence, wisdom, and cunning in Chapter 5.

Serve Your Constituency

This is an elementary rule of survival in electoral politics. It entails knowing one's base of support and providing what it takes to keep supporters content. In the United States, it is most apparent when elected legislators use their positions to steer government contracts or appropriations to their state or district and provide access for constituents seeking interpretations or rule exemptions from government agencies. A *Washington Post* report dealt with the accomplishments of then–Senate Majority Leader Trent Lott and other Mississippi representatives in serving state interests during 1999. What is notable about Lott and his conservative colleagues is that their often-expressed opposition to government spending does not apply when the issue is service to the constituency:

- $72.8 million added to defense bills for the purchase of items made in Forest, Mississippi.
- $375 million for a helicopter carrier to be built at Ingalls Shipyard in Pascagoula.
- $5.1 million for an electronic targeting system at the Army Reserve training facility at Camp Shelby, near Hattiesburg.
- $2 million for Mississippi State University's Engineering Research Center.
- $2 million for new computer labs at the University of Mississippi.
- $4 million to convert a flood control lake into a recreation site and conference center at Sardis, Mississippi.
- Items in the agriculture spending bill for at least seventeen Mississippi research programs.
- Money to support the Mississippi Space Commerce Initiative.[63]

There may be no more prominent example of constituency service than expenditures on rivers and harbors. Members of the Senate and House of Representatives trade their votes in order to obtain federal funding of water projects, typically implemented by the Army Corps of Engineers. The politicians promise jobs and economic development, and the corps cooperates for the sake of its budget and political connections. The corps' own data show little of the economic payoff that supporters promise. In the case of one river project touted at its inception as having a "positive impact [that] will be unmatched by any other endeavor in state history," the reality is much different. Compared with the 3.4 percent of funding for navigation-related projects that the river receives, the traffic generated has been less than 0.1 percent of the commercial traffic on the government-operated river system. When the Army Corps of Engineers was promoting the development of the Missouri

River in the 1930s, it predicted 12 million tons of annual barge traffic. Now the river sees only 1.8 million tons a year.[64]

Israel is a small country without legislative districts. When citizens go to the polls to elect members of the Knesset, they select one party slate from the thirty or so on offer. Each party ranks its candidates and receives a proportion of seats in the Knesset to match its percentage of the national vote. Constituency service means that legislators act in behalf of sectors that support them: Knesset members of religious parties promote issues with implications for religious doctrine or assuring financial support for religious institutions; Arab members pressure the government to aid Arab localities and accommodate Arab interests in international matters; Knesset members who have been supported by industrial, financial, or social welfare interests make their presence felt in deliberations relevant to those constituencies.

The corollary of serving one's own constituency is the simple rule described by the epithet "Beggar thy neighbor." The meaning is to save one's goodies for oneself, or those with a close relationship, at the expense of depriving others. An example of U.S. states seeking to beggar their neighbors with the help of their own legislatures and representatives in Congress appears in the political sparring concerned with the allocation of human organs. The Clinton administration proposed altering the procedures used by the United Network for Organ Sharing. This agency coordinates the distribution of donated human organs. Organs are typically used locally if suitable for someone on a waiting list, then are offered regionally, and only then nationally. An estimated 62,000 Americans are waiting for a heart, lung, liver, kidney, or pancreas. Some 4,000 people died waiting during 1998.The proposed reform would enlarge the definition of regions, make organs more widely available, and encourage their use in major transplant centers with better records of success than small transplant centers. Opposed to the idea is an organization called Patient Access to Transplant Coalition, representing thirty-one small and mid-sized transplant centers. They benefit from the existing patchwork of small regions within which most organs pass from donor to recipient.

The dispute over the distribution of organs is so intense that when the Department of Health and Human Services proposed its reform, a number of states responded by passing laws prohibiting organs from being sent out of state.[65] At a certain point in the congressional process, opponents inserted a provision, which would counter the Clinton administration's proposed reform of organ allocation, to another bill that the administration wanted enacted. The "camel" carrying the insert contrary to the organ reform would help disabled people get back to work and extend certain tax credits. This bill seemed likely to pass and to be signed into law by the president, despite the rider that would set back his concern for organ allocation.[66] In April 2000, congressional opponents of the administration's organ reform celebrated a tactical victory. According to a Florida Republican, a vote in opposition to the reform "keeps organ allocation out of the hands of federal bureaucrats and in the hands of local communities."[67]

Money and professional egos seem to be important in the turf wars surrounding human organs. The chief liver surgeon at the University of Nebraska described as "self-serving baloney" the claims of a physician intent on achieving transplant status for the Iowa Methodist hospital, which would compete with the University of Nebraska for available organs. The physician who was the target of the Nebraskan's accusation replied, "It's a tug of war, and the patients are the rope." By this time he was leaving Iowa for a more attractive opportunity in a Boston hospital, which in turn had lost a key surgeon who was moving across town to another hospital, and taking his entire transplant team of twenty-eight people and his waiting list of 2,000 patients.[68]

Do as Little as Possible

Doing less is a way of simplifying that may be cheaper as well as easier. The second-largest Health Maintenance Organization (HMO) in the United States simplified procedures that had required physicians to obtain advance approval of certain tests or treatments from administrators. Advance approvals had proved costly from a public relations point of view insofar as they generated complaints from physicians that they were not able to employ their own professional judgment and complaints from patients that they were not able to receive the care chosen by their physicians. The HMO also found that the approval procedures had been costly in direct outlays. When the HMO stopped requiring pre-approvals in two experiments, costs declined by close to 10 percent.[69]

A variant of doing as little as possible is "Don't be too strict," or "Do not demand more from a population than it is likely to provide." A common example appears in the enforcement of traffic regulations. Usually the police allow an extra few percent on the posted speed limit.

The Los Angeles School Board estimated that one-half of its pupils would be held back if it instituted state-mandated standards to end "social promotion," or automatically moving pupils from one grade to the next regardless of achievement. Not only would such a draconian move bring protests from parents, perhaps sharpened by charges of discrimination against African Americans, Hispanics, and other minorities. It would also overwhelm the programs being planned to provide supplementary teaching to students with low test scores. As a result, school officials considered ways to phase in the state requirements in order to lower the failure rates. In this, they resemble what their counterparts were doing in New York, Massachusetts, Virginia, and Arizona. They, too, declared themselves against social promotion but were pondering ways to limit the impact of their own policies.[70]

Passing the buck is one way of doing as little as possible. Putting problematic files on someone else's desk is a well-known trick of bureaucrats wanting to avoid work or responsibility. Politicians like to blame others for problems that occur during their tenure. President Harry Truman put a placard on his desk saying, "The buck stops here." The overt message was that there was no higher authority to whom he could assign responsibility. The motto did not prevent him from campaigning in 1948 by calling the Republican-controlled legislature the "do-nothing Congress."

Evasion was the theme of Texas Governor George W. Bush's presidential campaign swing through South Carolina when African Americans pressed him to say that the Confederate flag should be removed from the state capitol. It was easier for Bush to say that the flag was a state issue, to be decided by South Carolina's authorities. However, when was asked whether it was appropriate for a high school football team to use the Confederate flag in his own state of Texas, Bush seemed to feel that the state government had no role. He answered, "That's for the local school district to decide if they want to continue to use it."[71]

Evading difficult issues may lead a policymaker to declare a policy without worrying about its most obvious implications. In response to an attack on a New York street by an unknown assailant (who may or may not have been homeless), Mayor Rudolf Giuliani declared that all homeless people who refuse shelter would be arrested. "Streets do not exist in civilized societies for the purpose of people sleeping there," the mayor said. "Bedrooms are for sleeping." He added that the right to sleep on the streets "doesn't exist anywhere. The founding fathers never put that in the Constitution." To critics, the mayor's statement was strange in the context of problems with finding shelter for all who want them and an announcement only a month earlier that New York's homeless would have to work in order to qualify for shelter.[72]

Postpone the Unpleasant by Appeals and Other Tactics

This is another variant of simplifying by doing as little as possible. The hope is that as a result of postponement one's chances will improve. Savvy individuals and companies do not give in to the threat of government action or consumer suits. They pursue appeals in court and employ lobbyists and friendly officeholders to state their case in the forums most likely to help. We may give low marks on morality to the efforts of tobacco companies to delay admitting responsibility for cancer and other maladies and for employing legal technicalities to avoid unfavorable court decisions. Not only is it their right to do so, however, it also makes sense in the case of an industry with friends as well as opponents in high places. Several decades into the struggle, the Philip Morris Company is still one of the giants of Wall Street. It has diversified into foods and beverages, but tobacco still accounts for the largest category of its profits, and it is one of the companies included in the Dow Jones 30 Industrial Averages, which pay the highest dividend as a percentage of their stock prices. That by itself is a measure of success.

Postponement also has a role in difficult negotiations. Participants can agree to array the issues from the easiest to the most difficult and begin with the first. Hopefully, they can build trust in one another that will help when they reach the more difficult matters. Postponement was integral to the Oslo agreements between Israel and the Palestine Liberation Organization. The parties would begin with the transfer of land that Israel least wanted to hold and work their way up to more sensitive issues like the status of Jerusalem and the final boundaries of Palestine. To date, negotiations have featured several crises and chronic delays in the attainment of agreements.

Make a Moral Declaration

Making a declaration in behalf of a moral good is a simple way of seeking support. It may also induce people to behave in desirable ways, even if it does not include a clear plan of program implementation. The governor of Arkansas declared a state of family emergency and called for a 50 percent reduction in the divorce rate. Florida policymakers were a bit more specific. They instituted a three-day waiting period between applying for a marriage license and the ceremony, hoping that the rule change would give couples time to consider their marriage prospects. Wisconsin has established a state marriage counselor. Among other duties, this official works with local clergy to establish requirements that couples must meet for counseling before being married in a church. The program was funded with federal money diverted from welfare programs under changes in a 1996 act that allows spending in cooperation with faith-based groups in order to strengthen families. Predictably, these efforts have encountered opposition by those who see yet another breach in the separation of church and state and the involvement of the state in what should remain personal issues.[73]

Claiming the support of a moral authority is an old trick for politicians. They seek to establish a link between themselves and the public's affection for a great person, even if he or she is long dead. Eleanor Roosevelt plays well among liberal New York Democrats, and it was she that retiring Senator Daniel Patrick Moynihan proclaimed would be supporting Hilary Rodham Clinton on the day that Mrs. Clinton formally announced her candidacy for the Senate.

Create a Crisis

Creating a crisis is a simple tactic that a generation of public administrators learned from a popular textbook. Aaron Wildavsky's *The Politics of the Budgetary Process* was published first in 1964 and has seen several editions. The book is still required reading in numerous courses in political science, public administration, and policymaking, at bachelor's and master's degree levels, in the United States and numerous other countries.[74] It illustrates how formal learning can educate government officials in the use of simple actions as ways to deal with complex formal procedures and political competition for resources.

The *Washington Post* smelled such a tactic when the U.S. Army announced that two of its ten divisions were not ready for war. According to the *Post,* the claim did not sit well alongside other indications of army resources. Why declare now that divisions are not ready for war, asked the *Post,* except as a way to squeeze more funds out of the White House and Congress?[75]

The underside of creating a crisis is the problem of calling "wolf." Too many cries may dull the willingness of the target population to provide the desired response. These are especially problematic in the case of programs that cannot be specific yet need to warn that danger is possible. The prospect of California earthquakes and attacks by terrorists surfaces periodically, with experts admitting that they cannot be certain about the time or place. The State Department issued "worldwide cautions" about terrorist attacks on American citizens five times in the last three months of 1999.[76] Its warnings were no more specific after the attacks of September 11, 2001.

When Bargaining, Claim a Great Deal

A simple tactic used in bargaining is to demand a lot and offer little, in the expectation of having some room to maneuver and still profit. Yet if the demands are too great, the risk is ridicule. Richard M. Nixon and then his survivors sought payment from the federal government for items held after his resignation from the presidency. Pleading before a federal district court, the Nixon estate sought $213 million for the president's White House tapes, photographs, and papers. In response, government attorneys argued that the judge should "not reward them one red cent for the right to destroy a nation's legacy." The government asserted that Nixon's claim was not based on a realistic assessment of the material's worth; that some of the items for which payment was sought were mass-produced photographs ("grip and grin" pictures worth "a dime a dozen"); and that the former president had already exploited some of the materials to earn $2.3 million for his memoirs and $600,000 for a paid television interview.[77]

When Appealing for Support, Promise a Great Deal

Constituents expect that politicians will exaggerate in their promises. Those who are too honest or modest risk being outsiders and losers. To be sure, style is important. No politician will admit to lying. When caught in a likely exaggeration, a skilled campaigner may claim to be voicing aspirations. Few will go so far as the drafters of the Declaration of Independence, who promised the pursuit of happiness along with life and liberty. Some years later, the drafters of the Fifth Amendment to the Constitution moderated the promises to include the more attainable life, liberty, and property.

Claim Credit

Claiming credit for a success is a simple way to forward one's hopes for political success, whether or not it is deserved. Economics and historical analysis are inexact sciences that lend themselves to claims that cannot be disproved. Political competition provides conditions where contrasting claims come from opposing camps that do little more than provide material for the already committed to reinforce their beliefs. In the run-up to the 2000 presidential election, Democratic activists were optimistic about their chances against the conventional Republican concern for economic growth. Bill Clinton himself said that he had a "lot of sympathy" for the Republicans. "I mean, it's hard for them to figure out what to run on. They can't run against the longest economic expansion in history." However, some Republican commentators had an answer: The growth was the delayed result of economic policies put into place by the Reagan administration.[78] Lags do happen. Tax cuts from the 1980s could be linked to growth that occurred in the 1990s. As is noted in Chapter 2, however, the number of claimed contributors to a political or economic event is limitless. Which president, if any, should be given credit for whatever growth can be claimed for the Internet, e-commerce, and other innovations? Should globalization be linked to the Clinton administration, or the Reagan-Bush administrations (or their predecessors) that contributed to victory in the Cold War? Let the campaign proceed.

Take a Narrow View of Your Responsibilities

This is related to the rule that instructs activists to do as little as possible. Israeli soldiers who want to stay out of trouble speak about approaching their responsibilities with a "small head." It means to do your job, but no more, and to conceive of your job in the narrowest possible terms. An American example close to the peak of international banking appeared in an article about how Citibank treated large and questionable deposits made to accounts held by the president of Gabon, a former president of Venezuela, and the sons of a former president of Nigeria. When asked by a Senate committee why the bank had not reported the deposits, bank officials said that statutes concerned with money laundering required reporting only in the case of certain drug crimes, certain violent crimes, and fraud by or against a foreign bank. According to Citibank, the money in question may have been "derived from corruption or other improper acts against a foreign government." If so, they fall outside the bank's concerns.[79]

The reputable Underwriters Laboratory, whose UL label is widely used as a sign of safety on electrical appliances and other consumer products, has been accused of being too dependent on the industries that pay for its tests. Critics say that the laboratory does not inquire sufficiently whether items submitted for testing truly are assembly-line products, or specially made to be able to pass inspection. UL-approved space heaters, halogen lamps, baby monitors, and toasters have caused fires. A UL-approved fire sprinkler system failed 30 percent of the time. Smoke detectors and carbon monoxide alarms that had passed UL laboratory tests did not work in real-world situations.

Laboratory personnel raised the flag of reputation in their defense: "Our 4,000 employees live, eat and breathe safety for breakfast, lunch and dinner. If we see there's a problem, we investigate it thoroughly and responsibly."[80] Six months after the *Washington Post* published its exposé of the Underwriters Laboratory, the organization announced changes in its procedures that it said would open them more completely to consumer advocates.[81]

Ignore the Inconvenient Rules

There are limits to the willingness of officials and citizens even in orderly and democratic societies to follow all the rules all the time. What usually obedient citizen has not driven a bit over the speed limit or made an especially favorable interpretation of instructions on tax forms or other official documents? And what government official has not overlooked what are likely to be minor infractions, rather than push authority to the limit and annoy otherwise good people in the cause of complete enforcement? We have seen how Israeli employers and employees fiddle with the notion of fringe benefits in order to avoid the undesirable chain of events that would follow from granting increases in salary per se. In the United States, the director of the Office of Surveillance and Biometrics at the Food and Drug Administration said, "We have used what we call enforcement discretion not to go after them," in response to a query about the FDA overlooking rules that prohibit the reuse of needles, catheters, wires, balloons, and other devices that the manufacturers label as "single use only." Care providers claim that they save substantial resources by purchasing reprocessed devices from companies that collect used equipment and clean, sterilize, and repackage it. Original manufacturers complain that they lose money and that patients are at risk and not informed about the nature of devices used on them. The FDA admits that it has not so far entered this realm of regulation. To date it has relied on the reporting of reused equipment that has failed, but concedes that if an item labeled "single use only" failed during its reuse, the care provider might avoid making a report in order to avoid exposure to claims for damages.[82]

A review of a major accounting firm found that most of its senior members were overlooking rules meant to prevent conflicts of interest. As many as 87 percent of the partners failed to report a violation of rules against investing in companies being audited by the firm.[83]

Evading the rules is not as blatant as ignoring them, but at times the distinctions are small. A number of schools evade prohibitions against displaying the Ten Commandments by putting them together with the Magna Carta and the Declaration of Independence and calling them historic documents rather than religious doctrine. Others edit the Ten Commandments to exclude reference to God but display alongside the list pictures of a penny with its inscription "In God We Trust." Still others simply ignore the Court's rulings against displaying the Ten Commandments as religious doctrine, in the expectation that none of the pupils or their parents will complain.[84]

To be sure, some rules are cumbersome and inconvenient, and some may be unnecessary. However, a shortcut through the inconvenience may prove even more troublesome, and it may be dangerous. A Romanian proverb instructs us that the shortest route is the one we know. This cautions that simple expedients in policymaking may not be worth the short-run benefits when viewed from a longer perspective. Wisdom involves knowing the right road, or at least sensing the dangers in a shortcut. I shall probe the possibilities and the problems of simple rules in the final chapter.

Blame Someone Else

When caught ignoring the rules—or committing any other foul—it is tempting to blame someone else. In a world where numerous organizations interact in order to implement programs and share responsibility, there are many possibilities for using this way of getting out of trouble. Although the U.S. Department of Health and Human Services operates a National Practitioner Data Bank and requires HMOs and hospitals to report disciplinary actions against physicians for incompetence or misconduct, a government report found only 715 reports actually submitted over the period 1990 to 1999. The report stated that HMOs have evolved into "bill-paying organizations," and managed care plans "often have little incentive to devote many resources to quality assessment and improvement." Explanations are that hospitals and HMOs are concerned about costly suits from practitioners. It is simplest to deal with problems by allowing a physician to leave the organization quietly and to avoid the report required by law. In response to the department's report, individuals speaking for HMOs and hospital organizations sought to blame the government. If the government did more to make HMOs aware of their obligations, according to one statement, those organizations would take "whatever steps are needed to comply with federal law and regulations."[85]

Avoid Trouble

A simple rule is to avoid trouble. Speaking and writing in politically correct terms helps with this tenet. Do not offend women, ethnic or racial minorities, the aged, the handicapped, homosexuals, or other groups granted special status by law or current political fashions; protect children and animals, as well as other groups thought to be disadvantaged; honor religion in its various formulations; be respectful of different styles in art, music, theater, and other media. The problems with political correctness (PC) comes when there is less than full agreement about what is politically correct, or even intense dispute as to the posture that is appropriate toward one group or another. The agenda of problems includes:

• Disputes among whites, African Americans, and members of other favored groups about the merits of affirmative action, in one or another of its variations.

• Indications that children and adults lie to the authorities about being the victims of sexual or other forms of abuse, with the result that the persons they accuse suffer economically and personally and may be subject to unjust incarceration, loss of employability, and damaged relations with family and acquaintances.

• Differing perspectives on political correctness: One person's view of politically correct is another's view of abomination. Those opposed to birth control, abortion, and homosexuality find support in the Bible, which provides its own authority to individuals who see it as being timelessly correct. Those who support individual freedom have their own revered texts.

• Claims and counterclaims about justices and injustices in distant parts of the world: Were the Serbians just in seeking to put down a rebellion by Albanian separatists in Kosovo? the Russians in Chechnya? and the American Union against the Confederacy? All of these conflicts have led outsiders to claim that the stronger side was using unnecessary force and causing civilian casualties. And in all there was no shortage of others who claimed that the rebels themselves were violent toward civilians. The call to "higher values" often translates into "my values," and war crimes trials are more likely to be directed against the losers who committed atrocities than the winners who committed atrocities. News reports in January 2000 told of law professors who were pressuring the United Nations International Criminal Tribunal for the Former Yugoslavia to bring cases against NATO officials for the bombing of civilians.[86]

Beware of Fashions

This is a simple rule that can be expressed as "doubting the trend," or questioning what others see as PC. Fashions can mislead. What the media hype as a way of solving an intractable problem can actually make things worse. We shall see in Chapter 5 that the essence of political wisdom is knowing when to follow one simple rule over another. A test of that wisdom is knowing what is politically correct and the danger of the fashionable.

One failed fashion is the state-run boot camp to lead juveniles from a life a crime via tough discipline. The movement spread from one state to another and produced fifty-two camps housing 4,500 juveniles. Maryland shut down its program in response to a pattern of guards punishing inmates so severely as to have provoked investigations of civil rights abuses and be charged with child abuse. A report by the U.S. Justice Department found recidivism rates no less among graduates of the boot camps than other forms of juvenile justice programs and concluded that that "the paramilitary boot camp model is not only ineffective, but harmful." After several reports of inmate deaths traced to excessive discipline, Colorado, North Dakota, and Arizona as well as Maryland ended their programs. Florida and California cut back theirs.[87]

Try Again

Trying again is a simple way of dealing with failure. Many people practice it, but some are too upset by a lack of success. Education is competitive in Japan, the better neighborhoods of Manhattan, and other societies concerned about assuring the continued upward mobility of the younger generation. Selection among candidates for the limited number of prestigious school places begins in kindergarten. The wife of a Buddhist priest in an upper-class neighborhood of Tokyo went over the edge when a neighbor's two-year-old daughter won admission to a top kindergarten and her own child failed to pass the cutoff. The dis-appointed mother killed the successful child and turned herself in to police. "I was thinking of killing her for some time," the disappointed mother-murderer is reported to have said after surrendering. "I had various interactions with [the child's] mother. It was not something superficial, and there were psychological clashes over a long period of time. I cannot express it in words."[88]

It is probably futile to offer a simple rule to a person who is close to the edge of emotional stability. When the Japanese tragedy became known, newspapers reported receiving more than 1,000 letters, many of them expressing understanding of the pressures felt by the woman who killed. They noted that a housewife's identity is tied to the success of her children, that competition is intense for getting into prestigious primary schools, some of which are affiliated with prestigious universities, and that mothers of "winners" can be cruel in their relations with the mothers of "losers."[89] However, competition is part of education, business, and politics. Losses are likely to be more frequent than victories for individuals with high aspirations. Taking one's lumps and trying again is part of the game. Revenge may be sweet, but suffering disappointment is more honorable. Moreover, it permits competing yet another day, whereas deadly revenge will end the game.

Communicate with Care: Symbols May Be More Important than Substance

This rule is a close relative of being politically correct as well as the rule of evading problematic issues. They all involve sensitivity to the importance of historical events, places, and heroic figures. Symbols can be explosive in the context of religions and national movements.[90]

Hillary Rodham Clinton found herself in a no-win situation when she traveled to Israel as part of her New York Senate campaign. The prominence of Jewish voters in New York made the trip important, but the complexities of Israel and its disputes with the Palestinians turned the trip into a minefield of competing symbols. Jewish voters would expect her to visit the Western Wall, but it is in East Jerusalem, which Arabs consider conquered territory. U.S. officials, including Jews and non-Jews, have sometimes visited and sometimes avoided the Western Wall, depending on the winds of fashion in the State Department, and Mrs. Clinton was the president's wife as well as being a political candidate in New York State. A visit to the Yad Vashem Holocaust Memorial was safer insofar as it is clearly in West (Jewish) Jerusalem. Earlier Mrs. Clinton had tripped up in the eyes of Jewish voters when she expressed her support for an independent Palestinian state. More recently she had said that Jerusalem should be the united and undivided capital of Israel, and that the U.S. Embassy should be moved there from Tel Aviv. The latter part of that statement caused a problem for the State Department, but probably nothing too serious. Promising to move the embassy to Jerusalem is standard rhetoric in U.S. election campaigns and is just as routinely overlooked when the campaign is over.

Reporters indicate that a visit to the Western Wall was an on-again–off-again element of Mrs. Clinton's itinerary. She did go there and was pictured appropriately outfitted in a religiously correct hat alongside the wife of the Israeli prime minister. When she traveled to the Palestinian city of Ramallah, she lent her presence to a troublesome speech by Suha Arafat, the wife of the Palestine Authority chairman. Mrs. Arafat said that Israel had polluted the land, water, and air of Palestine and caused cancer, other illnesses, and death among Palestinian women and children. During this trip, Mrs. Clinton annoyed Palestinians by refraining to support their desire for a state and annoyed Jews by being present at what they viewed as inflammatory comments by Mrs. Arafat. After the trip, some commentators suggested that she should have stayed home.[91]

The visit of Pope John Paul II to Israel was no less infused with problematic symbols implied by what he said, what he did not say, and where he spoke or remained silent. "Diplomatic eggshells" was the term used by Jerusalem's correspondent of the *New York Times* in advance of the visit by John Paul II. Among the incidents were:

• The refusal of Islam's mufti of Jerusalem to meet with the pope along with Israel's chief rabbis.

• Israelis' response to the news that the ambulance that would accompany the pope would have its Star of David removed.

• Palestinians' efforts to equate the pope's visit to a refugee camp with his visit to the Yad Vashem Holocaust Memorial. Israelis worried that this would equate the Israelis' treatment of Palestinians with the Nazis' efforts to liquidate European Jewry. Israelis also pondered whether the pope's comments at Yad Vashem would address the feeling of many that the Church had not sufficiently accounted for the silence of Pope Pius XII with respect to the Holocaust that proceeded during his reign.

• A protracted strike of mostly Muslim workers in the Nazareth municipality resulted in piles of garbage accumulating near the Basilica of the Annunciation only days before the pope's visit and produced a last-minute infusion of cash to the municipality by the Israeli government in an effort to end the strike.

• Concern that the midday call to prayer at the Bethlehem mosque close to Bethlehem's Manger Square would interrupt the papal mass scheduled for late morning. When the loudspeaker proclaimed the muezzin's call to prayer, the pope paused in his prayers until the noise subsided.[92]

When all was finished and the pope was safely back in Rome, it appeared that he had skillfully maneuvered past a number of the potential problems. He neither completely satisfied nor completely disappointed the major groups monitoring his statements and actions. While he did not explicitly endorse the Palestinians' desire for an independent state, he did say that they deserved a homeland of their own. And although he did not call for a return of the Palestinian refugees to the homes they left (or were forced from) fifty-two years earlier, he did call for the countries of the region to provide them with humanitarian responses suitable to their misery. He did not admit wrong in the actions of Pope Pius XII for not condemning publicly the Nazis' murder of Jews while it was occurring, but at two sites especially meaningful to Jews—the Yad Vashem Holocaust Memorial and the Western Wall—he admitted to the wrongs done by Christians to Jews over the centuries, he asked God's forgiveness, and he called for reconciliation between Jews and Christians.[93]

At the same time that the pope was avoiding the troublesome symbols of the Holy Land, Israel's Jews were having their own tussle with loaded religious symbols. The rabbi who was the spiritual leader of the ultra-Orthodox political movement SHAS included in his sermon on the occasion of the festival of Purim the equation of a political rival with the evil Haman and the tribe of Amelek. Those who know the biblical books of Esther and First Samuel recognize these as powerful curses. Against the background of Yitzhak Rabin's assassination by a religious Jew, the rabbi's sermon could be interpreted as an endorsement of yet another political killing.[94] Over the next few days, the rabbi clarified that he was not calling for violence, only asking the Lord to punish his rival in His own way. In the eyes of numerous Israelis the rabbi had violated good sense and the law against incitement to violence. SHAS

controlled an important seventeen seats in the Knesset and was a partner in the government of Ehud Barak, so it was not easy to avoid a trap
made up of religious symbols and political realities. Israel's attorney
general took a week before deciding to order the police to investigate
the rabbi on charges of incitement with an eye to possible criminal
charges. The rabbi's party threatened to act against what they considered the insult of a police investigation, and Israelis girded themselves
for yet another chapter in their continuing *kulturkampf*. The apparent
end of the story was the receipt by the police of the rabbi's explanation
of his comments.

Elsewhere, the issue of South Carolina's flag was not only an issue
for presidential candidate George W. Bush. The state branch of the National Association for the Advancement of Colored People (NAACP)
had made the flag's removal from the state capitol the centerpiece in a
campaign that had escalated to an economic boycott of South Carolina
by African Americans. The governor, the state chamber of commerce,
and the religiously conservative Bob Jones University all asked the legislature to remove the flag.

When the controversy was at a boil, the discovery of Confederate
war graves under a sports stadium elevated tempers even further. Supporters of the state's Confederate heritage, with descendents of Confederate veterans prominent among them, organized an elaborate reburial
of the remains, together with assertions that the South's traditions must
be preserved against what one state legislator termed an NAACP that
does not care about the flag, but is "just doing this to raise money."[95]

Athletes must guard their mouths as well as their muscles. A star
pitcher of the Atlanta Braves who expressed nasty things about gays,
African Americans, and foreigners provoked a resolution of the Atlanta
City Council calling for his dismissal, and the baseball commissioner
declared that he must undergo psychological testing.[96]

Keep It Simple

Actions by popular referenda, courts, and legislatures against affirmative action put a severe strain on an imperfect but effective way to provide entry for disadvantaged minorities to higher education. In response, the states of Texas, Florida, and California moved to one or
another version of a simple rule: assuring the top percentage of each
high school's graduating class a place at a state university. Texas promised entry to the top 10 percent and allowed each student in that range

to choose among the state universities. Florida proposed admitting the top 20 percent of each school's class. California is more restrictive. It offers university admission to the top 4 percent of each high school class but does not assure the students' choice of campus. The appeal of this simple rule is that it is blind to race and ethnicity and avoids quotas, yet it helps minorities by virtue of their concentration in particular high schools.

The problems are somewhat beneath the surface, or yet to come. While giving students from poor high schools a chance at a quality higher education, the rule by itself does not assure success, or even a fighting chance, for someone beginning at a quality campus on the basis of poor preparation at a substandard secondary school.[97]

KISS (Keep it simple, stupid!) is an acronym taught to U.S. military officers and others who are charged with planning and executing actions that are important and dangerous. On one occasion when an Israeli military unit failed to capture the target in a commando action and managed to kill several of its own soldiers, the chief of staff concluded that the planning had been too complicated: The mission included too many units with too many assignments. Some of the soldiers lost track of their assigned locations and shot one another. The chief of staff admitted to overlooking a prime ingredient of good planning. His version of KISS is not as terse in the translation from Hebrew to English but is useful nonetheless: "What will not be simple, will simply not be."

Look Closely at the Emperor—He (or She) May Be Naked

This rule urges participants to suspect their adversaries of exaggerating their position and their status. There may be far less to the person than what he or she is claiming. Moral stature is one way to acquire political stature, but those claiming moral authority may be exaggerating their virtue. The exposures of immorality in high places, especially in the case of those claiming their own moral superiority, were common in the period of Bill Clinton's impeachment and its aftermath. Journalists advanced their own reputations, meanwhile, by demonstrating that individuals claiming the moral high ground were in fact similar to the president in their personal shortcomings.

• Important participants in the impeachment of the president, including Representatives Henry Hyde, Dan Burton, and Bob Livingston, had to endure the revelation of their own sexual indiscretions.

• Testimony from his divorce trial indicated that Newt Gingrich was having an extramarital affair while he was House Speaker. Gingrich had written about himself in 1992: "Gingrich—primary mission: Advocate of civilization/Definer of civilization/Teacher of the rules of civilization . . . Leader (possibly) of the civilizing forces."[98]

• George Roche, president of Hillsdale College and a prominent conservative leader, who foreswore federal aid as a statement of the college's conservative credentials, was accused of having had a nineteen-year affair with his own daughter-in-law. The woman reported the affair to her husband and committed suicide. Subsequently, present and former faculty members of the college accused Roche of being a cult leader in the guise of a college president, stifling free speech, and driving away good academics.[99]

• For some time, Senator John McCain has taken the high ground on campaign finance. This is ostensibly about limiting, and providing transparency to, donations to political parties and individual candidates by individuals or organizations wanting to buy influence. It is an issue made for hypocrisy, insofar as politicians recognize it as a topic of popular appeal (who is not against influence peddling?), but nonetheless they need lots of money to campaign. The history of campaign finance reform has seen one set of measures enacted against known ways of donating large sums of money, followed by the development of evasion mechanisms that well-heeled individuals, organizations, and needy candidates employ to fund campaigns. McCain has stood four-square in favor of reform, but he has also been caught doing favors for those who contribute to his campaigns. At one point he was judged by the Senate ethics committee as having "exercised poor judgment" when he pressured federal officials in behalf of a donor whose savings and loan failed at a cost to the government of $2 billion. During McCain's run for the 2000 Republican presidential nomination, the chair of the Federal Communications Commission took the unusual step of complaining about McCain's excessive intervention in behalf of a donor who wanted a favorable ruling about a television station.[100] Another report from the 2000 campaign indicated that the telephone company serving Arizona was McCain's largest corporate donor, and the chief executive of the company was cochair of McCain's presidential campaign finance committee and his biggest overall fund-raiser. Meanwhile, one group rated the company as the regional telephone provider with the worst customer service.[101]

An article in the *New Republic* about the hypocrisy in proposals to control campaign financing began with this paragraph:

> About a year after every presidential election, stories chronicling the campaign finance violations of the previous campaign start appearing. It's a hallowed quadrennial ritual, but it has two problems. First, the stories appear long after they could make any difference. Second, the stuff that's actually legal often makes the violations look tame by comparison.[102]

The article proceeded to describe some of the devices that candidates and their organizations use in order to evade the laws governing moneys that can be donated for political campaigns.

* * *

Complexity leads to simplicity. The many players and demands in politics and the uncertainties in predicting outcomes of policy options lead activists to avoid thorough analysis for actions that are simple and manageable. Citizens and political activists learn them by experience, from mentors, or from textbooks. Their aid in producing some accomplishments makes up for their lack of perfection.

Two of the simplifying mechanisms described in this chapter, political parties and incrementalism, are so pervasive that political science research overlooks how thorough they are and focuses on the times when they do not have their customary influence. Parties lead most people, most of the time, to their political decisions. They guide citizens to their opinions on public issues and their votes on candidates. They provide the principal framework for disputes involving the chief executive and the legislature as well as the votes in the legislature. They guide officials in selecting their aides and in choosing their postures with respect to policy options.

Incrementalism prevails in most decisions about budgeting and programming. What exists has the edge of legitimacy and acceptance by citizens and other policymakers. It is difficult to make radical changes but easier to change in stages, or increments.

Slogans simplify political campaigns in behalf of candidates and policies. At times they overwhelm those who use them. As we saw in the cases of the U.S. war against drugs and a united Jerusalem completely under Israeli control, slogans can acquire the status of policies so strongly supported as to resist change, even if officials indicate by some of their actions that they would prefer greater flexibility.

Coping is a way of avoiding the frustration of trying to solve a problem that has festered for years without solution. Making vague commitments may calm antagonists even if all know in their hearts that they will not get all that is promised. In a situation where violence is possible, of course ambiguity is better than killing. Not doing anything is the simplest of all possible responses. At times, in fact, inaction is ideal, as when there are opposing views but no one supports a position so intensely as to insist on it at all cost.

Beyond these widely used simplifications, policymakers learn about more specific simplifications to help them in difficult circumstances. None of them are useful all the time. If caught being too simple (or simple-minded), politicians suffer public embarrassment. "So what" may be part of the politician's defense in a situation where there are charges and countercharges, headlines changing several times each day. Judgment is necessary and wisdom helps. Choosing when to be simple, and how to be simple, is part of the skill that is essential to real creativity in politics or policymaking. It is to this topic that I turn in the final chapter.

Notes

1. Allen D. Hertzke and Ronald M. Peters Jr., eds., *The Atomistic Congress: An Interpretation of Congressional Change* (Armonk, N.Y.: M. E. Sharpe, 1992), p. 143.

2. Christopher J. Bailey, *The U.S. Congress* (Oxford: Basil Blackwell, 1989), p. 70.

3. Steven A. Shull, *Presidential-Congressional Relations: Policy and Time Approaches* (Ann Arbor: University of Michigan Press, 1997), p. 77.

4. Russel Dalton, *Citizen Politics in Western Democracies: Public Opinion and Political Parties in the United States, Great Britain, West Germany, and France* (Chatham, N.J.: Chatham House Publishers, 1988), p. 182.

5. Dalton, p. 197.

6. Dalton, p. 183.

7. Dalton, p. 184.

8. A classic description is Lincoln Steffens's *The Shame of the Cities* (New York: Hill and Wang, 1957).

9. Arnold J. Heidenheimer, ed., *Political Corruption: Readings in Comparative Analysis* (New York: Holt, Reinhart & Winston, 1970); James C. Scott, *Comparative Political Corruption* (Englewood Cliffs, N.J.: Prentice-Hall, 1972).

10. Sam Dillon and Julia Preston, "Political Reforms in Mexico Don't Halt Old-Style Tricks," *New York Times,* November 3, 1999. Internet edition.

11. Bradley Graham, "Pentagon's Antimissile Program Needs Defense," *Washington Post,* November 14, 1999, p. A1. Internet edition.

12. David E. Rosenbaum, "Gradual Expansion of Medical Benefits Puts Vermont in the Vanguard," *New York Times,* June 19, 2000. Internet edition.

13. Michael Crowley, "Dull and Duller," *The New Republic,* April 9, 2001. Internet edition.

14. Ellen Alderman and Caroline Kennedy, *The Right to Privacy* (New York: Alfred A. Knopf, 1995), p. 331.

15. Victoria Benning, "Fairfax Autism Program Ignites Battle over Access," *Washington Post,* June 30, 2000, p. A01. Internet edition.

16. See, for example, Gabriel Weimann, *The Influentials: People Who Influence People* (Albany: State University Press of New York, 1994); Leon H. Mayhew, *The New Public: Professional Communication and the Means of Social Influence* (Cambridge: Cambridge University Press, 1997); John R. Zaller, *The Nature of Mass Opinion* (Cambridge: Cambridge University Press, 1992); Michael L. Geis, *The Language of Politics* (New York: Springer-Verlag, 1987); Murray Edelman, *The Symbolic Uses of Politics* (Urbana: University of Illinois Press, 1964); Robin Tolmach Lakoff, *Talking Power: The Politics of Language in Our Lives* (New York: Basic Books, 1990); Anthony Pratkanis and Elliot Aronson, *Age of Propaganda: The Everyday Use and Abuse of Persuasion* (New York: W. H. Freeman, 1992); and William Riker, *The Strategy of Rhetoric* (New Haven: Yale University Press, 1996).

17. Thomas Sowell, *Inside American Education: The Decline, the Deception, the Dogmas* (New York: Free Press, 1993); Stephen Carter, *Reflections of an Affirmative Action Baby* (New York: Basic Books, 1991).

18. Steven A. Holmes, "Re-Rethinking Affirmative Action," *New York Times,* April 5, 1998. Internet edition.

19. Paul Van Slambrouck, "College Acceptance Season: Asian Students Struggle with High Rate of Success," *Christian Science Monitor,* March 18, 1999. Internet edition.

20. The Employment Policy Foundation, "AFL-CIO's Equal Pay Initiative Equals Comparable Worth" (Washington, DC, February 24, 1999). Available online at www.epf.org.

21. Roberto Michels, *Political Parties* (New York: Free Press, 1915).

22. P. Streeten, "Nongovernmental Organizations and Development," *Annals of the American Academy of Political and Social Science* 554, November 1997, 193–210.

23. Rene Sanchez, "A Movement Builds Against 'Three Strikes' Law: Tough Sentencing Rules May Face Challenge on Calif. Ballot; Nonviolent Crimes Draw 25-Year Terms," *Washington Post,* February 18, 2000, p. A03. Internet edition.

24. For example, Gregory Acs, Norma Coe, Keith Watson, and Robert Lerman, *Does Work Pay? An Analysis of the Work Incentives Under TANF (Temporary Assistance for Needy Families)* (Washington, DC: The Urban Institute, July 1998).

25. Details in this section come from Timothy Egan, "The War on Drugs Retreats, Still Taking Prisoners," *New York Times,* February 28, 1999. Internet edition; Elliott Currie, *Crime and Punishment in America* (New York: Henry

Holt, 1998); Steven Wisotsky, "A Society of Suspects: The War on Drugs and Civil Liberties," Policy Analysis No. 180 (Washington, DC: Cato Institute, October 2, 1992); Diana Jean Schemo, "In Colombia, Plan to Replace Coca Is Scorned," New York Times, August 20, 1998. Internet edition; David Johnston and Tim Weiner, "Seizing the Crime Issue as His Own," New York Times, August 1, 1996. Internet edition; Tim Golden, "Mexico and Drugs: Was U.S. Napping?" New York Times, July 11, 1997. Internet edition.

26. Sheryl Gay Stolberg, "Government Study Labels Marijuana a Useful Medicine," New York Times, March 18, 1999. Internet edition.

27. Ann Scott Tyson, "Anti-Drug Ad Blitz Criticized for Omitting 'Drug of Choice,'" Christian Science Monitor, June 11, 1999. Internet edition.

28. Kay Bailey Hutchison, "Truth About the Drug War," Washington Post, March 9, 1999, p. A15. Internet edition.

29. Tim Golden, "Cold Pursuit: A Special Report," New York Times, March 16, 1999. Internet edition.

30. Tim Golden, "Mexican Tale of Absolute Drug Corruption," New York Times, January 9, 2000. Internet edition.

31. Karen DeYoung, "U.S. Colonel to Plead Guilty in Colombia Drug Probe," Washington Post, April 4, 2000, p. A01. Internet edition.

32. Yahoo News Digest (www.yahoo.com), July 14, 2000.

33. Jesse Katz, "U.S. Prison Population Hits the 2 Million Mark: 1990s Is 'Most Punishing Decade on Record,'" International Herald Tribune, February 16, 2000, p. 1.

34. See Elliot Currie, Crime and Punishment in America (New York: Henry Holt, 1998).

35. Johnston and Weiner, "Seizing the Crime Issue as His Own."

36. Karen DeYoung, "U.S. to Give Colombia $1 Billion to Fight Drugs," Washington Post, January 8, 2000, p. A1. Internet edition.

37. "A Muddle in the Jungle," Economist, March 4–10, 2000. Internet edition.

38. Mike Tidwell, "American Misguided Drug War: Attacking Suppliers of Drugs Without Addressing the Demand Guarantees Drug Sales Will Continue," Christian Science Monitor, March 8, 1999. Internet edition.

39. Sheryl Gay Stolberg, "U.S. Eases Curb on Medical Marijuana Research," New York Times, May 22, 1999. Internet edition.

40. "Experiment with Drugs, Mr. Bush," Economist, May 3, 2001. Internet edition.

41. Timothy Egan, "A Drug Ran Its Course, Then Hid with Its Users," New York Times, September 19, 1999. Internet edition.

42. Anthony Lewis, "It Isn't Working," New York Times, July 1, 2000. Internet edition.

43. Johnston and Weiner, "Seizing the Crime Issue as His Own."

44. Egan, "The War on Drugs Retreats."

45. David A. Vise and Lorraine Adams, "Study: Local Drug 'Epidemics' Plague U.S.," Washington Post, December 16, 1999, p. A25. Internet edition.

46. For dispute as to cause or excuse for the war, see Norman Rich, Why the Crimean War? A Cautionary Tale (Hanover, N.H.: University Press of New England, 1985); Brison D. Gooch, ed., The Origins of the Crimean War (Lexington, Mass.: D. C. Heath & Co., 1969).

47. Michael Romann and Alex Weingrod, *Living Together Separately: Arabs and Jews in Contemporary Jerusalem* (Princeton: Princeton University Press, 1991); Abraham Ashkenasi, "Israeli Policies and Palestinian Fragmentation: Political and Social Impacts in Israel and Jerusalem" (Jerusalem: Hebrew University Leonard Davis Institute, 1988); and Ashkenasi, "Opinion Trends Among Jerusalem Palestinians" (Jerusalem: Hebrew University Leonard Davis Institute, 1990).

48. Meron Benvenisti, *Jerusalem: The Torn City* (Minneapolis: University of Minnesota Press, 1976); and Gerald Caplan with Ruth B. Caplan, *Arab and Jew in Jerusalem: Explorations in Community Mental Health* (Cambridge: Harvard University Press, 1980).

49. *Ha'aretz,* March 15, 1999, p. 6. Hebrew.

50. *Ha'aretz,* January 31, 2001, p. 3. Hebrew.

51. Lee Hockstader, "Jerusalem Is 'Individible,' Sharon Says," *Washington Post,* February 8, 2001, p. A01. Internet edition.

52. Ira Sharkansky and Gedalia Auerbach, "Which Jerusalem? A Consideration of Concepts and Borders," *Environment and Planning D: Society and Space* 18, no. 3, 2000, 395–409.

53. Timothy Egan, "In States' Anti-Drug Fight, a Renewal for Treatment," *New York Times,* June 10, 1999. Internet edition; Alexandra Marks, "With Jails Packed, More States Try Drug Treatment," *Christian Science Monitor*, January 5, 2000. Internet edition.

54. Baruch Kimmerling, ed., *The Israeli State and Society: Boundaries and Frontiers* (Albany: State University of New York Press, 1989); Kimmerling, *Palestinians: The Making of a People* (New York: Free Press, 1993).

55. Herbert Simon, *Administrative Behavior* (New York: Free Press, 1976).

56. William E. Connolly, *Politics and Ambiguity* (Madison: University of Wisconsin Press, 1987). For a discussion of other coping techniques, see Ira Sharkansky, *Ambiguity, Coping, and Governance: Israeli Experiences in Politics, Religion, and Policymaking* (Westport, Conn.: Praeger Publishers, 1999).

57. *Ha'aretz,* May 3, 1995, p. 1. Hebrew.

58. Peter Bachrach and Morton S. Baratz, *Power and Poverty: Theory and Practice* (New York: Oxford University Press, 1970).

59. My thanks to Professor Asher Friedberg, of the University of Haifa, for suggesting the importance of this topic. This section draws on our joint work currently under way.

60. Sharkansky, *Ambiguity, Coping, and Governance.*

61. *New York Times,* July 7, 2000.

62. "Recommendations," *Report* (Tel Aviv: Public Committee to Examine the Issue of a Casino in Israel, December 1995). Hebrew.

63. Dan Morgan and Juliet Eilperin, "Mississippi Lawmakers Keep Federal Dollars Flowing," *Washington Post,* November 9, 1999, p. A1. Internet edition.

64. Michael Grunwald, "Corps' Taming of Waterways Doesn't Pay Off," *New York Times,* January 9, 2000. Internet edition.

65. Sheryl Gay Stolberg, "Small Steps," *New York Times,* November 12, 1999. Internet edition.

66. Sheryl Gay Stolberg, "Deal to Revamp Organ Allocation Distribution Is at Risk," *New York Times,* November 19, 1999. Internet edition.

67. Eric Schmitt, "House Votes to Reject Revised Organ Donation System; Clinton Veto Is Urged," *New York Times,* April 5, 2000. Internet edition.
68. Sheryl Gay Stolberg, "Iowa Turf War Mirrors Thicket on Transplants," *New York Times,* December 29, 1999. Internet edition.
69. David S. Hilzenrath, "HMO to Leave Care Decisions Up to Doctors," *Washington Post,* November 9, 1999, p. A1. Internet edition.
70. James Sterngold, "Los Angeles May Ease Up on School Promotion Policy," *New York Times,* December 2, 1999. Internet edition.
71. Terry M. Neal, "In South Carolina, Bush Steps Gingerly Around Racial Issues: Texan Tries to Woo Minorities Without Offending Conservatives," *Washington Post,* November 11, 1999, p. A14. Internet edition.
72. Elisabeth Mulmiller, "In Wake of Attack, Giuliani Cracks Down on Homeless," *New York Times,* November 20, 1999. Internet edition.
73. Yvonne Zipp, "Wisconsin Hires a Marriage Counselor," *Christian Science Monitor,* November 16, 1999. Internet edition.
74. Originally published by Little, Brown.
75. Bradley Graham, "Up in Arms: Department of Defense Army's Unready Divisions: Budget Feint or Fact?" *Washington Post,* November 16, 1999, p. A21. Internet edition.
76. Amy Goldstein, "Warning Issued for Americans Abroad," *Washington Post,* December 12, 1999. Internet edition.
77. Bill Bill, "Final Arguments Heard on Nixon Materials' Value," *Washington Post,* November 17, 1999, p. A04. Internet edition.
78. Paul Krugman, "Reckonings," *New York Times,* February 23, 2000. Internet edition.
79. Jeff Gerth, "Hearings Offer View into Private Banking," *New York Times,* November 8, 1999. Internet edition.
80. Caroline E. Mayer, "UL: Still Safety's Symbol?" *Washington Post,* November 24, 1999, p. A1. Internet edition.
81. Caroline E. Mayer, "UL Opens Up Testing Process," *Washington Post,* June 16, 2000, p. E01. Internet edition.
82. Gina Kolata, "'Single Use' Medical Devices Are Often Used Several Times," *New York Times,* November 10, 1999. Internet edition.
83. Floyd Norris, "Report Says Some PricewaterhouseCoopers Partners Made Improper Investments," *New York Times,* January 7, 2000. Internet edition.
84. Dirk Johnson, "Schools Seeking to Skirt Rules That Bar Ten Commandments," *New York Times,* February 27, 2000. Internet edition.
85. Robert Pear, "Incompetent Physicians Are Rarely Listed as Law Requires," *New York Times,* May 29, 2001. Internet edition.
86. Charles Trueheart, "Professors Pursue War-Crimes Case Against NATO," *Washington Post,* January 20, 2000, p. A15. Internet edition.
87. Francis X. Clines, "Maryland Is Latest to Rethink Boot Camps," *New York Times,* December 19, 1999. Internet edition.
88. Kathryn Tolbert, "In Japan, Education Is Deadly Serious," *Washington Post,* November 27, 1999, p. A16. Internet edition.
89. Kathryn Tolbert, "Young Mothers in Japan Feel a Killer's Pain," *Washington Post,* March 7, 2000, p. A12. Internet edition.

90. The classic expression is by Murray Edelman, *The Symbolic Uses of Politics* (Urbana: University of Illinois Press, 1964).

91. Lee Hockstader, "Mideast Political Web Entangles First Lady," *Washington Post*, November 12, 1999, p. A27. Internet edition.

92. Deborah Sontag, "The Holy Land, in an Edgy Mood, Awaits the Pope's Visit," *New York Times*, March 19, 2000. Internet edition; Lee Hockstader, "Pope Will Need Solomon's Wisdom in the Holy Land," *Washington Post*, March 20, 2000, p. A1. Internet edition.

93. The only previous visit of a reigning pope to Israel had annoyed Israelis by what he did not say: Paul VI was in the country for twelve hours in 1964, and he did not say the word *Israel*.

94. See I Samuel 15:3.

95. David Firestone, "South Carolina Faces Storm over Its Flag," *New York Times*, November 13, 1999. Internet edition.

96. Jack Curry, "Baseball Orders Tests for Rocker," *New York Times*, January 7, 2000. Internet edition.

97. Jodi Wilgoren, "Texas' Top 10% Law Appears to Preserve College Racial Mix," *New York Times*, November 24, 1999. Internet edition.

98. David Brooks, "Scandals and Standard-Bearers," *The New York Times*, November 18, 1999. Internet edition.

99. David Brooks, "Scandals and Standard-Bearers," and Jennifer Frey, "The Toppling of an Ivory Tower: Hillsdale College Was a Conservative's Dream. Or Was It a Mirage?" *Washington Post*, November 18, 1999, p. C01. Internet edition.

100. Stephen Labaton, "McCain Urged F.C.C. Action on Issue Involving Supporter," *New York Times*, January 6, 2000. Internet edition.

101. Michael Grunwald, "Ties to Phone Company Leave McCain on a Fine Line: As Arizonans Fume About 'US Worst,' Firm Fares Well," *Washington Post*, January 18, 2000, p. A03. Internet edition.

102. Ryan Lizza, "Extra: The Hottest Campaign Finance Abuses," *New Republic*, January 31, 2000. Internet edition.

5

Intelligence, Cunning, and Wisdom in Politics and Policymaking

Previous chapters have specified the complexities in politics and policy-making and have identified a number of methods individuals use to simplify their activities. The choice of simple solutions is imperfect. The devices and rules for decisionmaking described in Chapter 4 do not solve one's problems once and for all time. Some of them contribute to problems more severe than those that invited their use. Wise policy-makers seek to minimize problems rather than make things worse. Sometimes they err in their choices of tactics. They may do more harm than good. However, the use of these devices testifies to their utility. They allow people to cope, manage stress, and deal with the burdens of too many options.

Use of these shortcuts through political choices does not signify an absence of intelligence or wisdom among the individuals who employ them. Indeed, recognizing the limits of making a comprehensive survey of one's options may be the essence of wisdom in politics and policy-making. The best that is possible with a level of inquiry tolerable to most participants most of the time may, in fact, be the ideal in real-world terms.

The ways of simplifying politics and policymaking are not suitable in all conditions. Adhering to the leadership provided by one's political party need not entail rigid loyalty to an organization or blind adherence to an ideology or a leader. Likewise, the perspectives of incrementalism are often useful but at times should bow to the desirability of making a large increment, or decrement, or departing from precedent entirely. Slogans are obvious ways to communicate in the competitive and noisy arenas of politics and policymaking, but we have seen the dangers of becoming prisoner to one's slogans. Conditions change, and the slogan useful at one time may hinder adaptation to a new situation. Ambiguity serves well in avoiding continued dispute about terms of agreement that may be impossible to define in any complete sense. However, a lack of sufficient clarity may render an agreement empty of meaning and lay the groundwork for continued demands, feelings of betrayal, and violent opposition to the arrangement.

The usefulness of any given approach to policymaking depends on the situation. The Book of Ecclesiastes expresses it in poetry. It reads best in Hebrew, but the King James translation is acceptable:

> To every thing there is a season, and a time to every purpose under the heaven: a time to be born, and a time to die; a time to plant, and a time to pluck up that which is planted; a time to kill, and a time to heal; a time to break down, and a time to build up; a time to weep, and a time to laugh; a time to mourn, and a time to dance; a time to cast away stones, and a time to gather stones together; a time to embrace, and a time to refrain from embracing; a time to get, and a time to lose; a time to keep, and a time to cast away; a time to rend, and a time to sew; a time to keep silence, and a time to speak; a time to love, and a time to hate; a time of war, and a time of peace.[1]

The key is knowing when to plant and when to reap, mourn or dance, make war or peace. Judgment is the essence of wisdom, which differs from the cunning of someone who knows how to maneuver but lacks the depth to know when to make concessions in the name of more important considerations. Cunning involves skill in using the tricks of a trade but lacks an understanding of the deeper meaning of these tricks, their significance, or their implications for further developments.

Learning When to Apply a Simple Rule

Reading about others' experiences may help, and for that reason I present in this chapter a number of cogent examples of difficult situations. All of them concern imperfect resolutions, but none lead to a complete solution widely applauded as the best of all possible options. Readers may quarrel with the details provided as well as with the way they are explained. However, quarrels are part of the accumulation and use of wisdom.

Problems of Party Loyalty: When Morality Becomes an Issue

People interested in politics judge officeholders and candidates constantly. Usually it is a matter of deciding who is more appealing, in the most general of terms, depending on one's view of the person's character, the person's postures toward policy issues, and the individual's political party. Most people make their judgments with something less than exhaustive inquiry. Much of the time, the party of the person being judged, and the party of the person doing the judging, have a great deal to do with the judgment. Where we sit, in terms of party affiliation, is likely to affect *what* we see, or at least *how* we see it.

Occasionally a politician's character and actions come to occupy the center of the political agenda and receive a prolonged examination and much commentary. Two prominent cases in recent U.S. history are Richard Nixon and Bill Clinton. Nixon became the first president to resign, a step that he took when it seemed inevitable that the House of Representatives would vote articles of impeachment. Clinton survived impeachment by the House when the Senate did not muster enough votes to convict.

Both men had been controversial from the time of their first national campaigns. Richard Nixon was targeted throughout his career for an excessively zealous anticommunism in his early campaigns for election to the House and the Senate and for slipping out of an accusation that he accepted questionable gifts in his famous "Checkers" speech defending his position as Dwight D. Eisenhower's running mate in the 1952 presidential campaign. (Checkers was a cocker spaniel given to Nixon's young daughter. He emphasized the dog as a trivial gift in his speech, but it was not the only gift at issue.) Twenty years later, "Tricky Dick" met his match in the Democratic members of Congress who took off against the Watergate scandal and in Republican members who lost the desire to defend Nixon once his lies became apparent.

As for Clinton, Jennifer Flowers was just one of the women linked to his sexual exploits. She came to prominence in the 1992 primaries eliciting from Clinton the claim that she was not telling the truth about an affair that she claimed had occurred over a period of twelve years.

When it came to the ultimate test of each man's presidency, there was considerable doubt as to whether they merited impeachment and conviction. The Constitution provides little guidance. Article 2, section 4 indicates, "The President, Vice President and all civil Officers of the United States shall be removed from Office on Impeachment for, and

Conviction of, Treason, Bribery, or other high Crimes and Misdemeanors." "High crimes or misdemeanors" may include everything from
murder or treason to a traffic ticket.

By one view, authors of the Constitution meant to give wide latitude to those who would be called upon to distinguish impeachment and
conviction from ordinary judicial procedures. They required a majority
vote in the House of Representative for impeachment, and a two-thirds
majority in the Senate for conviction and removal from office. For some
modern commentators, this extraordinary procedure meant that the
process would involve judgments by politicians that would be political
in their nature. That is, no ordinary offense would be sufficient; only
one that would somehow persuade those majorities of its seriousness
would justify impeachment. According to some commentators, that
means an offense that would threaten the working of the body politic.
This interpretation goes beyond the language of the Constitution, however, and competes with others in a setting where there is no agreed
standard for throwing a president out of office.

Among the reasons given for impeaching and convicting Clinton
were his violation of conventional morality, his perjury before a grand
jury with respect to his personal conduct, his obstruction of justice by
inducing others to lie in his behalf, and his abuse of power by virtue of
legalistic and evasive answers to questions put to him by the House Judiciary Committee. Prominent among the reasons for not impeaching or
convicting him were assertions that his behavior with Monica Lewinsky, while reprehensible, was a personal failing that did not affect his
conduct of public business. Moreover, the topic of extramarital sex was
one where lying and evasion should be expected and overlooked, even
if done in the context of a formal proceeding.

These arguments compress the points made in hours of debate by
members of the House and Senate as well as in countless more hours
and pages of commentary. They occurred in the context of wider allegations. Clinton's history of sexual adventures, as well as questions
about his and his wife's investments, had occupied critics and a special
prosecutor throughout his presidency. They recalled allegations about
his behavior as Governor of Arkansas and his evasion of the draft during Vietnam. "Slick Willy" was the nickname for a politician who had
slipped through one crisis of confidence after another concerned with
the legality or morality of his actions.

Against the claims of personal wrongdoing and violation of laws
concerned with perjury, obstruction of justice, and abuse of power were
assertions about Clinton's merits as a president. His accomplishments,

in the eyes of supporters, included a balanced budget and accumulated surplus, national prosperity measured by full employment and an absence of inflation, plus multiple-year, double-digit stock market growth that had provided riches to an increasing segment of the population.

Was the United States selling its moral soul in exchange for a few years of prosperity? A number of Republicans were certain of it. Democrats were no less certain that the Republican Party had been captured by religious fanatics and moral demagogues whose own personal behavior was not above reproach.

The votes in the House of Representatives with respect to charges of impeachment and in the Senate with respect to conviction pointed to the roles of political party in shaping the sentiments and votes of officials. Yet while majorities of the lawmakers voted with their parties, in no case was there a vote of all members of one party against all members of the other party. On December 19, 1998, the House of Representatives voted 228 to 206 to accept the first article of impeachment, accusing Clinton of perjury for misleading a federal grand jury about the nature of his relationship with White House intern Monica S. Lewinsky. Five Republicans voted against impeachment, while an equal number of Democrats supported it. A second article of impeachment, charging Clinton with obstruction of justice by inducing others to lie, passed on a vote of 221 to 212. Twelve Republicans voted no, while five Democrats voted yes. Two additional charges against Clinton lost. One accused him of perjury in the Paula Jones sexual harassment lawsuit, and another charged abuse of power due to his evasive answers to questions asked by the House Judiciary Committee.

Clinton's trial in the Senate reached its climax on February 12, 1999. Conviction required a two-thirds vote. No Democrat voted to convict on either charge. Ten Republicans voted against conviction on the perjury charge, and the final vote was 55 to 45 against conviction. The Senate split 50-50 on the charge of obstructing justice, with five Republicans voting against conviction.

The stories of Nixon and Clinton may not establish a clear role for morality in U.S. politics. What they do show, however, are the problems faced by party loyalists when they come up against a party leader whose moral shortcomings make it difficult to support him.

The Problems of Postponement: Deadlines Approach

The evolution of the Israeli-Palestinian peace process demonstrates both the attractions and the dangers of postponement. After many years of bloodshed, the Israeli government and the major Palestinian organization agreed in 1993 to settle their conflict in stages. The principle was to deal with the easy issues first and to move through the more difficult issues once a degree of confidence had been established.

It worked, more or less, for a number of years. There were incidents of violence, breakdowns in diplomatic contacts that won the designation of "crises," and delays in the agreed-upon timetable for subsequent agreements. Yet countless understandings and agreements were worked out. They include those that are informal and unwritten, between middle-level officials of Israel and the Palestinian Authority below the threshold of key politicians and the hoopla of public and mass media attention. A measure of public understanding seems to have been achieved that peace, even with animosity and unresolved issues, is better than violence.

The problem with postponement is that, sooner or later, it becomes necessary to deal with ever more sensitive and complex issues. As this is being written, we are in a period of violence. No end of the killing is in sight, and several major issues lack resolution. Hopefully, some will be dealt with by the time readers reach this point in the book.

• *Jerusalem.* Each side claims this city as its capital. While this is often described as the most difficult of the issues, it may be the easiest. Israel can maintain its definition of Jerusalem, and the Palestinians can place their capital building a few meters outside the Israeli municipality in a place that the Palestinians label Jerusalem, or, even better from an Israeli perspective, *Al Quds,* which is Arabic for Holy City. With respect to Arab neighborhoods within the Israeli municipality, Israeli authorities already recognize the dual or triple status of residents. They are Israeli residents for some purposes, Palestinians or Jordanians for other purposes. Palestinian authorities operate in Arab neighborhoods, sometime in formal violation of written agreements but with apparent acceptance by Israel. Muslim authorities have de facto control of Muslim holy places in the Israeli city, although there is some dispute between Jordanian and Palestinian religious officials as to which has the final say about particular issues. With a major surge in violence, however, both sides are hardening their position. Israel insists on controlling all of Jerusalem. Palestinians want the Israelis out of neighborhoods they created in 1967 and are demanding control of the Western (Wailing) Wall.

• *Palestinian refugees and Jewish settlers.* This is a twinned set of issues that involves an unresolved number of Palestinians (3 to 5 million) claiming the right to return to Israel or to the Palestinian area and perhaps 300,000 (depending on the areas at issue) Israeli Jews living on land that the Palestinian Authority claims as its own. Neither side wants the other's people, and neither cherishes the prospect of paying compensation to the large number of individuals who may be disappointed by whatever is agreed.

• *Water.* Whoever or whatever created the Land of Israel/Palestine produced confusion as to the location and ownership of underground water. Among the problems is that rain falling on the area claimed by one side seeps into the ground and settles in aquifers under the other's territory.

• *Borders.* Lots of Israelis and Palestinians prefer separation, and that is an easy formula for their leaders. Yet many Palestinians want to work in the Israeli economy, and several Israeli businesses want to profit from the low wages that they accept. Moreover, Israel and Palestine offer different opportunities for medical care, education, shopping, and family visits that will attract movement across boundaries. The geographical location of Israeli and Palestinian settlements, including neighborhoods in and around Jerusalem, render separation a supreme challenge for those who would define borders and establish fences, points of entry, and procedures for moving back and forth. Rather than clear lines of separation, it seems inevitable that enclaves of one jurisdiction will remain inside the other. Or at least ethnic and religious enclaves will remain in place, no matter what the formal designation of which jurisdiction is responsible for the territory, social services, and policing.

• *Conflicting claims with respect to security and sovereignty.* While Palestinians demand the full rights of statehood, including a military force and control over its borders and international relations, Israel demands a demilitarized Palestine, with only a lightly armed police force to control internal security. Israel also demands a strip along the Jordan Valley in order to guard against an invasion from the east as well as a military presence on the hills overlooking its coastal plain. All of these Israeli demands would not leave much by way of statehood for the Palestinians.

In what may be an overly optimistic Israeli view, the prospect of limited statehood for the Palestinians, as well as the differential economic and military capacities of the two sides, will lead the Palestinian leadership to accept a number of the Israeli demands, perhaps in exchange for access to Israel for Palestinian workers and a combination of formal and informal Israeli concessions on other issues. The sticking point is the sensitivity of each side to its own people. Thomas Friedman, a *New York Times* columnist with substantial experience in the Middle East, imagined what might be the ultimate conversation between Palestinian Authority chairman Yassir Arafat and Ehud Barak, who was then Israel's prime minister:

> Mr. Barak will say to Mr. Arafat: "If you want to get a state, you need to help me with my political problem, and that is the settlers. You've got to eat most of them. And anyway, that's the price you have to pay for launching a war against us in 1967." And Mr. Arafat will reply: "If you want me to help you with your political problem, you have to help me with mine. You have to radically reduce the number of settlers in the West Bank and the amount of territory you keep there for security so that I have room to settle the refugees. And you are going to have to take at least a symbolic number of refugees back into Israel proper—if I have to take some settlers. I can't help you solve your political problem if you can't help me solve mine."[2]

The artful use of ambiguities, or being more accommodating de facto than in the formal agreements, may help deal with the as yet unresolved issues between the Israelis and the Palestinians, as they have helped since the 1993 Oslo ceremony. Yet there is no assurance that the killing will stop and that efforts at accommodations will overcome the memory of recent violence.[3]

The Endless Problems of Health

All who are born are destined to die. Most of us want to postpone that fate as long as possible and to enjoy our years in the comforts of good health. Each year that option becomes more possible, thanks to medical progress. Enjoying the full benefits of medical science also becomes more expensive. Dealing with the allocation of medical science consumes a great deal of policymakers' time and energy and seems bound to produce frustration and anger along with well-being. If we were to look at each country's history of health policy, we could find examples of several simplifications in policymaking: incrementalism, evasion, postponement, political correctness, and other rules used to simplify responses to particular controversies. Insurance coverage has expanded incrementally. Policy advocates demand coverage of AIDS and abortions as politically correct, and yet denying those benefits is politically correct for those of different perspectives. Others seek to evade the sticky issues. Among the problems that remain are:

• Who will benefit, and how much, from medical care? This is a universal problem, but its nature varies from one country to another. Among Western democracies, the United States is an outlier in the high incidence of people who do not benefit from government-provided health services, or government-mandated health insurance. Elsewhere, the problem is more focused on how much each individual can benefit. This usually takes the form of treatments and medicines that are included in the basic package of coverage. Among the factors affecting the items included are money, the cost of particular drugs or treatments, the total sum allocated by policymakers to health, and the capacity of politicians to stand firm when those who cannot afford to treat themselves privately accuse policymakers of being hard-hearted and impervious to the suffering of the poor. Also involved are questions of ideology and religion, as when issues of the public health service paying for abortion, addictive drugs, or sex-change operations reach the agenda of policy dispute.

• Should presently illicit drugs be decriminalized, and if so, with what controls to prevent the spread of addiction?

• Should assisted suicide be permitted, and if so, how should it be regulated?

• What policies should be pursued with respect to mental health? This opens its own range of difficult issues, such as which categories of mental health care providers fall within the national service, provisions for involuntary hospitalization of the mentally ill, and the use of drugs to treat children with attention deficit or hyperactive disorders. After the surgeon general of the United States reported that 20 percent of Americans suffer from problems of mental health, the op-ed page of the *New York Times* carried a commentary from a psychiatrist that was critical of the wide conception of mental illness used by the surgeon general. The critic argued that many of those said to be ill were just people who "felt sad," whose problem would disappear without treatment. The critic feared that the surgeon general's remarks would cause health plans to treat many people with minor problems, with the result that there would not be resources available to focus on individuals with severe problems.[4]

Other Knotty Problems of Public Policy

We can test our wisdom on any number of knotty problems removed from the juicy exposés of presidential sex, complexities of peace in the Holy Land, and endless debates about how much health service the government should provide. Some of the issues I describe provoke some advocates and opponents to intensity, while they leave others indifferent or even generate ridicule at what seems trivial. Politics serves the entire community with different strokes for different folks.

At times policymakers think seriously, pursue simple treatments, or simply retreat in search of peace and quiet. For some of the issues considered here, the simplest solution is to ignore them. Readers will disagree, but at least a few will conclude that one or another issue is not worth the time of policymakers. Someone may have to respond, but the person most appropriate will be somewhere lower down in the hierarchy. Even there, it may be best to ignore an event. Appearance in the media does not signify importance. It may only mean that a reporter and editor sense the opportunity to humor their audience with a bizarre episode. Officials who take the mundane too seriously may become the subjects of a simple rule used in making promotions and identify themselves as unworthy of greater responsibility. People who make mountains out of molehills qualify for being passed over in the competition for higher positions.

The Slippery Slope

Some of the issues considered here involve a slippery slope. The image of the slippery slope is meant to stop a threatening action. In other words, something on a slippery slope needs to stop before it reaches a precipice of true danger. Yet there is a fundamental controversy about the notion of the slippery slope. We cannot be sure about the future, and it is likely to be complex. A step taken today might not lead to further steps in the same direction. And if it does, the threat may be perceived and halted closer to the point of real danger. Conversely, a trend may never develop. An unpleasant occurrence may be just that, with no implications for the spread of undesired behaviors. In short, we can often draw lines where we want them, without pondering implications for further development.

Campaigns against smoking involve a slippery slope. Opponents are so concerned with stopping the possibility of secondary smoking that they have acted against smoking in public buildings, in favor of mandatory no-smoking sections in restaurants, and for the end of smoking sections on airliners. Davis and Palo Alto, California, have local ordinances prohibiting smoking within twenty feet of a public building, which led an editorial writer for the *Economist* to view tobacco as the

U.S. substitute for the now-defeated evil empire of the Soviet Union and to inquire where there would be a pause in the concern to protect individuals from their own good times. Would the Big Mac be next in line, along with other fattening foods? Like cigarettes, junk food also has its secondary impacts, as felt by anyone unfortunate enough to sit next to an overweight person in the coach section of an airliner.[5] Perhaps the line of decency in opposing smoking is banning it in public buildings but not to worry how far a smoker must be from such a place before lighting up. Large people in airplanes are a problem, but keeping us all from eating fattening food sounds like too severe a solution.

Supreme Court Justice Oliver Wendell Holmes Jr. expressed his own doubts about the slippery slope in a case where plaintiffs argued against a tax on the grounds of the government's capacity to create great damage through the power of taxation: "The power to tax is not the power to destroy while this Court sits." Holmes's point was that the Court should intervene only at the point of real danger and not limit government authority simply on the prospect of danger at some time in the future.[6] In this, Holmes may have been thinking of a lesson taught by his father, who once wrote, "Insanity is often the logic of an accurate mind overtaxed."[7]

With or without bras. Toward the lighter side of the spectrum is a dispute that focused on the women's rugby team of Ohio State University. Several members of the team removed their shirts and their sport bras while touring the Lincoln Memorial in Washington, D.C. They claimed the action fit within the (men's) rugby tradition of removing one's shirt in ecstasy upon scoring a goal. At the moment, the women were not on a field of play, and even if they had been, university authorities might not have acted differently. They suspended university support for the team, imposed community service penalties on the offending players, and left unresolved the future of the women's sport at Ohio State.

Arguments went beyond the details of what the women had done and where they had done it. Comments extended from Ohio State University to the actions of high school officials who prohibited female athletes from practicing without shirts over their sport bras and prohibited male athletes from playing without their shirts in order to guard against charges of gender discrimination. This in turn brought complaints about the foolishness of prohibiting boys from taking off their shirts on a sports field in order to guard the domain of equality.[8]

Women on submarines. Should women be allowed as members of submarine crews? The principles of political correctness and equal opportunity suggest a positive answer, but the small size of the vessels, limited arrangement of bunks, the few toilets, and the intensity produced by crowding argue against it.

Males in the most senior positions of the U.S. Navy refused even to discuss the issue. The commander of one nuclear submarine said, "I only know one way, the way I was brought up. I've been doing this for eighteen years, and it works well." The most senior admiral said, "For us, for me as chief of naval operations, I do not intend to change."[9] Such attitudes may reflect a society that is ignorant of women attendants in men's washrooms. European men seem inured to the problems of urinating while a female cleans a nearby facility. And even Americans use dual-sex toilets in airplanes. To the extent that the issue is the prospect of sex under the sea, one has to perceive the unspoken in order to understand that what is tolerable in the expanse of an aircraft carrier or even much smaller ships might not work as well in the extreme confines of a submarine.

Sex, football, and the Holocaust. Israelis woke one day to the news that their national football (soccer) team, which had lost a humiliating one-sided contest with the Danish national team, might have been weakened by spending the pregame evening in the company of call girls. As if that were not sufficiently shocking, a day later Israelis learned that a class of high school students on a trip to a Holocaust death camp in Poland arranged evening entertainment consisting of female and male strippers.

Israelis may think of themselves as more inured to sexual adventures than puritanical Americans. For some, however, the tarnishing of a Holocaust remembrance trip put their indifference to a test. Both the football players and the high school students had their defenders. One player defended the party with call girls as a harmless way of relieving tensions. A female high school student said that the party with a male stripper was "no big deal." It would take an expert to determine if there was more—or less—tongue-clucking directed at the football players or the high school students.

Sex and gambling at the airport. With brothels set to become legal in the Netherlands, the operators of an existing exclusive establishment applied for permission to open a branch at the Schiphol international airport. Authorities refused, saying that the service would not fit with their overall philosophy. But the airport already has a casino. Why one and not the other? asked the brothel operators. The dispute continues, with the applicants indicating that they would limit their services to hors d'oeuvres and nonsexual massages for travelers facing long layovers.[10]

ATM fees. Somewhere close to the issues of sports bras and the sexual temptations of submarine crews, athletes, high school students, and air travelers on the scale of policy complexity are the fees charged by automated teller machines (ATMs). Charges levied on each use by one's own bank, and by another bank owning the machine being used, have infuriated patrons, who ask, "Should we be charged for withdrawing our own money?" Against this is the banks' response that the machines and their servicing cost money and provide convenience to customers and that fees represent a legitimate way to recover costs and make a profit.

Politicians have smelled an issue. Local councils in Santa Monica and San Francisco legislated local bans against the charges, which have so far produced court challenges and the closure of some ATMs against individuals who are not customers of the banks operating the ATM. New York Senator Alfonse D'Amato and Vermont Congressman Bernard Sanders introduced legislation banning certain charges nationwide, so far without clear prospects of an enactment. The *New York Times* seemed to be seeking balance in its reports on the controversy. It ended one article by quoting a resident of Santa Monica who damned all the participants:

> I think Santa Monica is overstepping its rights trying to impose business practices on the banks, and I think the banks are being vindictive and hasty in trying to make a statement back to the city of Santa Monica (by restricting ATM machines to a bank's own account holders). I just think it's childish.[11]

Just where one puts issues on a scale of moral complexity depends on personal perspective and intensity. Some readers might agree that the foundations of a secure nation are not shaken by issues of braless women athletes, mixed submarine crews, the mixture of call girls and athletes, high school exposure to strippers, airport massage parlors, or ATM charges. Others might see them as a step toward the slippery slope that would lead to full public nudity, orgies, widespread exploitation by the plutocrats who run the banks, and God knows what next.

Humans and Other Creatures

The Student Organization for Animal Rights (SOAR) and the Animal Liberation Front (ALF) at the University of Minnesota have targeted university scientists who feed controlled substances to monkeys in order to study drug addiction and carry out research on animals for a cancer vaccine to be used by humans who suffer from brain tumors. "Stop animal torture now" is one slogan used by activists who have trashed laboratories, distributed pictures of scientists with the words "You are looking into the eyes of an animal abuser," and distributed leaflets on the streets near another scientist's home urging residents to keep their dogs on leashes "because there was an animal murderer in the neighborhood."[12]

Though justice might seem clearly on the side of serious researchers seeking cures for human illness by experimenting on monkeys and other animals, it is not always clear that a researcher is serious, pursuing a fruitful line of inquiry, or working in a way to minimize animal suffering. Some university faculty members may be concerned only with publishing enough to acquire tenure or a promotion. Even the most dedicated may produce a lot of suffering among animals without approaching a cure for a human disorder. Less attractive still are corporate scientists who test cosmetics on the eyes of rabbits. What about psychologists who drive rats crazy for the sake of learning something that might apply to humans? And high school biology students who butcher frogs in their teacher's hopes that they will learn something about biology?

Scientific funding agencies and university officials insist that committees of scientists screen applications for research that involves animal (and human) subjects for appropriate treatment of the subjects and guard against projects that are trivial or that can be conducted with less pain or danger to the subjects. However, proposals that pass muster may still involve confinement, pain, and eventual death for the animal subjects.

The mayor of Assisi, like numerous other Italian (and non-Italian) cities, finds himself with a pigeon problem. There are too many, and they make too much of a mess that endangers the facing of historic buildings. Yet Assisi was the site where Saint Francis is reported to have preached to the pigeons about human love for all creatures. The mayor supports a new ordinance that bans feeding the birds, and this has provoked protests that it is an anthropocentric violation of the town's ethos. The issue is likely to simmer for some time, with observers giving the ordinance little chance of enforcement. Meanwhile, the mayor has said, "Saint Francis was a saint; I'm just a humble mayor. . . . I have no interest in becoming a saint. I am trying to apply common sense and pragmatism."[13]

Who Owns Genetic Material Found in Poor Countries?

This issue is less concerned with the feelings of the creatures and plants that supply the genetic material than with the compensation of poor countries where the material is found. A number of countries have awakened to the profits that Western pharmaceutical companies have made from discoveries among their fauna and flora. The 1992 Earth Summit in Rio de Janeiro approved a Convention on Biological Diversity. This endorsed the principle that nations have sovereignty over their genetic resources and are entitled to "fair and equitable sharing of the benefits." It is no longer a simple matter for scientists to wander freely through the jungles in search of exotic genetic materials. Several countries demand formal applications and payments in exchange for their plants and animals. One scientist has received a death threat from Amazonian activists on account of work he had done, and a number of drug companies have warned that bureaucratic procedures will hamper the search for lifesaving compounds.[14]

When Is Legal Not Just?

Unjust laws have a long history in the literatures of revolutionaries and social critics. The label of an unjust law may describe blatant examples of exploitation in the name of law, the state, or the current elite. It also serves in usually orderly democratic societies to describe instances when particular actions seem to fall outside the scope of laws, or when the application of law is shown to be unjust. There are cases of the conviction and incarceration of individuals for crimes later found to have been committed by someone else. Laws meant to punish severe crimes may be used against individuals who seem to engage in acts that seem trivial, or even not improper. The U.S. Immigration and Naturalization Service, for example, has acted to deport individuals who committed minor crimes years ago on the basis of laws meant to guard the country against international trafficking in drugs. Gays and lesbians suffer on account of laws that criminalize private actions among consenting adults. Antiabortion activists view the laws protecting women's choice to end a pregnancy to be a prime case of legalized injustice. "Legality" and "justice" are terms used in debates about allowed and prohibited behavior, rather than clearly articulated standards having wide agreement. The concept of "state crime" is especially slippery. It is used to condemn the actions of rogue states that do evil as well as to condemn actions thought to be politically incorrect by states widely viewed to be within the normal range.[15]

When Is Enough Enough?

How thorough should government regulators be in minimizing all possibility of danger? If a product offers both risks and benefits, how far must policymakers concern themselves with both the bad and the good? There is no clear answer to these questions. It depends on circumstances and the result is not likely to please all who are interested in the outcome.

One case presents a medicine that offers relief from an unpleasant, but usually not fatal, condition against a small risk of complications and even death. A prescription medicine used against nighttime heartburn has been linked to 270 significant negative reactions and 70 deaths during the period 1993 to 1999, when it was prescribed some 30 million times. Is the incidence of danger too great or negligible? A representative of the company making the drug emphasized the rarity of the problems. The FDA strengthened its warnings to both physicians and patients, adding more cautions to label requirements already detailed in terms of the conditions when the drug might cause problems. A citizens' group that has criticized FDA procedures said that the agency's response was a good example of what is wrong with government regulation and that the drug should be taken off the market except for limited research uses.[16]

Is the Policy Enforceable? Is It Likely to Be Fair?

We saw in Chapter 2 that it is easier to declare policies than to implement them. The knowledge is widespread among political scientists but has not kept legislators from trying to fix problems quickly with new laws, while many existing provisions are enforced only haphazardly, if at all. The problem is even more serious in an authoritarian regime, where authorities can enforce laws selectively against those it deems to be uncooperative or enemies of the government. The prospect arose when the Chinese government issued what seemed to be draconian declarations against the transmission of unapproved material via e-mail or the Internet. Enforcement is likely to be uneven. The state hardly has the capacity to check everyone's messages. The worry of dissidents is that electronic snooping will focus on those the regime wants to punish and that penalties will be severe.[17]

Factory Conditions: How Much Must Poor Workers Endure?

Economic competition in wealthy markets make for low prices and high quality. Manufacturers search out the cheapest ways to produce their goods, while also worrying about the control of quality. Often this means that workers come from the poorest countries of the world, or the lowest strata of one's own society, and endure the regime of intense work and marginal surroundings that management provides. Typically people line up for the jobs. They receive much less than the average wage in the consuming society but more than the workers are likely to obtain elsewhere in their own society.

"Cheaper is better" is a simple rule of purchasing and policymaking, especially when it comes along with high-quality control, but at what cost in less-than-decent wages, safety, and other working conditions for the workers? If the industrial plants are in the wealthy countries, there is some prospect of government supervision over wages and working conditions. Yet even in these countries, supervision may be lessened by a concern not to discourage investments and jobs. In poor countries, the definition and application of decent standards are likely to depend on the industries themselves. Some are more humane than others.

Rights for the Homeless
Versus Rights for Merchants and Visitors

The problem of homelessness reflects several causes: a lack of cheap housing in cities concerned with removing areas of blight and replacing them with up-scale housing and shopping; the poverty of those who cannot afford available housing despite what had been record levels of low unemployment and high average incomes; the efforts of state governments to release the mentally ill from costly hospitals, relying on the ill to monitor their own medication; and drug abuse and alcoholism.

A number of cities have acted against the homeless and in support of citizens and merchants who complain about filth, persistent panhandling, and other disturbances:

• Of forty-nine cities surveyed in 1998 by the National Law Center on Homelessness and Poverty, 73 percent were enacting or enforcing measures against the homeless, up from 26 percent in 1994.

• In Sacramento, officials give homeless people one-way bus tickets out of town. The Downtown Sacramento Partnership, which represents about 550 businesses, employs about twenty people it calls city guides to patrol sixty-five blocks. The patrols, concentrating on tourist areas and shopping zones, call the police when they find someone sleeping on the street or panhandling.

• In Roseville, a suburb about twenty-five miles east of Sacramento, the police go undercover to catch panhandlers in the act.

• In Santa Ana, it is illegal to sit in the Civic Center with belongings that occupy more than three cubic feet.

• In Atlanta, a person who asks for money more than twice from a passerby who ignores the request can be arrested.

• In Seattle, those caught sleeping in parks can be banned from them.

• The San Francisco police issued more than 20,000 citations in 1999 for violations of ordinances like trespassing, camping, carrying an open container, and violating park curfews, compared with 17,500 in 1998 and 15,700 in 1997.

• The New York City police have arrested volunteers for handing out food to homeless people without having a permit to do so. Moreover, the city will not grant such permits for high-visibility locations.[18]

New York's mayor proclaimed a policy that would refuse shelter to homeless people who had refused to work. A state court judge delayed implementation of the policy. Against claims by city officials that the judge lacked jurisdiction, the judge responded, "It's winter. It's cold. . . . Christmas is just around the corner."[19]

Privacy for the Mentally Ill Versus the Sale of Guns to Dangerous People

How do policymakers protect the privacy of the mentally ill while also enforcing laws against the sale of guns to dangerous people? The issue puts liberal privacy advocates on the same side as conservative gun advocates: against law enforcement personnel who worry about faults in screening programs that do not indicate that a gun purchaser has a history of mental illness. Utah, New Jersey, and Connecticut changed their laws to provide access to mental health records after people with records of illness were able to purchase guns that they used in widely publicized killings.

The problem is made serious by the incidence of mentally ill people who seek to purchase weapons. An Illinois study found 3,699 people rejected as gun purchasers on account of histories of mental illness from 1996 to 1998 and another 5,585 people with histories of mental illness who already had gun permits during the same period.

This is a situation where technical fixes may address the balance of personal rights and public safety. Instead of simply turning over medical records to the police, a number of states have left them in the hands of health authorities and given them the task of checking for episodes that would disqualify a potential gun purchaser.[20]

Genetic Modification

Europeans accuse Americans of being overly sensitive to food safety, environmental protection, and other matters that enter the realm of the politically correct. Yet a curious exception to the pattern is the U.S. tendency to accept the benefits of genetically modified (GM) foods while Europeans bristle at the threat. Advocates point to increased yields for genetically modified foodstuffs as well as to plants that can be engineered to fend off potential pests and thus minimize the need for insecticides that have negative consequences for the environment. Genetically engineered medicines can be more effective with fewer side effects, and genetically engineered humans may be less inclined to pass on deformities or tendencies to disease. Some opponents to GM express their arguments in terms of a slippery slope. Others say that research has already brought us to the edge of the chasm and must be stopped now.

Concerns include the possibility that the crops produced will be harmful to humans or animals; that new species will escape from the fields where they are planted and affect the genes of related species; that the new creations can trigger a process whereby pests become immune to insecticides; and that the new varieties of plants will render farmers dependent on industries that produce vegetation whose seeds will not germinate, thereby requiring farmers to buy new seeds for each successive planting.

Most sensitive are fears about genetically engineered people. For some critics, this issue threatens the status of the Almighty to affect what is born to each of us. The concern also includes a Frankenstein syndrome of human tinkering with what should remain a mystery. For some, the major concern is "cloning," or reproducing individuals who are especially attractive, talented, or wealthy enough to pay for some measure of eternal life via a clone.

The problem of human safety has gained prominence in a Europe made sensitive to high-tech afflictions after the "mad cow disease" scare associated with beef from Great Britain, which was thought capable of infecting humans with Creutzfeldt-Jakob disease, a form of encephalitis. Also involved are reports of human deaths associated with the poorly supervised testing of genetically modified medicines.[21]

A public hearing concerned with genetic engineering by the Food and Drug Administration may have been more circus than a forum for the collection of useful information. Demonstrators outside the hearing room displayed signs claiming "Genetically engineered food is poison." Among those who expressed themselves during the two-minute time allowed each speaker in a small conference room were those who claimed that the "meeting has excluded most of the public." Others noted, "This format lends itself to sound bites," and that the FDA's presentation "sounds like promotional literature of the [food] industry."[22]

Aid for Poor Countries in the
Face of Inappropriate Spending

How much aid should be given developing countries when their rulers spend income from national resources on warfare and send substantial sums to private bank accounts? The United States and a number of other Western aid providers have cut back on their assistance to poor countries. Except for Denmark, Norway, the Netherlands, and Sweden, none of the twenty-one well-to-do members of the Organization for Economic Cooperation and Development (OECD) live up to their 1996 agreements to provide aid in the amount of seven-tenths of one percent of gross national product. Fifteen of the OECD members fail to provide even one-half of the agreed amounts.

The irony is one of falling aid in a time of unprecedented prosperity among the rich countries. In 1997, the U.S. government spent about $7 billion on nonmilitary foreign aid, or less than one-tenth of 1 percent of its GNP. That was the lowest percentage of any donor country and less than half the proportion that the United States spent ten years earlier. Overall international foreign assistance dropped 21 percent in inflation-adjusted terms between 1992 and 1997.

Representatives of African governments accuse the major powers of racism in their disregard for the suffering of blacks. However, Western governments have no shortage of reasons for declines in aid. They include dismay at the frequent and endless wars within and among poor countries and widespread corruption among aid recipients. According to the World Bank, nearly 40 percent of Africa's aggregate wealth has fled to foreign bank accounts. UN Secretary-General Kofi Anan conceded, "There are, in short, places where the widely held view of Africa as a region in perpetual crisis is not just an image, but an all-too-grim and painful reality."[23] Also working against international charity is the end of the Cold War. Western countries and the Soviet Union no longer compete for poor countries' voting support in the United Nations.

The weight of difficult choices may fall on charities as well as governments. When a prominent rebel group in southern Sudan, the Sudanese People's Liberation Army (SPLA), demanded that aid groups work according to its terms, thirteen organizations decided to pull out of the region, while twenty-six others agreed to go along with the SPLA. Those pulling out said they were being forced to choose sides in an ongoing civil war, a political demand that could compromise their efforts at a later time or in another place. The European Community also indicated that it would cease its aid to the region if the SPLA did not drop its ultimatum.[24]

Prayer in Schools and Other Religious Issues

No one concerned with issues of policymaking in the United States and Israel can reach the conclusion that issues of religion are trivial. They are in another league altogether from women athletes who doff their shirts, mixed-sex toilets, or the rights of laboratory animals. Religion is the stuff of shrill intensity affecting masses of people with the prospect of violence. Yet like other issues noted here, the state's involvement in religion involves fine distinctions in highly nuanced decisions. Issues are open to continuing controversy, and there is the prospect of a slippery slope.

U.S. courts have yet to clarify exactly and completely what is permitted and forbidden with respect to prayers in schools or other public facilities. The Supreme Court ruled by a vote of five to four in 1992 that faculty-organized, clergy-led prayer at graduation was unconstitutional. The Court opinion said that school-led prayers might lead students to feel coerced. After that decision, some lower courts allowed student-organized prayer at graduations on account of their "singularly serious nature." However, the same courts forbid student-led prayers at football games.

One case in Texas reflects the importance of both high school football and religion in that state. Students have smuggled their own public-address systems into the stands in order to lead unsanctioned prayers, school authorities have sought court permission for prayers in behalf of good sports behavior and safety, and antiprayer activists have challenged prayers both at sports events and graduations.[25] A decision by the Supreme Court against a student-led prayer at football games led the general counsel of the National School Boards Association to advise school districts to regard student-led prayers at graduation ceremonies as unconstitutional as well.[26]

The observance of religious holidays is no less confusing. Different federal courts have ruled on both sides of the question as to whether public schools may close in observance of Good Friday. As late as January 2000, the Supreme Court refused to rule in a case that might have clarified the principles involved.[27]

Highway crosses are another issue. Friends and relatives of people killed in road accidents have erected homemade crosses at the death sites, only to have them removed by state workers. Others have been defaced or replaced by swastikas and satanic signs.

Religion can set up blinders to social problems close at home. The conservative Christian clergy's discomfort with issues of homosexuality, promiscuity, and drugs may have contributed to the spread of AIDS among African Americans. Churches are prominent sources of leadership in the African American community, and many of these communities are religiously conservative. Of those in the United States who died from AIDS in 1998, 49 percent were African American, up from 29 percent in 1990, according to figures from the Centers for Disease Control and Prevention. Fifty-four percent of new cases of HIV infections in 1999 occurred among African Americans, even though they make up less than 15 percent of the population. Yet for some clergy, it was not until members of the choir began dying from AIDS that they saw the illness as a problem that must be addressed.[28]

Advantages and Disadvantages of Population Pressure

Population growth in the Palestinian community of Gaza may be among the highest in the world. Moreover, health services contribute to relatively low rates of infant mortality and long life expectancy when compared to other third world locales. Palestinian leaders encourage population growth as a weapon against the Israelis. The policy was especially prominent during the uprising against Israeli occupation from 1987 to 1993. The hope was that a continually growing population of Palestinians would force concessions or withdrawal from Israel. Women in Gaza average 7 children; Palestinians in the West Bank average 5.6; and Israelis 2.7. The policy is less understandable since the Palestinians themselves have acquired responsibility for governing increasing parts of Gaza and the West Bank. Now physical crowding and high rates of unemployment are likely to cause problems for Palestinian authorities before they cause problems for Israelis. However, a policy in behalf of large families is not easy to reverse. Palestinian leaders both encourage families and provide clinics that help with family planning. Islam is ambivalent. It encourages fertility and a quality of life to be shared by parents and children. Clerics oppose permanent solutions like sterilization but support increasing the number of years between births.[29]

When the Politically Correct
Meets Inconclusive Anecdotal Evidence

Insofar as religion is politically correct among large numbers of Texans and other Americans, it should be no surprise that Governor George W. Bush promoted the national application of "Inner Change," a fundamentalist program for bringing prisoners to Christ and away from crime. On the side of the program are numerous stories of prisoners who testify to their rebirth and their commitment to decency. Somewhat troubling are the Muslims among the prisoners who feel kept on the outside of a program that does not speak to them. More disturbing are reports by guards that the prisoners who have found Christ present no fewer disciplinary problems than other prisoners. It is too early for conclusive evidence of what happens to the prisoners once released. However, their assertions of faith have not proven to be a complete cure. Of the ninety-five program graduates who have been released, sixteen have been rearrested. Skeptics worry about prisoners' exploitation of their "jailhouse religion," where "inmates talk Jesus as long as they're incarcerated, then leave the Bible in the trash can." Israelis also notice that a number of their own inmates exhibit increased religiosity. It may make a good impression on the committees that decide on early release.[30]

Prolife and the Death Penalty

When he was a candidate for president, Governor George W. Bush's critics made a case against his wrapping himself in mantles of Christianity and "prolife" (antiabortion), along with his reigning in the state that makes the greatest use of the death penalty. According to one article that soon became outdated with respect to the numbers of the executed,

> This pro-life governor has executed 113 people in his five-year tenure, more than a sixth of all the Americans executed since 1976. . . . The question here is not the rights and wrongs of the death penalty. The question is whether Bush has the right, figuratively speaking, to his title of pro-life. And whether these actions, by a man who claims Jesus Christ as his greatest political influence, can be called Christian. . . . The strongest theme of Jesus's ministry was that we should not piously announce our great devotions, like the Pharisees he saw as hypocritical and rule-sodden, but quietly devote ourselves to repentance—and forgiveness.[31]

The case against Bush was not only that he had not worked to end the death penalty but that he had not done enough to assure adequate counsel for individuals accused of crimes that may lead to the death penalty, not to mention the casual way in which state authorities rule against appeals. One case in which Bush evaded involvement and the death penalty was carried out involved a person represented by an alcoholic defense lawyer who drank heavily during the time of the trial and did not pursue lines of inquiry thought to be obvious and crucial by lawyers who examined the case later. The defense attorney in question had been disbarred and found guilty, and he served a prison term for illegal and unethical conduct involving another case.[32] On another occasion, Governor Bush did grant a stay of execution for a convicted rapist and murderer who claimed that newly available DNA testing would clear him of the crime. When the tests were performed, however, they indicated that he was the source of the semen and pubic hair found with the victim. State authorities rescheduled his execution, and the governor said the test outcome "demonstrates the safeguards present in our system."[33]

Simple Rules and Their Opposites

One danger in simple rules is that they may be too simple. There are bromides offered by self-proclaimed experts, or homilies purveyed as truth, without reference to the situations that would make them more or less helpful. While we have focused on simple actions in politics and policymaking, the problems associated with them are not limited to these fields.

Investors have a host of rules to guide their buying and selling of securities. They appear simple only insofar as one does not perceive that their list includes some contradictions as well as recommendations whose simplicity is more apparent than real:

• Sell after a security has had a substantial run-up in price. It is probably inflated in value.

• Buy after a security has had a substantial fall in price. It is probably undervalued.

• Measure value by the ratio between the price of the security and the earnings of the company issuing it. The lower the price/earnings ratio, compared to other companies in its sector, the more attractive the security.

• Measure value by the ratio between the dividend associated with the security and the current price of the security. The higher the dividend or price ratio, compared to other companies in its sector, the more attractive the security.

• Know what is occurring inside the company. Corporate officials may be hyping its shares, perhaps paying inordinately high dividends, in order to hide weaknesses in the company's performance.

• Know what is likely to occur in terms of the government's regulatory actions. The prospect of the central bank increasing interest rates will have a depressing effect on shares in the financial sector.

• Know what is likely to occur in the international economy. The prospect of increasing energy prices will have a positive effect on shares in the energy sector. International crises are likely to depress share prices generally as investors panic and sell.

• If events portend increasing or decreasing share prices, buy or sell accordingly, early, before the movement that is predicted gets under way.

These rules for smart investing do not ensure accuracy in predicting movements in international events or government policy that can affect the stock market, and the rules do not clarify action in the case of conflict between the rules. What should one do when a share has a low price or earnings ratio (a sign to buy) but a low dividend? Or a high dividend along with the high price or earnings ratio? International crises

may cause the price of energy to increase, which suggests that it is time
to buy oil and gas stocks but threatens interruptions in the supply of oil
and gas from areas likely to be affected by the tensions.

Likewise, interest groups also follow simple rules in policymaking:

• Promote the bills favored by your members.
• Oppose the bills that your members do not want enacted.
• When your members disagree on an issue, sit out the struggle.
• Politics is the happy science. Economics is the dismal science. Do
not say no. Do not offend. Leave it to others to say what the govern-
ment cannot afford.

Like investors' rules, any one of these rules may be too simple to
help in specific cases. What happens when a well-regarded, well-to-do,
and otherwise powerful member wants a group to take a position, while
other members see the same position as harmful to them? We have already seen that politicians and other policymakers know how to say no
without using the word. They postpone, evade, do as little as possible,
take a narrow view of their responsibilities, and emphasize the positive
while leaving to others the unpleasant tasks.

Teaching, policing, social work, and other fields of public service
also have their rules, taught either formally in training sessions or informally as older workers mentor the younger. In some cases, the informal rules stand in sharp contrast to what is taught officially. Racism
passed on from one generation of white police recruits to the next gains
public awareness in the case of spectacular abuses, as in the Los Angeles police beating of African American Rodney King on the occasion of
what began as a traffic incident, and the sodomizing by New York City
police of a Haitian immigrant, Abner Louima, with the handle of a toilet
cleaner when he was being interrogated. Additionally, uncounted numbers
of anonymous teachers and social workers relate to minorities as incorri-
gible, uneducable, or undeserving their best efforts at counseling.[34]

Tough Choices

Politicians cannot please everyone. Tough choices define the limits of
the happiness they wish to purvey. Some options involve the tricky manipulation of symbols that can excite intense feelings. Should George
W. Bush, a Republican presidential candidate seeking conservative support, have met with the Log Cabin Republicans, the organization of gay

party activists? How far should he have gone to alter his state's miserly policies with respect to providing competent attorneys that affect the chances of poor defendants to receive the death penalty?

Such options appear to be small change in contrast to the tough choices facing black officeholders in South Africa. They must balance on a daily basis the aspirations of their majority constituency for improved living conditions against the concerns of whites for guarding their own living standards in the context of limited resources and the prospect of white flight that would strain the country's resources even further. The black majority came to power in 1994 with the promise of housing, jobs, education, and health. Recent official statistics indicate that 20 percent of the population lives in dwellings without running water, more than one-half without indoor sanitation, and even more without paved roads close to their dwellings. More than half the population in numerous localities is unemployed and does not pay taxes or service fees. Optimists count the number of houses built and those connected to running water, electricity, and sewers. Pessimists emphasize what remains to be done as well as high crime rates and the emigration of white professionals and entrepreneurs.[35]

One problem faced by a wealthy country is not quite so draconian but still serious: A government panel estimated that 98,000 Americans die each year on account of medical errors. This is more than die from highway accidents, breast cancer, and AIDS. Many others suffer lesser consequences because of mistakes by care providers. They receive the wrong medication or the wrong dosage, receive incorrect diagnoses due to mislabeled blood tubes, or do not receive the prescribed treatment as a patient gets passed from one physician, nurse, or therapist to another and instructions are misunderstood.

Currently there are no mandatory reports or follow-ups in place for medical errors. This puts them outside the networks that exist for nuclear reactor accidents, highway crashes, industrial accidents, and airline disasters. It might be simple to require the reporting of errors to a central registry, but the mechanism is likely to provoke opposition and lack of compliance from care providers and hospitals concerned about patient lawsuits. A report by the Institute of Medicine, associated with the National Academy of Sciences, suggests that minor medical errors that have not resulted in serious injuries or death be collected in a confidential database, not available for public review. Reducing health care providers' legal exposure might give the nation a chance to learn from their mistakes.[36] While the issue was still in the headlines, the New

York State Health Department levied a fine of $80,000 on a hospital that provided a concrete illustration of the problem. According to the Health Department, the chief of neurosurgery had operated on the wrong side of patients' brains twice in five years and had improperly affixed screws to a device implanted in a patient's spine. The department fined the hospital for failing to monitor and discipline the surgeon and for failing to report the cases to state authorities as required.[37]

It did not take long for the report about medical errors to provoke charges of exaggeration. Critics said that the report had counted deaths due to drug abuse as "medication errors" and had not distinguished between errors in treatment and "adverse events" or bad outcomes, as in the case of surgery that failed to help a patient but not necessarily as the result of an error. The report also provoked a political standoff. Congressional Republicans and Democrats responded with competing bills addressing how hospitals should deal with errors, neither of which seemed likely to be enacted.[38]

When Are Simplifications Worthwhile?

This book has not been simplistic in preaching simple solutions to the complexities of politics. It has been explicit in placing the emphasis on the *description* of simplifying devices that individuals employ. Rather than justifying some simplifications over others, I have indicated that the utility of simplifications appears in their use. This and earlier chapters have warned about the costs that one or another simplification may entail.

Pursuing simplicity is not only a way of dealing with complexity. It also contributes stresses that add to the problems of policymaking. My discussion of slogans showed how Americans suffer from legislation and enforcement that risk civil rights without having a noticeable impact on drug use. Israeli and Palestinian leaders have stumbled through a cumbersome peace process by avoiding sensitive issues concerned with Jerusalem. If they would only admit to having learned how to fudge the slogan "Jerusalem must remain united under Israeli control," Israeli and Palestinian negotiators might actually move closer to a resolution and further from violence.

Following simple rules that are appropriate in the midst of many options and political pressures is not for the innocent. Its techniques involve subtle distinctions, well-crafted appeals to individuals with different perspectives, and perhaps some degree of guile, trickery, mendacity, and skill in outright deception. Judging one's political and policymaking activity is also not for the innocent. It is incumbent on the observer who separates symbolic from substantial actions and admits that long-range goals may be rendered secondary to the accumulation of lesser accomplishments.

The workability of simple rules assumes a willingness to profit from a lack of fullness and finality. Individuals using the rules must be able to take some chances. Allies and antagonists are likely to be pursuing their own simplifications in order to work through the options that are possible. Among political activists and policymakers there are few philosophers who truly worry about all the implications of their actions. All who participate may gain from the simplifications, and all may lose something. Individuals of different perspectives will reach contrasting conclusions as to the balance between losses and gains. To paraphrase the passage of Ecclesiastes quoted earlier, there is a time for simplicity and a time for thorough research and extensive deliberations, or a time for dispatch and a time for delay.[39]

Democratic politics necessitates imperfect decisions. Contending organizations and individuals want the power of government to advance their purposes. Usually the agenda of government is controversial. Issues that do not provoke argument can find their solutions in individuals or companies without official involvement. Pressures for or against government decisions involve competing arguments, research findings, and sometimes implications for the high values of justice and morality. "You can't please everyone" and "You can't please anyone" are simple ways of summarizing the political workload.

Participants must assess their own feelings as well as larger economic and political conditions. The gains of simplification will be worth its risks as long as one feels comfortable with the situation. How should one read the signs of support for the process amidst the feelings of insecurity within oneself and complaints from others? These are questions to be judged by experience. Such interpretation may require assessing delicate signs in the political atmosphere, together with some daring. The clues of what should be done are seldom without ambiguities.

It would be nice to end this book with a simple set of rules that guide individuals in the matter of choosing simplicity or thorough analysis. Unfortunately, there are none. Politics and policymaking are too dependent on local and personal considerations to support clear do's and don'ts. Readers in search of guidelines should consult the subheadings of Chapter 4. They provide a partial list of simple rules that might be useful when making decisions for the public sector. I maintain that most individuals will often choose a simple rule—perhaps without thinking about it or recognizing it—when they encounter political options. The trick is deciding when to forgo a simple option and analyze the situation thoroughly instead.

The problem that evades simple prescription is one of judgment. None of the devices mentioned in the previous chapter offer ideal solutions to the complexity of politics or policymaking. Party loyalty is widespread and easy, but the risks of supporting a weak candidate or a weak issue are likely to be masked by campaigners beating the drums and insisting that their judgment is certain. Others among the simple rules reveal what seems like contrary bits of advice. When should you serve your constituency, and when should you do as little as possible? When do you want to threaten, and when do you want to postpone? When should you be politically correct, and what if different groups of potential supporters have contrasting views of what is politically correct? When should you evade difficult issues? Pursue a trade-off with the least cost? Activists must judge what is suitable to the situation at hand. A few rules may be learned, but knowing the utility of each comes from experience. Choices are likely to be intuitive.

"It depends" is a crucial aspect of judgment. A device that works in a setting of likely cooperation, or, in contrast, when clients are likely to be passive, may not work where the atmosphere is charged with confrontation. Also important is the amount of information available, though it is important to distinguish a lack of details from a situation of uncertainty. A sense of leisure or the heavy pressure of a deadline can render further thought more or less practical. The availability of political allies and supporters can support careful experimentation, while a condition of animosity may produce a felt need to decide firmly in a way to protect one's future. The list of relevant conditions can go on and on. It may not be easy to evaluate the context. Political judgment is best done by feeling with one's fingertips, rather than by swinging from the waist. Being subtle is usually better than overreacting, but sometimes it is necessary to use force. As we have seen before, uncertainty is one of the conditions that leads to simplicity. Often there is no time or no patience in a busy setting to consider fully all the ways of looking at a situation.

As I am finishing this book in my Jerusalem apartment, I occasionally hear the sounds of heavy machine guns and tank cannons as well as military helicopters bringing the wounded to the nearby hospital. For the time being, the simple rules of politics have not succeeded in dealing with dispute; instead, the rules of violence continue to dominate. The Israeli example is extreme but not beyond the range of what can happen. It cautions that being simple should not mean being sloppy. It also cautions that if one side in a dispute cannot assure its minimum conception of success, it may be necessary to prepare for a disaster.

In all of politics, the context is vital for deciding appropriate actions. Most readers will be far from the toughness to which political competition might lead. Intuition will be sufficient to deal with the vast majority of decisions they face. By providing a list of options and brief descriptions, this book may help some activists improve their intuition and may help observers better understand the widespread pursuit of simplicity amidst the complexities of politics and policymaking.

Notes

1. Ecclesiastes 3:1 to 3:8.

2. Thomas L. Friedman, "The Price," *New York Times,* November 10, 1999. Internet edition.

3. See Ira Sharkansky, *Ambiguity, Coping, and Governance: Israeli Experiences in Politics, Religion, and Policymaking* (Westport, Conn.: Praeger Publishers, 1999).

4. Sally L. Satel, "Metally Ill or Just Feeling Sad?" *New York Times,* December 15, 1999. Internet edition.

5. "Rout of the New Evil Empire," *Economist,* November 6–12, 1999. Internet edition.

6. *Panhandle Oil Co. v. Knox,* 277 U.S. 223 (1928).

7. *The Autocrat of the Breakfast Table* (Boston: L. C. Page, 1858), chapter 2.

8. Donna St. George and Angela Paik, "Rugby Stunt Signals Shift in Women's Sports," *Washington Post,* November 6, 1999, p. A1.

9. Steven Lee Myers, "New Debate on Submarine Duty for Women," *New York Times,* November 15, 1999. Internet edition.

10. "Brothel Sues to Offer Airport 'Relax Service,'" *International Herald Tribune,* February 3, 2000, p. 2.

11. Andrew Pollack, "Debate Intensifies over A.T.M. Surcharges," *New York Times,* November 16, 1999. Internet edition.

12. Will Woodward, "On Campus, Animal Rights vs. Animal Research," *Washington Post,* November 5, 1999, p. A1. Internet edition.

13. Alessandra Stanley, "When in Assisi, Don't Feed Saint's Flock," *New York Times,* January 8, 2000. Internet edition.

14. Andrew Pollack, "Biological Products Raise Genetic Ownership Issues," *New York Times,* November 26, 1999. Internet edition.

15. Jeffrey Ian Ross, ed., *Controlling State Crime* (New York: Garland Publishing Company, 1995).

16. Marc Kaufman, "FDA Links 70 Deaths to Heartburn Drug," *Washington Post*, January 25, 2000, p. A01. Internet edition.

17. Elisabeth Rosenthal, "China Issues Rules to Limit E-Mail and Web Content," *New York Times*, January 27, 2000. Internet edition.

18. Evelyn Nieves, "Cities Try to Sweep Homeless Out of Sight," *New York Times*, December 7, 1999. Internet edition.

19. Nina Bernstein, "State Court Halts Giuliani Plan to Make Homeless Families Work for Shelter," *New York Times*, December 9, 1999. Internet edition.

20. Fox Butterfield, "The Mentally Ill Often Skirt a Landmark Federal Gun Control Law," *New York Times*, April 11, 2000. Internet edition.

21. Deborah Nelson and Rick Weiss, "Gene Research Moves Toward Secrecy," *Washington Post*, November 3, 1999, p. 1A. Internet edition.

22. William Claiborne, "A Biotech Food Fight," *Washington Post*, November 19, 1999, p. A3. Internet edition.

23. Karen DeYoung, "Generosity Shrinks in an Age of Prosperity," *Washington Post*, November 26, 1999, p. A01. Internet edition.

24. Steven Mufson, "International Relief Groups Pull Out of Sudan," *Washington Post*, February 29, 2000, p. A15. Internet edition.

25. Joan Biskupic, "Religion at School Revisited," *Washington Post*, November 17, 1999, p. A03. Internet edition.

26. Linda Greenhouse, "Student Prayers Must Be Private, Court Reaffirms," *New York Times*, June 20, 2000. Internet edition.

27. Joan Biskupic, "Justices Reject Church-State Case: Md. Law, Closing Schools on Good Friday, Was Challenged by Former Teacher," *Washington Post*, January 19, 2000, p. A06. Internet edition.

28. Jennifer Steinhauer, "Shift in Money and Message as Minorities Take On AIDS," *New York Times*, December 17, 1999. Internet edition.

29. Deborah Sontag, "Gaza Adding Children at an Unrivaled Rate," *New York Times*, February 24, 2000. Internet edition.

30. Hanna Rosin and Terry M. Neal, "Converting Convicts to Christians," *Washington Post*, November 27, 1999, p. A01. Internet edition.

31. James Wood, "Playing God," *New Republic*, February 21, 2000. Internet edition.

32. Paul Duggan, "Defense Lawyer's Lapses Stir Doubts on Fairness Toward a Woman Facing Execution," *Washington Post*, February 22, 2000, p. A03. Internet edition.

33. Paul Duggan, "Texas Prisoner Gets New Execution Date," *Washington Post*, August 16, 2000, p. A02. Internet edition.

34. Michael Lipsky, *Street Level Bureaucracy: Dilemmas of the Individual in Public Services* (New York: Russell Sage Foundation, 1980).

35. Rachel L. Swarns, "Apartheid's Legacy Leaves Poorest Adrift," *New York Times*, November 30, 1999. Internet edition.

36. Rick Weiss, "Thousands of Deaths Linked to Medical Errors," *Washington Post*, November 30, 1999, p. A1. Internet edition.

37. Jennifer Steinhauer, "Albany Says Surgical Error Was Doctor's 2nd in 5 Years," *New York Times*, March 1, 2000. Internet edition.

38. Rick Weiss, "Researchers Challenge Data on Medical Errors," *Washington Post*, July 5, 2000, p. A02. Internet edition.

39. See Ecclesiastes 3:1–8.

Bibliography

Anderson, Charles W., *Prescribing the Life of the Mind: An Essay on the Purpose of the University, the Aims of Liberal Education, the Competence of Citizens, and the Cultivation of Practical Reason* (Madison: University of Wisconsin Press, 1993).

Bachrach, Peter, and Morton S. Baratz, *Power and Poverty: Theory and Practice* (New York: Oxford University Press, 1970).

Benvenisti, Meron, *Jerusalem: The Torn City* (Minneapolis: University of Minnesota Press, 1976).

Berg, Robert J., and David G. Gordon, eds., *Cooperation for International Development: The United States and the Third World in the 1990s* (Boulder, CO: Lynne Rienner, 1989).

Bernstein, Peter L., *Against the Gods: The Remarkable Story of Risk* (New York: John Wiley & Sons, 1996).

Birkland, Thomas A., *After Disaster: Agenda Setting, Public Policy, and Focusing Events* (Washington, DC: Georgetown University Press, 1997).

Bloom, Allan, *The Closing of the American Mind* (New York: Simon and Schuster, 1987).

Bloom, Harold, *The American Religion: The Emergence of the Post-Christian Nation* (New York: Simon and Schuster, 1992).

Carter, Stephen, *Reflections of an Affirmative Action Baby* (New York: Basic Books, 1991).

Chelimsky, Eleanor, *Program Evaluation: Patterns and Directions* (Washington, DC: American Society of Public Administration, 1985).

Coelho, George V., David A. Hamburg, and John E. Adams, eds., *Coping and Adaptation* (New York: Basic Books, 1974).

Cohen, Michael D., and James G. March, *Leadership and Ambiguity: The American College President* (New York: McGraw-Hill, 1974).

Coleman, James S., with David Court, *University Development in the Third World: The Rockefeller Foundation Experience* (Oxford: Pergamon, 1993).

Connolly, William E., *Politics and Ambiguity* (Madison: University of Wisconsin Press, 1987).

203

Dearing, James W., and Everett M. Rogers, *Agenda-Setting* (Thousand Oaks, CA: Sage, 1996).

Dery, David, *Problem Definition in Policy Analysis* (Lawrence: University of Kansas Press, 1984).

———, *Data and Policy Change* (Boston: Kluwer Academic Publishers, 1990).

Dror, Yehezkel, *Public Policymaking Reexamined* (San Francisco: Chandler Publishing Company, 1968).

———, *Crazy States: A Counterconventional Strategic Problem* (Lexington, MA: D. C. Heath, 1971).

———, *Policymaking Under Adversity* (New Brunswick, NJ: Transaction Books, 1986).

Edelman, Murray, *The Symbolic Uses of Politics* (Urbana: University of Illinois Press, 1964).

Elazar, Daniel, and Chaim Kalchheim, eds., *Local Government in Israel* (Lanham, MD: University Press of America, 1988).

Epstein, Leon D., *Governing the University: The Campus and the Public Interest* (San Francisco: Jossey-Bass Publishers, 1974).

Foucault, Michel, *Discipline and Punish: The Birth of the Prison*, translated by Alan Sheridan (New York: Vintage Books, 1979).

Geis, Michael L., *The Language of Politics* (New York: Springer-Verlag, 1987).

Gerston, Larry N., *Public Policy Making: Process and Principles* (Armonk, NY: M. E. Sharpe, 1997).

Gibson, J. L., J. M. Ivancevich, and J. H. Donnelly Jr., *Organizations: Behavior, Structure, Process* (Homewood, IL: Irwin, 1991).

Gideron, B., R. Kramer, and L. M. Salamon, eds., *Government and the Third Sector* (San Francisco: Jossey Bass, 1992).

Green, Donald P., and Ian Shapiro, *Pathologies of Rational Choice Theory* (New Haven: Yale University Press, 1994).

Groof, Jan De, Guy Neave, and Juraj Svec, *Democracy and Governance in Higher Education* (The Hague: Kluwer Law International, 1998).

Heidenheimer, Arnold J., ed., *Political Corruption: Readings in Comparative Analysis* (New York: Holt, Rinehart & Winston, 1970).

Hofferbert, Richard I., *The Study of Public Policy* (Indianapolis: Bobbs-Merrill, 1974).

Jacob, Herbert, *The Frustration of Policy: Responses to Crime by American Cities* (Boston: Little, Brown, 1984).

Johnson, Stephen D., and Joseph B. Tamney, eds., *The Political Role of Religion in the United States* (Boulder, CO: Westview, 1986).

Kerr, Clark, *The Uses of the University* (Cambridge: Harvard University Press, 1982).

Kimmerling, Baruch, ed., *The Israeli State and Society: Boundaries and Frontiers* (Albany: State University of New York Press, 1989).

Kingdon, John W., *Agendas, Alternatives, and Public Policies* (Boston: Little, Brown, 1984).

Kramer, R., and L. M. Salamon, eds., *Government and the Third Sector* (San Francisco: Jossey Bass, 1992).

Lacey, Michael J., ed., *Religion and Twentieth-Century American Intellectual Life* (New York: Cambridge University Press, 1989).

Lakoff, Robin Tolmach, *Talking Power: The Politics of Language in Our Lives* (New York: Basic Books, 1990).

Lasswell, Harold D., *Politics: Who Gets What, When, How?* (New York: Mc-Graw Hill, 1936).

Laver, Michael, *Private Desires, Political Action: An Invitation to the Politics of Rational Choice* (London: Sage, 1997).

Leege, David C., and Lyman A. Kellstedt, eds., *Rediscovering the Religious Factor in American Politics* (Armonk, NY: M. E. Sharpe, 1993).

Light, Paul C., *Thickening Government: Federal Hierarchy and the Diffusion of Accountability* (Washington, DC: Brookings Institution, 1995).

Lindblom, Charles E., and David K. Cohen, *The Intelligence of Democracy: Decision-Making Through Mutual Adjustment* (New York: Free Press, 1965).

———, *The Policy-Making Process* (Englewood Cliffs, NJ: Prentice-Hall, 1968).

———, *Usable Knowledge: Social Science and Social Problem Solving* (New Haven: Yale University Press, 1979).

Lipsky, Michael, *Street Level Bureaucracy: Dilemmas of the Individual in Public Services* (New York: Russell Sage Foundation, 1980).

Lodge, David, *Changing Places: A Tale of Two Campuses* (New York: Penguin Books, 1978).

———, *Small World: An Academic Romance* (New York: Warner Books, 1991).

Marsden, Gordon M., and Bradley J. Longfield, eds., *The Secularization of the Academy* (New York: Oxford University Press, 1992).

Martin, William, *With God on Our Side: The Rise of the Religious Right in America* (New York: Broadway Books, 1996).

Mayhew, Leon H., *The New Public: Professional Communication and the Means of Social Influence* (Cambridge: Cambridge University Press, 1997).

Mazmanian, Daniel A., and Paul A. Sabatier, *Implementation and Public Policy* (Glenview, IL: Scott, Foresman and Company, 1983).

Miller, Henry D. R., *The Management of Change in Universities: Universities, State and Economy in Australia, Canada and the United Kingdom* (Buckingham, UK: The Society for Research into Higher Education & Open University Press, 1995).

Moore, R. Laurence, *Selling God: American Religion in the Marketplace of Culture* (New York: Oxford University Press, 1994).

Morris, Edmund, *Dutch: A Memoir of Ronald Reagan* (New York: Random House, 1999).

Moynihan, Daniel P., *Coping: On the Practice of Government* (New York: Vintage Books, 1975).

Nakamura, Robert T., and Frank Smallwood, *The Politics of Policy Implementation* (New York: St. Martin's, 1980).

Neustadt, Richard, *Presidential Power: The Politics of Leadership* (New York: Wiley, 1976).

Pfeffer, J. *New Directions for Organizational Theory: Problems and Prospects* (New York: Oxford University Press, 1997).

Pratkanis, Anthony, and Elliot Aronson, *Age of Propaganda: The Everyday Use and Abuse of Persuasion* (New York: W. H. Freeman, 1992).

Quade, S., and Grace M. Carter, *Analysis for Public Decisions* (New York: North-Holland, 1989).

Radford, John, Kjell Raaheim, Peter de Vries, and Ruth Williams, *Quantity and Quality in Higher Education* (London: Jessica Kingsley Publishers, 1997).

Riker, William, *The Strategy of Rhetoric* (New Haven: Yale University Press, 1996).

Romann, Michael, and Alex Weingrod, *Living Together Separately: Arabs and Jews in Contemporary Jerusalem* (Princeton: Princeton University Press, 1991).

Ross, Jeffrey Ian, ed., *Controlling State Crime* (New York: Garland Publishing Company, 1995).

Safire, William, *The First Dissident: The Book of Job in Today's Politics* (New York: Random House, 1992).

Salamon, L. M., *Partners in Public Service: Government–Non-Profit Relations in the Modern Welfare State* (Baltimore: John Hopkins University Press, 1995).

Scott, James C., *Comparative Political Corruption* (Englewood Cliffs, NJ: Prentice-Hall, 1972).

Sharkansky, Ira, *Governing Jerusalem: Again on the World's Agenda* (Detroit: Wayne State University, 1996).

———, *Rituals of Conflict: Religion, Politics and Public Policy in Israel* (Boulder, CO: Lynne Reinner, 1996).

———, *Ambiguity, Coping, and Governance: Israeli Experiences in Politics, Religion, and Policymaking* (Westport, CT: Praeger Publishers, 1999).

———, *The Politics of Religion and the Religion of Politics: Looking at Israel* (Lanham, MD: Lexington Books, 2000).

Simon, Herbert, *Administrative Behavior: A Study of Decision-Making Processes in Administrative Organization* (New York: Free Press, 1976).

Smith, Rathgreb, and Michael Lipsky, *Nonprofits for Hire: The Welfare State in an Age of Contracting* (Cambridge: Harvard University Press, 1993).

Sneeding, Timothy M., Michael O'Higgins, and Lee Rainwater, eds., *Poverty, Inequality and Income Distribution in Comparative Perspective: The Luxembourg Income Study (LIS)* (New York: Harvester Wheatsheaf, 1993).

Snow, C. P. *The Masters* (Harmondsworth: Penguin Books, 1956).

Sowell, Thomas, *Inside American Education: The Decline, the Deception, the Dogmas* (New York: Free Press, 1993).

Steffens, Lincoln, *The Shame of the Cities* (New York: Hill and Wang, 1957).

Trowler, Paul R., *Academics Responding to Change: New Higher Education Frameworks and Academic Cultures* (Buckingham: The Society for Research into Higher Education & Open University Press, 1998).

Urbach, Ephraim E., *The Sages: Their Concepts and Belief,* translated by Israel Abrahams (Cambridge: Harvard University Press, 1987).

Wald, Kenneth D., *Religion and Politics in the United States* (Washington, DC: CQ Press, 1992).

Weber, Max, *Max Weber on Universities: The Power of the State and the Dignity of the Academic Calling in Imperial Germany,* translated and edited by Edward Shils (Chicago: University of Chicago Press, 1973).

Weimann, Gabriel, *The Influentials: People Who Influence People* (Albany: State University Press of New York, 1994).

Wuthnow, Robert, *The Restructuring of American Religion* (Princeton: Princeton University Press, 1988).

Zaller, John R., *The Nature of Mass Opinion* (Cambridge: Cambridge University Press, 1992).

Index

About the Book

Social scientists have constructed elaborate theories involving policy-makers as rational actors and purporting to predict and explain policy outcomes. In contrast, this provocative book paints a picture of policy-makers who—coping with the uncertainty of constantly changing constraints—must simplify, taking shortcuts rather than surveying all of their options and pursuing carefully thought-out plans.

Sharkansky draws on wide-ranging examples to illustrate the conditions that make simplification *the* necessary constituent of political life as well as the various ways in which policymakers navigate the maze of possibilities they confront. While acknowledging the shortcomings of the approach, he demonstrates that, considered in context, simplifications may in fact be more rational and effective than traditional rational models of decisionmaking.

Ira Sharkansky is professor of political science and public administration at the Hebrew University of Jerusalem. His numerous publications include *The Routines of Politics* and *The Politics of Religion and the Religion of Politics.*